MACMILLAN
WORK OUT
SERIES

# Work Out

# Economics

# 'A' Level

R. Young
and
S. Grant

MACMILLAN

First published 1989

Published by
THE MACMILLAN PRESS LTD
Houndmills, Basingstoke, Hampshire RG21 2XS
and London
Companies and representatives
throughout the world

British Library Cataloguing-in-Publication Data
Young, Richard, 1955–
Work out economics 'A' level.
1. Economics. Questions and answers — For schools.
I. Title. II. Grant, S. III. Series.
330′.076
ISBN 0–333–45873–7

Printed in Hong Kong

To our families

# Contents

# Preface

This book has been primarily designed to prepare students for the 'A' level examination in economics. In addition, it should also provide a useful reference for Scottish Higher Certificate examinations; for the first year of undergraduate studies; and for professional papers which contain economics. We hope that students revising or following self-study, distance learning courses will find benefit in following through a series of structured worked examples.

*Work Out Economics 'A' Level* is based on a thorough analysis of all the syllabuses set by the examining groups listed in the Acknowledgements. It has been structured to enable *effective* revision. Each chapter begins by setting out a summary of the essential economics that students need to know. Students are then presented with examples of past data response and essay questions set by examining groups, together with complete solutions. Where appropriate, new questions reflecting recent developments in the subject have also been included. All multiple-choice questions have been set by the authors, and solutions explain not only why a particular answer is correct, but also why other options are wrong.

All answer guidelines are our sole responsibility and have not been provided or approved by any examining group.

*Witney, Oxfordshire, 1989*                                                      R. Y.
                                                                                 S. G.

# Acknowledgements

The authors and publisher would like to thank the following boards who have given permission for the use of copyright material:

Associated Examining Board
Joint Matriculation Board
Northern Ireland Schools Examination Council
Scottish Examinations Board
Southern Universities' Joint Board
University of Cambridge Local Examinations Syndicate
University of London School Examinations Board
University of Oxford Delegacy of Local Examinations
Welsh Joint Education Committee

All examining groups would wish to point out that worked examples included in the text are entirely the responsibility of the authors and have neither been provided nor approved by the board. They may not constitute the only possible solutions.

The University of London School Examinations Board accepts no responsibility whatsoever for the accuracy or method of working in the answers given.

The authors and publisher would also like to thank the following, who have also given permission for the use of copyright material:

*The Guardian*
*The Independent*
Times Newspapers Ltd

Every effort has been made to trace all copyright holders but if any have inadvertently been overlooked, the publishers will be pleased to make the necessary arrangements at the first opportunity.

We are most grateful to the following Heads of Economics for their careful reading and correction of some or all of the original typescript:

Clarrie Haynes, Marlborough School, Woodstock, Oxfordshire
Danny Myers, New College, Swindon, Wiltshire
Brian Sangster, Burford School, Oxfordshire
Jonathan Townsend, Abingdon School, Oxfordshire
Laurence Whitehouse, Farnborough Sixth Form College, Hampshire

A particular thanks to Robert Ackrill for the long hours of invaluable assistance given freely in shaping the initial stages of the book. Past students of

West Oxfordshire Technical College, Corrina Boreham, Angela Frost, Clare Guy and Robert Prior-Wandesforde, and Sally Trego, formerly of Matthew Arnold School, corrected many early errors. We also owe a huge debt to the many other students who have painstakingly worked through the examples. Robert Sulley of Macmillans has given the most helpful support.

Since this is a joint venture, both authors thank their families for their sacrifices, patience and understanding throughout.

Any failings which remain are entirely our own.

The cover illustration is courtesy of Camera Press London and Benoit Gysembergh.

## Examination Boards for Advanced Level

Syllabuses and past examination papers can be obtained from:

**The Associated Examining Board (AEB)**
Stag Hill House
Guildford
Surrey GU2 5XJ

**University of Cambridge Local Examinations Syndicate (UCLES)**
Syndicate Buildings
Hills Road
Cambridge CB1 2EU

**Joint Matriculation Board (JMB)**
78 Park Road
Altrincham
Cheshire WA14 5QQ

**University of London School Examinations Board (L)**
University of London Publications Office
52 Gordon Square
London WC1E 6EE

**University of Oxford (OLE)**
Delegacy of Local Examinations
Ewert Place
Summertown
Oxford OX2 7BZ

**Oxford and Cambridge Schools Examination Board (O&C)**
10 Trumpington Street
Cambridge CB2 1QB

**Scottish Examination Board (SEB)**
Robert Gibson & Sons (Glasgow) Ltd
17 Fitzroy Place
Glasgow G3 7SF

**Southern Universities' Joint Board (SUJB)**
Cotham Road
Bristol BS6 6DD

**Welsh Joint Education Committee (WJEC)**
245 Western Avenue
Cardiff CF5 2YX

**Northern Ireland Schools Examination Council (NISEC)**
Examinations Office
Beechill House
Beechill Road
Belfast BT8 4RS

# Introduction

## How to Use This Book

This book has been designed to help you prepare for your 'A' Level examination in economics. Simply buying a revision text does not guarantee examination success. However, by working from this book over the months leading up to the final examination, you will improve your ability to understand and apply key economic concepts.

*Work Out Economics 'A' Level* is not intended as a textbook but as a comprehensive revision manual. If there are topics which you have not covered in class, refer to a good textbook and make notes from the relevant chapter. Key economic terms are in *italic* type for emphasis and are clearly defined in the text.

The book is divided into self-contained chapters each covering a major topic. At the beginning of a chapter you will find a summary of the essential economics you need to know. Make sure you become thoroughly familiar with the material in these summaries.

Each chapter contains a number of worked examples of the type of question you can expect in the final examination. For data response and essay-type questions, suggested solutions are given. It is absolutely essential that you do *not* treat solutions given as 'model' answers to be memorised and then copied out in the examination. In economics there is almost always more than one 'correct' solution to a given problem. This is particularly true in macroeconomics, where professional economists are divided as to the causes and cures for problems such as inflation and unemployment. Use the solution given as an indication of the sort of analytical skills of evaluation and judgement that you should be using yourself.

The section on objective questions gives you a chance to test your own knowledge and understanding of a topic. Do these questions without looking at the answers provided. If you give an incorrect solution to one of the questions, refer back to the relevant section in the fact sheets.

## Revision

Most courses in 'A' Level economics are over two years. Ideally, preparation begins six months before the final examination! You cannot hope or expect to sustain intensive concentration for twenty-six weeks. Start by obtaining a copy of the syllabus from the appropriate examining group listed in the acknowledgements. Use the syllabus to write out a study plan, listing the topics you are going to revise each week. Spend most time studying those concepts and issues central to the subject. For instance, you may find that some topics such as indifference curves or welfare economics are covered in more depth in *Work Out Economics 'A' Level* than is required by your syllabus.

Build up to a period of intensive revision during the last four weeks before the exam. Many people find it helpful to write as they revise. Make notes on one side of loose-leaf paper. Leave generous margins in case you want to add new ideas. In particular, make sure that when you have finished a topic, you can:

(a) define economic terms;
(b) list key points;
(c) apply important concepts;
(d) draw relevant graphs.

It is important to be able to draw graphs quickly and accurately, and a little practice will be needed.

The number of hours you put in is far less important than what you put into those hours. Most students find that they can concentrate better and learn faster if they work in bursts of thirty minutes with regular breaks. Avoid uninterrupted three-hour slogs. Promise yourself a special 'treat' at the end of a successful revision session.

Try to review material covered shortly after you have studied it and again a few days later. At the beginning of the revision programme have a look at past questions and write down the main points you would make in an answer. Draw and label relevant graphs. Make sure you can explain in your own words important concepts such as crowding out and inferior goods. It may help to draw up your own glossary of key economic words. Find time to familiarise yourself with current economic trends in the UK by reading economic articles in the quality newspapers and journals. For instance, do you know the present rate of inflation or the balance of payments trend? Similarly, you should be aware of the current government's policy. Are you aware of the Chancellor's strategy for demand management of the economy?

As the final exam approaches, practise answering questions in full and under examination conditions. You will soon find that your ability to apply economics has improved beyond all measure.

Make sure your study programme is balanced and allows time for enjoyment and relaxation. Work hard, do your best and look forward to the long summer holiday when you can take a well-earned break.

## The Examination

You are bound to be slightly nervous on the day of the exam. So is everyone else. Remember, with careful revision and good examination technique picked up by reading this book, you should do well. Arrive in good time. Do not forget to take the appropriate equipment for each paper. There are three main types of question in the final examination.

### (a) Essay Questions

For this paper you are going to need two pens, a ruler, a pencil, a rubber and a watch. Correcting fluids such as Tipp-Ex are *not* allowed! Essay questions test the ability to evaluate arguments and express viewpoints. Most students find this type of question the hardest to tackle and, on average, marks earned in the essay paper are generally lower than those for data response and objective test papers.

Start by reading through the paper and decide the topic covered by each question. Check the phrasing, noting particularly the key words. These will indicate what the examiner is looking for. For instance, '*compare and contrast*' means discuss similarities and differences, while '*elucidate*' means explain. Only answer questions on topics you have revised. Only attempt questions where you can answer each part. Once you have decided to attempt a question, briefly plan your answer. Many candidates like to gain confidence by tackling their best question first. Remember, there are two main reasons why capable students underachieve when writing essays:

(i) Candidates decide a question is about one topic (e.g. inflation) and then write all they know about that topic.
(ii) Candidates copy out a memorised answer to a similar past question.

You will do much better if you make an answer a well-reasoned explanation which is relevant to the set question. Develop a line of argument which has a beginning, a middle and an end. Try starting an essay by defining important economic terms given in the question. Then make clear any assumptions you are going to make. For example, suppose a question asked ' *"In the long run, all firms earn normal profits, only." Discuss.*' You might begin by defining firms and normal profits and then continue by initially assuming a perfectly competitive market structure. After establishing that the ability of firms to leave or enter the industry ensures that only normal profits are earned in perfectly competitive markets, in the long run, end the essay by evaluating an industry assuming imperfect competition.

Some questions, such as the one just discussed, lend themselves to a graphical analysis. Clear, neat and labelled graphs which are relevant to the set question can save a hundred words of explanation. It is always better to draw a series of graphs to advance an argument than to use one diagram for all stages of an argument. Avoid simply drawing diagrams and then ignoring them in your answer. Any graph should be an integral part of the essay. Draw the examiners' attention to a diagram by, say, stating 'in Figure 1 the firm sets output at $Q_1$'.

Write in clear, simple, short sentences. Often arguments are best developed by stating a point, explaining that point and then giving a real-world example. For instance, suppose part of a question asked, '*Explain the meaning of* ad valorem *taxes*'. You might write:

An *ad valorem* tax means value added tax [statement]. A given percentage is added to the selling price of a good and the resulting tax is passed on to the government by the seller [explanation]. For example, 15% VAT on the sale of a £200 camera would increase its market price to £230 and raise £30 of tax for the government [example].

Once a point has been fully developed, start a new paragraph. Try to relate your theory to the real world. Examiners are always impressed if a candidate can display an understanding of how economics influences the world around us. Remember, too, that good candidates avoid narrow interpretations and recognise that there is more than one approach which is valid.

Do *not* use unacceptable abbreviations — for example, 'gov' instead of government. When using acceptable abbreviations, first write out the word or phrase in full with the abbreviation following in brackets. For instance, 'International Monetary Fund (IMF)'. Thereafter, you may use the abbreviation.

It is absolutely essential that you complete the required number of questions. If you are running out of time and cannot complete an answer, do a full essay plan, including graphs where appropriate.

Be careful to avoid irrelevant answers, which not only earn no marks, but also waste valuable time which could have been used to earn marks from another

3

question. No marks are earned by waffle or by repeating points made earlier in the essay. Do not spend too much time on one particular question. Set out your work clearly and neatly. Use your economics. Above all, make sure that what you are writing is relevant and answers the set question.

## (b) Data Response Questions

For this paper you are going to need two pens, a ruler, a pencil, a rubber and a watch. Bring a calculator along. Remember to check that the batteries are not on the verge of running out.

Data response questions are especially good at testing the ability to apply economics and to quantify. There are two types of data response questions: *statistical* data, displayed as graphs, tables, charts or diagrams, and *literary* prose extracts from newspapers, journals, etc.

Each examining board tends to have its own 'house' style of data response question. Make sure you have familiarised yourself with examples drawn from previous papers. In the actual exam, allocate sufficient time for a careful study of the entire question. Here is a check-list of points to consider when tackling statistical data response questions:

(a) Ask yourself what key economic concepts are being tested by the question.
(b) Look at how the data have been obtained:
   (i) Are there any hidden assumptions or unsupported statements?
   (ii) Is the evidence used selective or biased?
   (iii) Is the survey *complete* (all the appropriate population have been included) or a *sample* (only some of the population have been included)?
(c) Identify major variables in the data:
   (i) Are the figures shown as absolute values; percentages; index numbers; billions of £s; thousands of people; etc?
   (ii) Which is the largest item?
   (iii) How do other items compare?
   (iv) Which variables are *stock values* (i.e. an amount at a given moment in time) or *flow values* (i.e. an amount per time period)?
(d) Observe any trends (patterns) in the data:
   (i) Which variables are rising, falling or stable?
   (ii) What is the percentage change in a variable? Use the equation

$$\text{percentage change} = \frac{(\text{present value} - \text{previous value})}{\text{previous value}} \times 100$$

   (iii) Are any variables cyclical?
(e) Is there a direct relationship between any variables in the data? Look out for:
   (i) *Causal relationships*, where the value of one variable determines the value of a second variable. However, remember that *unrelated variables* sometimes move closely together.
   (ii) *Lagged relationships*, where the current value of one variable is related to the previous value of a second variable.
(f) Relate your knowledge of theory to the data. Can you give reasons for relationships, trends or cycles observed?
(g) Always look for relevant data to explain your assertions.

Gain confidence in handling and interpreting statistical data by familiarising yourself with typical examples. Much of the data used by economists is presented as *time series* which show the value of a particular variable such as national income at different points in time. Great use is made of official statistics issued by the Central Statistical Office (CSO). Try to find time to look at CSO publications such as the 'Blue Book' (UK National Accounts) or the 'Pink Book' (Balance of Payments Statistics), held in the reference section of most public libraries.

Literary data response questions set a passage and sometimes supporting tables for analysis. Spend time reading the section of prose carefully. Many of the check-list of points given for use with statistical data can equally be applied to prose.

You are almost certainly going to be asked to identify and express *in your own words* the main features of the data. Try to avoid making sweeping or vague statements which are unsupported by evidence. Instead, explain essential features of the passage, quoting relevant phrases from the text only to support a point made in your own words. Always indicate such phrases by 'quotation marks'.

Many literary data response questions ask candidates to apply economic concepts. You are expected to relate relevant theories such as supply-and-demand or theory of the firm to the passage given. Remember that a variety of approaches may be required. Diagrams should be used if appropriate.

You may be asked to evaluate the data and then predict future trends or outcomes. Look back at the passage and identify key variables, relationships and economic concepts. Use these as the basis of your predictions. Avoid making a series of random predictions unsupported by information contained in the data provided.

## (c) Objective Questions

For this paper you are going to need a pencil, rubber, ruler, watch and calculator.

Objective questions are well suited to testing knowledge and understanding of theories, and deal with 'certainty' areas of economics. Hence, objective questions are set on topics where economists are agreed that there is a single correct answer. There are four types of objective question used in 'A' Level economics.

### (i) *Multiple-choice questions*

Multiple-choice questions contain a stem and a number of possible answers of which only one is correct.

**Example 1**

STEM      Industrial inertia occurs when:

DISTRACTORS
- A   labour is geographically immobile
- B   the share of manufacturing in national output declines
- C   firms fail to exploit economies of scale
- D   industry gains no cost advantage from any one site

KEY
- E   the initial reasons for location have disappeared

OPTIONS

The *stem* sets the question and then candidates have to choose between a number of incorrect *distractors* and the correct option, called the *key*. Some questions can be answered quickly. Look at the options and see whether there are any which can be immediately eliminated or accepted. If not, it is important not to be delayed by those questions requiring deep thought or lengthy calculations. Remember: each question, whether easy or difficult, carries the same number of marks. Make a note of such questions for later consideration and carry on working through the paper.

### (ii)  *Multiple-completion Questions*

Multiple-completion questions are similar to multiple-choice except that one or more of the options may be correct. The need to sort out which *options*, rather than which single option, may be correct means that multiple-completion take more time than multiple-choice. Each board has its own option code. If you can establish that one option is definitely a distractor, this reduces the number of answers possible from the option code.

### (iii)  *Matching-pairs Questions*

Matching-pairs questions are another variation on multiple-choice questions, where the same set of options are used for several questions. It is important to remember that the same option can be the correct answer for more than one question.

### (iv)  *Assertion–Reason Questions*

Candidates are given an assertion (first statement) followed by a reason (second statement). Consider the assertion and decide whether it is a true statement. Consider the reason and decide whether it is a true statement. If *both* the assertion and the reason are true, consider whether the reason is a correct explanation of the assertion. Each board then supplies its own option key.

Start by studying each statement *separately*. Mistakes usually follow from looking at both statements at the same time. Remember: it is quite possible for both statements to be correct and yet unrelated.

A range of strategies can be used when tackling the objective question paper. Only one rule must be followed: answer all the questions. Some candidates prefer to work through the paper, answering each question in turn, irrespective of the amount of time or degree of difficulty involved. However, we have already suggested that it may be better to hold over time-consuming questions until you have worked through all other questions. Be sure to treat each question carefully and not to give a wrong answer through carelessly misreading the stem or options. Questions with 'not' in the stem are particularly dangerous! For this type of question, the option to which you can answer 'no' is the correct solution.

If you begin to run out of time, work through the remaining questions allowing yourself a maximum of, say, 20 seconds per question. If time is about to run out completely, make sure you scribble down some answer and hope that at least one or two will be right.

In any case, DON'T PANIC. Both the authors wish you all the best and good luck in the final exams!

# 1 The Economic Problem

## 1.1 Fact Sheet

### (a) The Economic Problem

(i) Wants and needs are satisfied through the *consumption* (use) of goods and services.

(ii) *Outputs* (goods and services) are produced from inputs (resources) sometimes called *factors of production*. The four factors are land, labour, capital and entrepreneurs.

(iii) The *economic problem* arises because, while our resources are finite, our wants and needs are infinite.

(iv) All societies have to decide: what goods and services to produce; how to produce them; and who is to receive them.

- *Resource allocation* refers to a particular use of land, labour, capital and entrepreneurs.
- Economics studies the allocation of scarce resources between alternative uses.

### (b) Economic Methodology

Economics is a social science and uses scientific methods:

(i) A *hypothesis* (prediction) is constructed about economic behaviour which may be right or wrong.

(ii) A *model* is built describing the behaviour of economic variables (influencing factors) involved in the initial hypothesis.

(iii) The hypothesis is tested against *empirical* (real-world) evidence by use of the model.

(iv) If the hypothesis cannot be disproved, it becomes an accepted *theory*.

- Economists isolate the relationship between two variables by assuming *ceteris paribus* — i.e. that all other influencing factors are held constant.
- *Positive economics* deals with statements of fact which can be proved or disproved, and shows how the economy actually works.
- *Normative economics* deals with statements of opinion which cannot be proved or disproved, and suggests what should be done to solve economic problems.
- *Microeconomics* considers the behaviour of an individual consumer, firm and industry, and is mainly interested in resource allocation and relative prices.

● *Macroeconomics* considers the behaviour of the economy as a whole, and is mainly interested in national output, employment, the balance of payments and general prices.

### (c) Opportunity Cost

The decision to produce or consume one product involves the sacrifice of another product. The real or opportunity cost of an action is the next best foregone alternative.

● An *economic good* is in limited supply and possesses an opportunity cost — e.g. a car.
● However, a *free good* is not scarce and has no opportunity cost — e.g. sunshine.

### (d) Production Possibility Curves

A *production possibility curve* (*PPC*) is sometimes called an opportunity cost or transformation curve, and shows the combination of two goods a country can make in a given time period with resources fully employed (Figure 1.1). A PPC is drawn assuming a country has a fixed amount of resources and a constant state of technology.

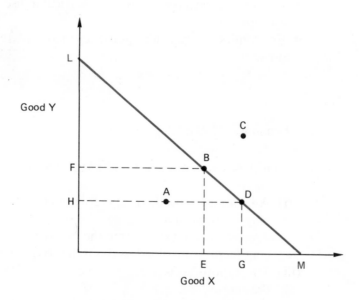

**Figure 1.1** A production possibility curve

  (i) LM is a PPC.
 (ii) Points under the PPC (e.g. A) imply resource underutilisation.
(iii) Points along the PPC (e.g. B) indicate a full employment of resources.
(iv) Points outside the PPC (e.g. C) are beyond the current productive capacity of the economy.
 (v) The opportunity cost of producing E amount of good X is LF of good Y.
(vi) The opportunity cost of reallocating resources from B to D is FH of good Y.

## (e) Economic Growth

*Economic growth* typically refers to an increase in a country's output of goods and services, and occurs following:
- (i) an increase in resources through:
    - (1) net investment;
    - (2) the discovery of natural resources;
    - (3) an increase in the labour force.
- (ii) a better use of existing resources through:
    - (1) using previously unemployed factors;
    - (2) training of the labour force;
    - (3) innovations which increase productivity;
    - (4) a reallocation of factors from low-productivity (e.g. agricultural) to high-productivity (e.g. manufacturing) sectors.

**Table 1.1**   The benefits and costs of economic growth

| Potential benefits of economic growth | Potential costs of economic growth |
| --- | --- |
| Improved standard of living | The opportunity cost of additional investment |
| Poverty can be reduced | Resulting externalities, including pollution |
| Opportunities for more leisure time | The depletion of non-renewable resources |
| A rise in people's expected life-spans | Alienation and stress on the labour force |

## (f) Types of Economic Systems

An *economic system* is the network of organisations used by a society to resolve the economic problem. There are three categories of economic system.

### (i)  *Free market economy*

- Resources are owned by households.
- Markets allocate resources through the *price mechanism*. An increase in price encourages firms to switch additional resources into the production of that good.
- Income depends on the market value of a resource. Factors in scarce supply and high demand are best rewarded.

### (ii)  *Planned* or *command economy*

- Resources are owned by the state.
- The state allocates resources, and sets production targets and growth rates according to its own view of peoples' wants.
- Income distribution is decided by the state, and ignores the scarcity value of a particular factor.

### (iii)  *Mixed economy*

In practice all economies are mixed where:
- Some resources are owned by the *public sector* (i.e. the government).
- Some resources are owned by the *private sector* (i.e. households).

**Table 1.2**  Problems of different economic systems

| Market economy can result in | Planned economy can result in |
|---|---|
| The non-production of public goods | Production not satisfying consumers' real wants |
| Monopolies reducing competition | |
| Production ignoring externalities | Reduced consumer sovereignty |
| An unequal distribution of income and wealth | Shortages and surpluses of products |
| | The forgone output of administrators |
| High unemployment | Reduced incentives lowering individual effort |

See also Section 10.1 (d) on *market failure*.

## 1.2  Data Response

**Worked Example 1.1**

One of the most fateful errors of our time is the belief that 'the problem of production' has been solved. Not only is this belief firmly held by people remote from production and therefore professionally unacquainted with the facts — it is held by virtually all the experts, the captains of industry, the economic managers in the governments of the world, the academic and not-so-academic economists, not to mention the economic journalists. For the rich countries, they say, the most important task now is 'education for leisure' and, for poor countries, the 'transfer of technology'.

Modern man does not experience himself as part of nature but as an outside force destined to dominate and conquer it. He even talks of battle with nature, forgetting that, if he won the battle, he would find himself on the losing side.

The illusion of power is based on the failure to distinguish between income and capital where this distinction matters most. Every economist and business-man is familiar with the distinction and applies it conscientiously and with considerable subtlety to all economic affairs — except where it really matters: namely the irreplaceable capital which man has not made, but simply found, and without which he can do nothing.

A businessman would not consider a firm to have solved its problems of production if he saw it was rapidly consuming its capital. How, then, could we overlook this vital fact when it comes to that very big firm, the economy of Spaceship Earth and, in particular, the economies of its rich passengers?
Source: E. F. Schumacher, *Small is Beautiful — A Study of Economics As If People Mattered* (London: Abacus, 1974), pp. 10–11

(a) From the passage distinguish between income and capital.  **(4 marks)**
(b) Explain the major problems which the author identifies nations are facing.
 **(8 marks)**
(c) What are the implications of the passage for government policies promoting economic growth?  **(8 marks)**

*Solution 1.1*

(a) Income is a flow value, and is the amount of money, goods or services received by an individual, firm or economy in a given time period, usually one year. Capital is a stock value; is one of the four factors of production and refers to producer goods used to manufacture other goods. However, the author is using a broader definition of capital than is generally employed by economists to include the Earth's natural resources. Tra-ditional economists count gifts of nature as land.

(b) The passage advances two points of view concerning the problems facing rich nations. Most traditional economists argue that great advances in technology have allowed rich countries to produce such a surplus of goods and services that the bulk of human wants and needs can now be satisfied. The problem is not so much one of scarcity as of knowing what to do with the large number of workers now no longer needed in the manufacturing process and who require training in the use of free time. Schumacher argues that the major problem facing rich nations is the over-rapid consumption of irreplaceable natural resources such as metals and minerals. Hence, economic growth is only achieved by running down our 'capital' — that is, our stock of finite natural resources.

Poor countries, it is argued, do not have a sufficient infrastructure to allow for capital accumulation through net investment, either because there is no surplus after output has been used to satisfy basic needs or because the nation lacks the technology to generate such surpluses. A transfer of 'production know-how' from rich to poor nations would overcome this last problem.

(c) Economic growth is typically taken to mean an increase in a country's output of goods and services, and occurs through either an increase in the amount of resources available or the better use of existing resources. Measures which encourage increases in production have been advanced by successive governments because output increases allow more wants and needs to be satisfied. Measures to encourage economic growth through net investment include subsidies to firms building new factories, particularly in depressed areas, and tax incentives to firms buying new machinery.

The passage highlights the concern of some economists for what they see as an unpleasant side-effect of economic growth: the unacceptably high level of consumption of resources which are gifts of nature and which once used cannot be replaced. Sustained economic growth implies an accelerating rate of consumption for non-renewable natural resources. Governments may be concerned to ensure that the system of resource allocation used takes full account of such negative externalities, as well as any pollution generated by high growth.

For instance, the price mechanism does not immediately take account of the depletion of finite resources such as oil. As the world's resources begin to reach exhaustion, restricted supply would then result in higher prices. But, in the immediate term, governments might want consumers and producers to pay some penalty for using irreplaceable resources, by imposing an indirect tax on their consumption. For example, substantial taxes on petrol reduces consumption but encourages conservation.

Alternatively, the government might want to encourage conservation of scarce gifts of nature by offering subsidies to firms which recycle waste products. For example, some local authorities convert refuse collected from households into electricity by burning waste at plants.

Finally, government energy policy can be adjusted. One man-made source of energy is nuclear power, the use of which avoids the depletion of finite resources such as oil, coal and gas. The government might want to achieve economic growth in the energy sector by building more nuclear power stations. However, this in itself creates more problems because of the high long-term economic and social costs of disposing of radioactive waste.

## 1.3 Objective Questions

**Example 1.2**

A worker is currently earning £200 for a 40 hour week. The management offer a 12% wage increase or a basic wage of £205 and a reduction in the working week to 38 hours. What is the opportunity cost if the worker opts for a 38 hour week?

**A**  2 hours      **B**  38 hours      **C**  £5      **D**  £19      **E**  £24

**Example 1.3**

The production possibility frontier for a market economy will necessarily shift immediately following a change in:

**A**  income distribution      **B**  wealth distribution      **C**  the stock of capital
**D**  population size      **E**  resource allocation

*Examples 1.4–1.6 refer to the following diagram, which shows a range of production possibilities for a country.*

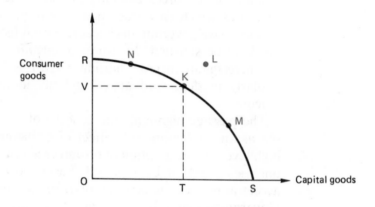

**Example 1.4**

An economy operating at point K can eventually reach point L:

**A**  by moving to point M      **B**  by moving to point N
**C**  by improving its standard of living      **D**  by employing idle resources
**E**  never

**Example 1.5**

A movement from point K to point N results in:

**A**  constant returns in the production of both goods
**B**  decreasing returns in the production of consumer goods
**C**  constant scale economies in the production of both goods
**D**  decreasing scale economies in the production of consumer goods
**E**  an improvement in social welfare

**Example 1.6**

If the economy is currently producing 0V consumer goods, the opportunity cost involved is:

**A**  OR consumer goods      **B**  0S capital goods      **C**  VR consumer goods
**D**  TS capital goods      **E**  0T capital goods

## Example 1.7

The production possibility boundary for a country producing only two goods, X and Y, is given by the formula $Y = 100 - 20X$, where 100 is the maximum amount of Y that a country can make. Assuming the full employment of resources, the opportunity cost of producing one extra unit of X is:

**A** 1/100Y     **B** 1/20Y     **C** 1/5Y     **D** 5Y     **E** 20Y

## Example 1.8

The essential characteristic of a market economy is:

**A** consumer sovereignty   **B** consumer surplus     **C** producer surplus
**D** marginal cost pricing   **E** public corporations

## Example 1.9

Only in a pure command economy does production:
- **A** reflect the preferences of households
- **B** reflect the preferences of firms
- **C** experience diminishing returns
- **D** respond to directives
- **E** respond to prices

## Example 1.10

Which of the following measures is most likely to encourage economic growth, directly?

**A** redistributing income        **B** increasing taxation
**C** increasing consumption     **D** improving the state of technology
**E** reducing the rate of inflation

*Select your answers to Examples 1.11–1.13 by means of the following code:*
**A** *if 1, 2 and 3 are all correct*
**B** *if 1 and 2 only are correct*
**C** *if 2 and 3 only are correct*
**D** *if 1 only is correct*

## Example 1.11

Normative statements in economics:
**1** can be tested empirically      **2** make policy recommendations
**3** depend on value judgements

## Example 1.12

Economics studies the allocation of:
**1** economic goods only    **2** consumer goods only    **3** free goods

## Example 1.13

Economic growth usually results in:
**1** an increase in living standards      **2** a depletion of natural resources
**3** positive externalities

# 1.4 Essays

**Example 1.14**

Explain the basis on which economists in classifying economic systems distinguish between 'market' and 'command' economies. On what basis, if any, is it possible to say which type of economy is superior?

(JMB 1987)

- Establish criteria such as resource ownership, for comparing market and command economies.
- Explain how welfare criteria can be used to judge the success of an individual economic system.
- One economic system is superior to another only if it is better able to satisfy welfare criteria. Discuss the evidence.
- Avoid making subjective, political statements of opinion.

*Solution 1.14*

A market economy is an economic system where resources are owned by individuals and allocated by the price mechanism without government intervention. In a command economy, the government owns resources and decides on the type and quantity to be made. A study of comparative economic systems will try to identify and contrast characteristics common to both types of economy. For instance, *property rights* are the rules that define the use to which resources may be put. In market economies, individuals are free to buy and sell land, labour and capital, provided that they do not infringe the legal property rights of others. In a command economy, individuals can own consumer goods but they are not allowed to own industrial plant or machinery. All non-labour resources are owned by the state.

Different economic systems have different methods of resolving the problem of scarcity. Market economies use the *price mechanism* to allocate resources. All goods, services and resources have a market price. An increase in consumer demand raises price and encourages a firm to increase production of that good by transferring resources out of the manufacture of less profitable products. In command economies, the state allocates resources according to its own view of what people want. A body of central planners decide what proportion of resources to devote to consumer and producer goods. They then set production targets and arrange for the supply of necessary inputs. Firms aim not to make a profit but to meet production targets.

It can be seen that the decision-making process in command economies is collectivist and centralised. The government is the single most important economic institution. On the other hand, decision-making in market economies is highly individualistic and decentralised. The role of the state is limited to collecting taxes to pay for public goods such as defence, and enforcing property rights.

The method of motivating economic agents varies between the two systems. In market economies, jobs in high demand but short supply command high wages. Successful entrepreneurs receive profits for taking on the risk and responsibility of organising production. Hence, income and wealth distributions are unequal. In command economies, limited wage differentials do exist to reward extra effort. However, it is the sense of 'shared purpose' springing from the common ownership of resources that is meant to act as the prime 'moral' incentive to work.

The success of an economic system lies in its ability to use resources to satisfy as many wants as possible. Welfare economics supplies a number of tests which can be used to judge the absolute efficiency of an economic system. There are two main tests:

(a) is it possible to reallocate resources and increase output?
(b) is it possible to reallocate resources and make a consumer better off without making anyone else worse off?

The system which best meets those conditions will be superior. Before considering empirical evidence, it is important to note that real-world examples such as the USA and the USSR only approximate to theoretical market and command models.

Economic theory suggests that a competitive market economy automatically brings about an optimal resource allocation. However, *market failure* occurs when some private-sector firms in the USA do not take full account of the spill-over effects of production such as pollution. Frictions in factor markets have resulted in mass unemployment and a general depression. Moreover, efficiency criteria make no statement about the 'fairness' of an uneven distribution of income and wealth in the USA.

Data suggest that there is hardly any unemployment in the USSR. However, critics argue that this has only been achieved by massive overmanning. Productivity and standards of living could be raised following a reallocation of resources. Modern economies are highly specialised, interdependent and complex. In the absence of market prices, planners have insufficient information on which to make welfare-maximising decisions. Distorted information stops planners taking full account of production and consumption externalities.

In conclusion, it can be seen that comparison of market and command economies is difficult and complex. Final judgement depends on the importance placed on a particular measure. For example, in terms of productivity, evidence suggests that market economies are superior to command economies; in terms of unemployment levels, evidence suggests that command economies are superior to market economies.

**Example 1.15**

What do you understand by 'opportunity cost'? Why is this concept relevant to the allocation of resources of a market economy?                    (NISEC 1987)

- This question tests your understanding of the relationship between opportunity cost and the economic problem.
- Use examples to explain the link between opportunity cost and resource allocation.
- Production possibility curves can be used to illustrate the opportunity cost of resource allocation at a macroeconomic level.

*Solution 1.15*

Humans have material wants and needs which are satisfied by consuming goods and services. At any moment in time, a country has a fixed amount of resources available for the creation of goods and services. Scarcity exists because a nation cannot produce sufficient products to satisfy *every* want and need. Therefore, society has to decide which wants and needs will be met.

In short, the 'economic problem' hinges on the concept of scarcity and choice. Society must choose what is to be produced, but the decision to make one good necessarily results in the loss of an alternative product. This is the concept of opportunity cost, which states the cost of obtaining one product in terms of the forgone quantity of another product that could have been made instead.

In a market economy, resource allocation is based on the free movement of prices. Comparing the prices of two products allows consumers and producers to calculate the opportunity cost of different goods. For example, it follows that if the price of apples is 20p and of pears 10p, the opportunity cost of one apple is two pears. A change in relative price affects the opportunity cost of a product.

Opportunity cost, then, is a key economic concept which focuses the attention of producers and consumers on the consequences of decision-making. The particular relevance of opportunity cost to resource allocation in a market economy at a macro level can be illustrated by using production possibility curves.

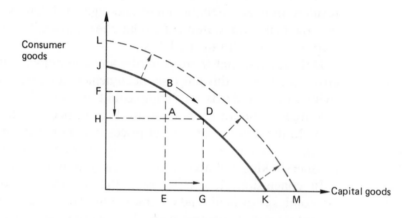

The production possibility curve, JK in the diagram, shows the combinations of consumer goods and capital goods that a country can produce in one year with resources fully employed. The shape of the curve is due to the existence of decreasing returns in production. Points under the curve, such as A, imply an underutilisation of resources. Points above the curve are beyond the current productive capacity of the economy. Assume that the country is at point B. The opportunity cost of producing F consumer goods is the extra amount of producer goods, K − E, that could be made instead.

Consider now the opportunity cost of a reallocation of resources which results in economic growth. It is not possible to increase the output of producer goods without reducing the manufacture of consumer goods. The expansion along the production possibility curve from B to D increases the amount of producer goods by G − E at an opportunity cost of F − H fewer consumer goods.

In the next time period, the extra plant and machinery now available increases the ability of the economy to manufacture both consumer and capital goods. Economic growth shifts the production possibility curve to the right, to LM. However, the production and consumption of extra goods and services may cause negative externalities such as pollution and congestion. These should also be included when calculating the true opportunity cost of economic growth.

Opportunity cost is a key economic concept which reminds us that, for any given resource allocation in a market economy, there is an alternative forgone. This essay has considered the particular example of the opportunity cost involved in economic growth.

# 1.5  Solutions to Objective Questions

*Solution 1.2   Answer:* **D**

A 12% wage increase on a 40 hour week results in a pay increase of £200 × 12/100 = £24. A worker opting for a 40 hour week now earns £200 + £24 = £224. Therefore, if the worker elects to work 38 hours and earn £205, he will be forgoing £19.

*Solution 1.3   Answer:* **C**

A production possibility curve (PPC) is sometimes called a production possibility frontier. A PPC is drawn, assuming that a nation's stock of resources, including capital, is fixed. A change in the stock of capital affects the ability of a country to produce goods and services and so shifts the PPC.

  **A** and **B** ⇒ Changes in income and wealth distribution may affect patterns of consumption and production, which may *eventually* affect the PPC.

  **D** ⇒ The increase in population size could be the result of an increase in dependants, such as children, which does not immediately increase the country's ability to produce goods.

  **E** ⇒ A change in resource allocation, where factors are moved out of the production of one type of consumer good and into another, will not affect the position of the PPC.

*Solutions 1.4–1.6 refer to the following diagram:*

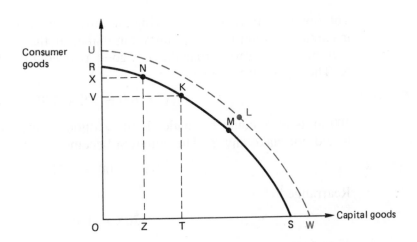

*Solution 1.4   Answer:* **A**

The movement from point K to point L can only come about if the production possibility curve (PPC) shifts to the right, to UW. This requires an increase in the productive capacity of the economy. Moving along the PPC from K to M shifts resources out of the production of consumer goods and into the production of capital goods. Additional capital goods can be used to make more consumer and producer goods and the economy can now be at point L. Other options are wrong because:
**B** ⇒ reduces the productive capacity of the economy;
**C** ⇒ is the *effect* of moving to L and not the *cause*;
**D** ⇒ point K lies on the PPC, so that there are no idle resources available.

*Solution 1.5   Answer:* **B**

Because the PPC is non-linear, resources moved out of the production of capital goods produce fewer and fewer additional consumer goods — i.e. decreasing returns in the production of consumer goods. For instance, the movement from point K to point N along the initial PPC reduces capital goods by TZ and increases consumer goods by VX. A similar movement from N to R reduces capital goods by the same amount as when moving from K to N, but, because of decreasing returns, there is a much smaller increase in consumer goods of XR.

Other options are wrong because:

**A** ⇒ is true only if the PPC is linear;

**C** and **D** ⇒ scale economies are a long-run concept (see Table 5.4);

**E** ⇒ there is insufficient information to deduce whether or not society prefers N to K.

*Solution 1.6   Answer:* **D**

If the economy devotes all of its resources to producing capital goods, then it could produce 0S. Similarly, if it devotes all of its resources to producing consumer goods, then it could produce 0R.

If the country produces 0V consumer goods, then it is also producing 0T capital goods and forgoing TS capital goods. Since opportunity cost is measured in terms of the forgone alternative, TS capital goods is the opportunity cost of 0V consumer goods.

*Solution 1.7   Answer:* **E**

The opportunity cost of producing an extra unit of X is found by dividing the maximum amount of Y a country can make, by the total amount of X.

If the economy were to make only good Y, it would make zero amount of good X. The equation becomes:

$$Y = 100 - 0X = 100$$

100 units of Y could be made. If the economy were to make only good X, it would not make any Y. The equation becomes:

$$0Y = 100 - 20X$$

Rearranged,

$$20X = 100$$

Therefore,

$$X = 5$$

The opportunity cost of producing an extra unit of X is 100Y/5X — i.e. 20 units of Y. (Note that the opportunity cost of additional Y can be calculated by dividing total X by total Y.)

*Solution 1.8   Answer:* **A**

In a market economy, households have consumer sovereignty and determine what is produced, by 'voting' with their purchases. For instance, if consumers demand more of a product, price rises and more is supplied. Other options are wrong because:

**B** ⇒ consumers do not necessarily enjoy consumer surplus;

C $\Rightarrow$ firms do not necessarily enjoy producer surplus;
D $\Rightarrow$ some firms will not use a marginal cost pricing policy;
E $\Rightarrow$ public corporations are nationalised industries and a feature of *mixed* economies.

*Solution 1.9   Answer:* **D**

A planned economy is run by the state and *directives* (instructions) are used to organise production. Other options are wrong because:
C $\Rightarrow$ all types of economic system experience diminishing returns;
E $\Rightarrow$ prices are not used as a method of regulating production in a *pure* command economy.

*Solution 1.10   Answer:* **D**

Economic growth occurs following an increase in, or better use of, resources. An increase in technology improves a country's ability to produce goods and therefore results in economic growth.

A $\Rightarrow$ An income redistribution from poor to rich would tend to reduce demand and so hinder economic growth.

*Solution 1.11   Answer:* **C**

Normative economics involves statements of opinion which cannot be proved or disproved against real-world (empirical) evidence. Therefore, option **1** is incorrect.

*Solution 1.12   Answer:* **D**

Economics studies the allocation of *scarce* resources between alternative uses. Economic goods are scarce, while free goods are not scarce and are therefore not usually studied by economists.

**2** $\Rightarrow$ Is incorrect because it implies that other types of scarce goods such as producer goods are *not* studied.

*Solution 1.13   Answer:* **B**

Externalities are the spill-over effects of consumption or production. Economic growth involves additional production, which usually causes negative externalities such as pollution. Option **3** is incorrect.

# 2 Demand

## 2.1 Fact Sheet

### (a) Definition of Demand

- *Demand* is the amount of a good consumers are both willing and able to buy at a given price.
- *Consumer surplus* is the difference between the maximum a consumer would pay for the good and the price actually paid.
- A *demand curve* shows the amount of a good consumers are willing and able to buy at different prices.
- The amount of a good demanded depends on:
    - (i) price;
    - (ii) the conditions of demand.

### (b) Movements along a Demand Curve

- A change in price results in a movement along a demand curve, resulting in a change in *quantity demanded*.
- A change in the price of a good *NEVER* shifts the demand curve for that good.
- In Figure 2.1 an increase in price causes a *contraction* in demand, and a decrease in price results in an *expansion* in demand.

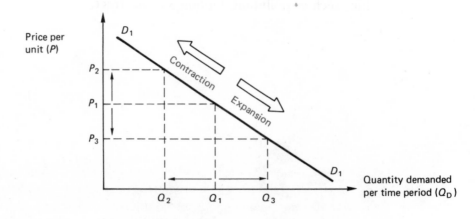

**Figure 2.1** Movements along a demand curve

## (c) Increases and Decreases in Demand

- A demand curve is drawn assuming *ceteris paribus* — i.e. that all factors influencing demand are being held constant except price. The *conditions of demand* refer to those factors held constant, and include:
  - (i) the real income of consumers;
  - (ii) the price of other goods:
    - (1) in competitive demand (substitutes);
    - (2) in joint demand (complements);
  - (iii) consumer taste;
  - (iv) advertising;
  - (v) expectations about the economy;
  - (vi) the population size and structure.
- A change in one of these conditions affects the level of demand at all prices and results in a shift in the demand curve.
- Figure 2.2 illustrates the effect of a decrease in demand.

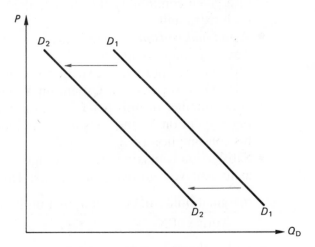

**Figure 2.2**   A decrease in demand

*Cause*:
a decrease in real income;
or an increase in the price of a complement;
or a decrease in the price of a substitute;
or an adverse movement in consumer taste;
or a reduction in advertising for this good;
or reduced expectations about the economy;
or a decrease in the population.

*Effect*:
the demand curve shifts to the left.

## (d) Income and Substitution Effects

- The *income effect* occurs when the price of a good falls and the consumer can maintain current consumption for less expenditure. Provided that the good is normal, some of the resulting increase in real income is used to buy more of this product. If the good is inferior, an increase in income is used to buy more of a superior substitute and less of this product.

- The *substitution effect* occurs when the price of a good falls and the consumer substitutes more of this product for others.
- The demand curve of a *giffen good* (a good whose demand falls as its price falls) such as potatoes slopes upwards from left to right because the income and substitution effects work in opposite directions and the income effect outweighs the substitution effect.

### (e) Utility

- *Utils* are used to measure satisfaction.
- *Total utility* is the amount of satisfaction obtained by consuming units of a good.
- *Marginal utility (MU)* is the extra satisfaction obtained from consuming one more unit of a good.
- The *law of diminishing marginal utility* states that the more a consumer has of a given commodity the smaller the satisfaction gained from consuming each extra unit.
- A *rational consumer* spends his income in order to maximise satisfaction. The consumer compares:
  (i) the utils per extra £ spent on X, using the equation $MU_X/P_X$, with
  (ii) the utils per extra £ spent on Y, using the equation $MU_Y/P_Y$.
- If the number of utils per £ spent on X is greater than the number of utils per £ spent on Y, the consumer can increase his satisfaction by increasing his consumption of X.
- Satisfaction is maximised by arranging expenditure among commodities so as to achieve *equi-marginal returns*. This occurs when:

$$\frac{\text{marginal utility of X}}{\text{price of X}} = \frac{\text{marginal utility of Y}}{\text{price of Y}}$$

- Utility theory requires consumers to be able to measure satisfaction.

### (f) Indifference Curves

- An *indifference curve* shows the combinations of two goods whose consumption yields equal total satisfaction to the consumer.
- A *budget line* or *income line* shows all the combinations of two goods the consumer can buy, given a fixed income and constant prices.
- A rational consumer maximises satisfaction by adjusting his expenditure between two goods so as to be at the point on the budget line tangential (just touching) to an indifference curve furthest from the origin — i.e. point A in Figure 2.3.

  In Figure 2.3, JK is the budget line of the consumer, and $I_1$ and $I_2$ are indifference curves. $I_2$ is further from the origin and yields a higher level of satisfaction than does $I_1$. To maximise satisfaction, the consumer will select point A and buy B amount of good X, and C amount of good Y.
- An increase in income would result in a parallel shift to the right in the budget line JK.
- An increase in price of good X would pivot the budget line around point J towards the origin.
- Indifference curves can be used to isolate the income effect and substitution effect of a change in price. See Example 2.11.

Good Y

J

C - - - - - - - - - - - A

$I_2$
$I_1$

Good X

B          K

**Figure 2.3**  Consumer equilibrium

## 2.2 Data Response

**Worked Example 2.1**

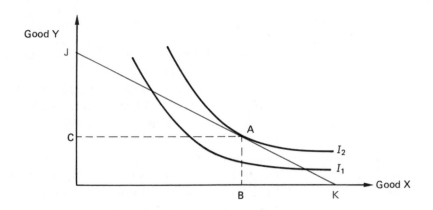

| AVERAGE HOUSE PRICES | Detached House | Semi-det House | Terraced House | Change in Quarter | Annual Change |
|---|---|---|---|---|---|
| UNITED KINGDOM | £59,480 | £39,300 | £31,380 | +4% | +12% |
| NORTHERN IRELAND | £41,320 | £25,550 | £18,100 | +2% | +5% |
| NORTH WEST | £47,990 | £29,020 | £19,730 | +2% | +6% |
| WALES | £44,640 | £28,120 | £22,310 | +3% | +8% |
| SCOTLAND | £47,490 | £34,540 | £31,490 | +2% | +5% |
| WEST MIDLANDS | £45,430 | £28,130 | £21,070 | +2% | +4% |
| SOUTH WEST | £57,530 | £38,560 | £32,870 | +4% | +13% |
| NORTHERN | £44,260 | £27,310 | £20,290 | -1% | +3% |
| YORKSHIRE & HUMBERSIDE | £43,510 | £26,420 | £18,550 | +1% | +6% |
| EAST MIDLANDS | £43,450 | £27,630 | £22,270 | +2% | +11% |
| OUTER SOUTH EAST | £67,820 | £46,110 | £37,890 | +5% | +16% |
| EAST ANGLIA | £52,860 | £35,520 | £30,860 | +1% | +10% |
| GREATER LONDON | £100,820 | £71,630 | £58,800 | +7% | +21% |
| OUTER MET. AREA | £88,160 | £58,210 | £47,290 | +6% | +16% |

House prices increased by 4% in the third quarter of the year, the same rise as in the previous quarter, and giving an annual increase of 12% to the end of September, according to the latest house price survey by the Nationwide Building Society. The society says the 4% increase for the UK showed that rises were not abating. The annual rate of house price increase, 12%, was 2% higher than in the second quarter, and if the present high level of housing activity continued it was likely that the annual rates of rises would be close to 15% by the end of the year. As the rate of increase continues well in excess of the increase in average earnings (7.5%), the Nationwide points out that the house price/earnings ratio has increased to 3.54, compared with the long-term average of 3.25.
Source: 'House prices', by Christopher Warman, *The Times*, 13 October 1986

(a) What evidence is there for believing that the real price of housing is rising?
(b) Describe the regional variations in house prices.
(c) Suggest causes for the regional variations you have described.
(d) What are the economic implications of the regional variations you have described?

23

*Solution 2.1*

(a)   (i)  The annual rate of house price increases (12%) is greater than increase in average earnings (7.5%).

     (ii)  The price of an average house has risen from 3.25 times average yearly income to 3.54 times annual earnings.

(b)  Taking semi-detached as an example, the average UK house costs £39 000.

     (i)  Only house prices in the outer south-east, outer metropolitan and Greater London areas exceed the national average. In general, the further an area from London the lower the price of housing.

     (ii)  The rate of change in house prices conforms to the same pattern, except that the annual change in the south-west (13%) also exceeds the average (12%).

(c)  The price of houses is determined by the local conditions of supply and demand.

     (i)  For instance, house prices in the south-east are highest because:

        (1)  the 'green belt' (planning restrictions) around London means that the supply of land for housing is limited and expensive;

        (2)  average earnings are higher than elsewhere;

        (3)  a larger percentage of the working population is in work than elsewhere.

     (ii)  Low average earnings and high unemployment in the midlands, the north, Northern Ireland and Wales means that house prices are below the national average in these areas.

(d)   (i)  The geographical mobility of labour from north to south may be reduced if workers are unable to afford higher house prices.

     (ii)  Moreover, since the annual rate of change in house prices is higher in the south than in the north, this barrier to labour immobility will increase over time.

     (iii)  Houseowners who have paid off their mortgage will have a more valuable asset if their house is in the south-east than elsewhere. The distribution of wealth becomes more regionally uneven.

     (iv)  First-time buyers in the south-east are likely to have a larger mortgage than are those in other areas.

# 2.3  Objective Questions

### Example 2.2

Which one of the following is not held constant when a demand curve is drawn?

A  households' real income         B  households' taste
C  the prices of competing goods     D  the price of the good itself
E  the prices of complementary goods

### Example 2.3

The demand curve for a normal good shifts to the left when:

A  prices of complementary goods rise  B  the price of this good rises
C  prices of substitutes rise         D  unit cost rises
E  the tax on this product is decreased

## Example 2.4

A basic assumption of all demand theories is that consumers allocate their incomes so as to maximise:

**A**  their wealth          **B**  total utility          **C**  their savings

**D**  marginal utility       **E**  current consumption

## Example 2.5

The table shows the total utility gained from consuming each of three goods:

| Units of good | X | Y | Z |
|---|---|---|---|
| 1 | 40 | 16 | 10 |
| 2 | 48 | 30 | 20 |
| 3 | 52 | 42 | 30 |
| 4 | 54 | 52 | 40 |
| 5 | 52 | 60 | 50 |

The consumer experiences diminishing marginal utility in the consumption of:

**A**  X alone          **B**  Y alone          **C**  Y and Z alone

**D**  Z and X alone      **E**  Y and X alone

## Example 2.6

| Good | Price | Quantity | Marginal utility |
|---|---|---|---|
| A | 20p | 6 | 10 |
| B | 30p | 2 | ? |

If a consumer buys the quantities of A and B shown above and is maximising his satisfaction, what is the marginal utility derived from good B?

**A**  3.33      **B**  5      **C**  6      **D**  10      **E**  15

## Example 2.7

A consumer has the following demand schedule for chocolate:

| Number of bars | 1 | 2 | 3 | 4 | 5 |
|---|---|---|---|---|---|
| Price | 60p | 50p | 40p | 30p | 20p |

If the price of chocolate is 40p and the consumer buys three bars, what is his consumer surplus?

**A**  30p      **B**  40p      **C**  50p      **D**  60p      **E**  70p

## Example 2.8

The diagram shows a demand curve for journeys over a toll bridge.

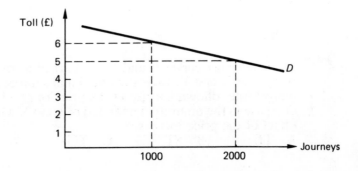

A reduction in the toll from £6 to £5 increases consumer surplus by:
A  £500      B  £1000      C  £1500      D  £6000      E  £7500

Example 2.9

Following a fall in the price of an inferior good:
A  the substitution and income effects are both positive
B  the substitution and income effects are both negative
C  the substitution effect is zero
D  only the income effect is positive
E  only the income effect is negative

Example 2.10

The diagram below shows a consumer's indifference map. RS is the consumer's budget line, and points J, K, L, M and N show different combinations of goods Y and X.

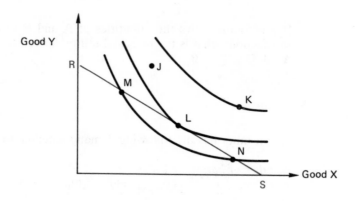

It can be seen that the consumer would prefer:
A  no one combination to all others      B  combination M to combination N
C  combination N to combination J         D  combination L to all others
E  combination K to all others

Example 2.11

The indifference curves $I_1$ and $I_2$ are part of a consumers' indifference map for two goods X and Y. JK is the individual's initial budget line, and JL is his new budget line following a rise in the price of good X. Which distance shows the decrease in the quantity demanded of good X which is the result of the income effect of the price increase?
A  TL          B  ST          C  TU          D  RT          E  RS

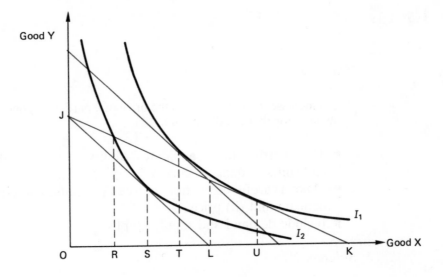

*Select your answers to Examples 2.12–2.15 by means of the following code:*

**A** if *1, 2* and *3* are all correct
**B** if *1* and *2* only are correct
**C** if *2* and *3* only are correct
**D** if *1* only is correct

## Example 2.12

The demand for apples is likely to increase following:
1 a fall in the price of apples
2 a rise in the price of pears
3 an increase in income

## Example 2.13

A good in composite demand has:
1 many uses
2 many substitutes
3 a high price elasticity of demand

## Example 2.14

The law of diminishing marginal utility states that the more a consumer has of a given commodity the:
1 lower the satisfaction from each extra unit consumed
2 lower the price of each extra unit consumed
3 lower the total level of satisfaction enjoyed

## Example 2.15

A fall in the price of a giffen good results in:
1 a negative income effect
2 a positive substitution effect
3 a negative price effect

## 2.4 Essays

**Example 2.16**

'An increase in demand raises the price of a particular good. An increase in price cuts demand for that good'. Discuss.

- The question tests candidates' ability to distinguish between movements and shifts in demand curves.
- Make a careful distinction between the cause and effect of an increase in (i) demand and (ii) price.
- Include demand and supply graphs.

*Solution 2.16*

Demand refers to the amount of a good consumers are willing and able to buy at a given price. The amount of a good consumers are initially willing and able to buy at different market prices is shown by the demand curve $D_1$ in Figure 1.

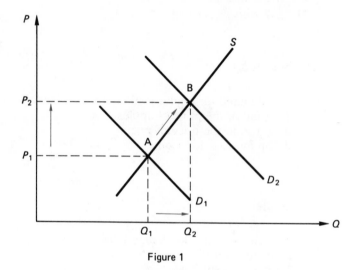

Figure 1

Assume that the good in question is apples. The demand curve $D_1$ is drawn, assuming that all factors influencing the demand for apples are held constant, except price. A change in a condition of demand invalidates this *ceteris paribus* assumption. For example, a rise in the price of a substitute good, such as oranges, encourages consumers to switch to alternative commodities, such as apples. Hence, the demand for apples increases at all prices. The increase in demand has the effect of shifting the demand curve $D_1$ to the right, to $D_2$. The price of apples rises from $P_1$ to $P_2$, causing an expansion along the supply (S) curve from A to B. Initial analysis suggests that 'an increase in demand raises the price of a particular good'.

An increase in the price of a good also affects the amount demanded by consumers. However, unlike an increase in demand, an increase in price does not shift the demand curve for the good. Again using apples as an example, an increase in price results in a fall in the quantity demanded, causing a contraction along the demand curve from A to B in Figure 2.

In fact, the fall in the quantity demanded in Figure 2 can only have been caused by a decrease in supply causing the supply curve to shift to the left and the price to rise. In these circumstances, 'an increase in price cuts demand for that good'.

28

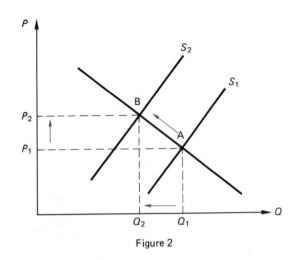

Figure 2

Analysis has so far supported both statements given in the question. By itself, an increase in demand does raise the price of a good. However, the price increase is the effect and not the cause of the increase in demand. By itself, an increase in price does cut demand. However, the price increase is now the cause and not the effect of the fall in demand.

In conclusion, it can be seen that the two statements in the question are correct if considered separately but are incorrect if linked together.


**Example 2.17**

How does a rational consumer allocate a fixed income between the purchase of two commodities? Would the consumer always use an increase in income to buy more of both goods?

- The question can be answered, using one of three consumer demand theories: marginal utility; revealed preference; or indifference curves. Use only one.
- Establish an initial position of consumer equilibrium.
- Illustrate the effect of an increase in income.
- Distinguish between normal and inferior goods.

*Solution 2.17*

A rational consumer is one who attempts to maximise satisfaction. A number of consumer demand theories, including marginal utility and revealed preference theory, explain how the consumer allocates income. This answer uses indifference curves.

An indifference curve (IC) shows combinations of two goods whose consumption yields equal total utility to the consumer. Figure 1 shows an indifference map — i.e. a large number of ICs. ICs further from the origin involve larger quantities of goods and give more satisfaction than do ICs close to the origin. In Figure 1, the budget line (JK) shows combinations of goods A and B the consumer can buy, given a fixed income and constant prices. The consumer can select any combination of A and B lying on or below the budget line. A consumer selecting point L is irrational, because by buying more of good B and less of good A the consumer can move to point M, which is on a higher IC, offering a greater level of satisfaction.

While the consumer would prefer to be on an even higher IC at point N, he

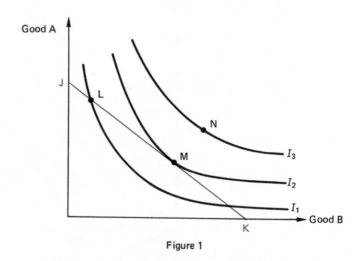

Figure 1

cannot afford to buy this combination. Therefore, satisfaction is maximised at point M, where the budget line is just touching the highest attainable IC.

An increase in income does not affect the position of the ICs. An increase in income means that the consumer is able to buy more of both goods, and so the budget line shifts to the right. In Figures 2 and 3, the new budget line is RS.

If A and B are normal goods, the consumer will use the extra income to buy more of both. In Figure 2, the new position of equilibrium is point N, where the budget line, RS, touches the highest attainable IC.

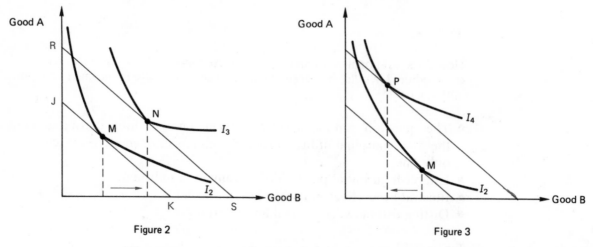

Figure 2          Figure 3

However, some goods are inferior, and an increase in income results in a fall in the amount of the good bought. Assume that good B is inferior. Initially the consumer buys good B only, because the superior substitute, good A, is beyond his means. The increase in income means that he can now afford to reduce his consumption of B and buy more of A. The new position of equilibrium is shown by point P in Figure 3.

It has been shown that a consumer will not always use an increase in income to buy more of both goods if one product is an inferior good.

## 2.5 Solutions to Objective Questions

*Solution 2.2   Answer:* **D**

When drawing a demand curve, all the factors influencing demand are held constant except price. Options **A**, **B**, **C** and **E** are incorrect, because they are all examples of conditions of demand held fixed when a demand curve is drawn.

*Solution 2.3   Answer:* **A**

If prices of complementary goods increase, the demand for this good decreases, resulting in the demand curve shifting to the left. Other options are incorrect because:

**B** ⇒ causes a movement (contraction) along the demand curve;
**C** ⇒ increases demand for the product;
**D** ⇒ shifts the supply curve to the left;
**E** ⇒ results in the price of the good falling and demand extending.

*Solution 2.4   Answer:* **B**

While consumers are interested in all the options stated, rational consumers seek to maximise their total utility or satisfaction.

   **D** ⇒ Is incorrect because consumers maximise their total utility by ensuring that the marginal utility per penny or pound spent for each good is equal.

*Solution 2.5   Answer:* **E**

This question requires students to calculate the marginal utility (MU) for each product. Marginal utility is the change (Δ) in total utility (TU) resulting from consuming one extra unit (Q) and is found, using the equation $MU = \Delta TU / \Delta Q$.

| Units of good | X | | Y | | Z | |
|---|---|---|---|---|---|---|
| | TU | MU | TU | MU | TU | MU |
| 1 | 40 | 40 | 16 | 16 | 10 | 10 |
| 2 | 48 | 8 | 30 | 14 | 20 | 10 |
| 3 | 52 | 4 | 42 | 12 | 30 | 10 |
| 4 | 54 | 2 | 52 | 10 | 40 | 10 |
| 5 | 52 | −2 | 60 | 8 | 50 | 10 |

The calculations show that while the marginal utility of Z is constant, the marginal utilities of X and Y decline as consumption increases. Indeed, in the case of X disutility occurs — i.e. the consumption of the fifth unit causes total utility to decline.

*Solution 2.6   Answer:* **E**

A consumer will not change his pattern of expenditure if he is at present enjoying maximum total satisfaction. This occurs when the marginal utility (MU) of each good divided by its price (P) is equal so that in each case:

$$\frac{MU \ of \ A}{P \ of \ A} = \frac{MU \ of \ B}{P \ of \ B} \quad \text{so that} \quad \frac{10}{20} = \frac{?}{30}$$

Therefore,

$$\frac{10}{20} = \frac{15}{30} \quad \text{so that } 0.5 = 0.5$$

*Solution 2.7   Answer:* **A**

Consumer surplus occurs when people are able to buy a good for less than they were willing to pay. The price of a chocolate bar is 40p, so:

consumer surplus on first bar      = 60p − 40p = 20p
consumer surplus on second bar = 50p − 40p = 10p
consumer surplus on third bar     = 40p − 40p =   0p
Total consumer surplus is:              20p + 10p = 30p

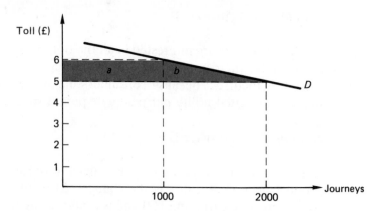

*Solution 2.8   Answer:* **C**

In the diagram, consumer surplus is shown by areas *a* + *b*. Those consumers who previously paid £6 now only have to pay £5. 1000 journeys are made at £1 less than people would have paid, so the increase in surplus is area *a* — i.e. £1000.

In addition, a further 1000 journeys are undertaken. The resulting increase in consumer surplus equals area *b*. Area *b* is given by the equation

$$\tfrac{1}{2}(P_1 - P_2) \times (Q_2 - Q_1)$$

$$= \tfrac{1}{2}(\text{£6} - \text{£5}) \times (2000 - 1000)$$

$$= \tfrac{1}{2}(\text{£1}) \times (1000) = \text{£}0.5 \times 1000 = \text{£}500$$

Therefore, the total increase in consumer surplus is area *a* + area *b* = £1000 + £500 = £1500.

*Solution 2.9   Answer:* **E**

A fall in the price of an inferior good results in two effects:
   (a) a positive substitution effect — i.e. the consumer buys *more* of this good, because it has become relatively cheaper;
   (b) a negative income effect — i.e. the consumer uses the increase in purchasing power brought about by the fall in price to buy *less* of the good.

*Solution 2.10   Answer:* **E**

Consumers will always prefer the point furthest away from the origin — i.e. K. Other options are incorrect because:
**A** ⇒ point K is furthest away;
**B** ⇒ the consumer is indifferent between point M and point N, because the two are on the same indifference curve;

**C** ⇒ point J is further from the origin than is point N;
**D** ⇒ while combination L is the consumer's point of equilibrium, the question asks which combination the consumer *prefers*.

*Solution 2.11   Answer:* **B**

The income effect arising from a price change can be found on an indifference map by drawing a budget line parallel with the new budget line. The gap between where this new budget line just touches the original indifference curve (at T) and the new quantity demanded (S) represents the income effect.

*Solution 2.12   Answer:* **C**

The demand for apples will increase following a rise in the price of a substitute (pears) and an increase in income.

   **1** ⇒ Option 1 is incorrect. A fall in the price of a good *never* increases the demand for the good. Provided that the good is normal, there would be an *extension in quantity demanded*.

*Solution 2.13   Answer:* **D**

A good in composite demand has many uses — e.g. apples can be demanded for cider or juice. Other options are incorrect because:
**2** ⇒ a good in composite demand may or may not have many substitutes;
**3** ⇒ goods with many uses tend to be price-inelastic and have low elasticity of demand.

*Solution 2.14   Answer* **D**

Diminishing marginal utility means that the satisfaction gained from consuming extra units declines as consumption increases. Other options are incorrect because:
**2** ⇒ the individual consumer is actually unable to influence the price at which the product is bought;
**3** ⇒ given overconsumption, marginal utility can be negative, so that additional consumption decreases total satisfaction. However, this possibility is not a necessary feature of the law of diminishing marginal returns.

*Solution 2.15   Answer* **A**

All options are correct. A fall in price allows an individual to buy a superior substitute and reduce consumption of the giffen good, so that the income effect is negative. The substitution effect is still positive. However, for giffen goods the negative income effect is always greater than the substitution effect, so that the overall price effect is negative.

# 3 Supply and Prices

## 3.1 Fact Sheet

### (a) Definition of Supply

- *Supply* is the amount of a good which producers are both willing and able to sell at a given price.
- *Producer surplus* is the difference between the minimum price a producer would accept to supply a given quantity of a good and the price actually received.
- A *supply curve* shows the amount of a good which producers are willing and able to sell at different prices.
- The amount of a good supplied depends on:
  - (i) price;
  - (ii) the conditions of supply.

### (b) Movements along a Supply Curve

- A change in price results in a movement along a supply curve, resulting in a change in the quantity supplied.
- A change in the price of a good *NEVER* shifts the supply curve for that good.
- In Figure 3.1 an increase in price causes an *expansion* in supply and a decrease in price results in a *contraction* in supply.

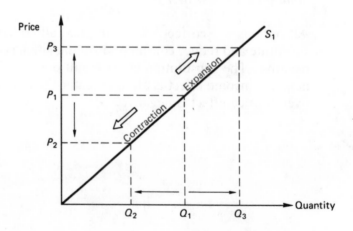

**Figure 3.1** Movements along a supply curve

### (c) Increases and Decreases in Supply

- A supply curve is drawn assuming *ceteris paribus* — i.e. that all factors influencing supply are being held constant except price. The *conditions of supply* refer to those factors held constant and include:
  - (i) *average* (or *unit*) *costs* of production;
  - (ii) the current state of technology;
  - (iii) the price of other goods:
    - (1) in *competitive supply* (i.e. alternative products which the firm could make);
    - (2) in *joint supply* (i.e. by-products from manufacture);
  - (iv) unforeseen circumstances (e.g. a drought ruining a wine crop);
  - (v) the number of firms in the industry;
  - (vi) the goals of producers.
- A change in one of these conditions affects the level of supply at all prices and results in a *shift* in the supply curve.
- Figure 3.2 illustrates the effect of an increase in supply.

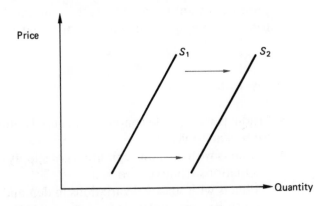

**Figure 3.2** An increase in supply

*Cause*:
a decrease in unit costs of production;
or improved technology;
or a fall in the price of a good in competitive supply;
or a rise in the price of a good in joint supply;
or beneficial unforeseen circumstances;
or new firms entering the industry;

*Effect*:
the supply curve shifts to the right.

### (d) Price Determination

- In Figure 3.3, excess supply occurs at prices above $P_1$, because producers are prepared to sell more than consumers are willing to buy. Attempts to maintain a *minimum price* above the market price (e.g. *Common Agricultural Policy*) results in *structural surpluses*.
- *Excess demand* occurs at prices below $P_1$, because consumers want to buy more than producers are prepared to sell. Attempts to maintain a *maximum price* below the market price (e.g. *rationing*) results in *artificial shortages*.

35

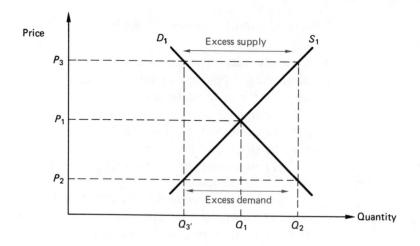

**Figure 3.3** Equilibrium and non-equilibrium prices

- *Equilibrium* is a state of balance — i.e. a situation where there is no tendency for change. There is only one market price where the amount that producers want to sell equals the amount that consumers want to buy. The forces of supply and demand ensure that $P_1$ is the *equilibrium market price*.

### (e) Price Instability

- Products with stable conditions of supply and demand will have stable prices from year to year.
- Products with unstable conditions of supply or demand will experience price fluctuations from year to year.
- Products with seasonal variations in demand, such as hotel accommodation, tend to be price-unstable.
- Agricultural prices tend to be unstable because:
  - (i) supply changes from one time period to the next because of variable weather conditions;
  - (ii) the effect of changes in supply is amplified by price-inelastic demand (see Chapter 4);
  - (iii) the effect of changes in demand is amplified by price-inelastic supply;
  - (iv) *supply lags* (delays) between decisions to produce and the product coming onto the market. The resulting *cobweb* model is explained in Example 3.18.

### (f) Indirect Taxation

An *indirect tax* $(T_i)$ is a surcharge on price imposed on the sale of goods and services by the government and can be:
  - (i) *specific* — i.e. a fixed amount per unit;
  - (ii) *ad valorem* — i.e. a percentage of the selling price.

- The effect of an indirect tax is shown by adding the amount of the tax to the supply curve.
- Tax *incidence* refers to the burden of a tax. The more price-inelastic the demand for a good the greater the incidence falling on the consumer.

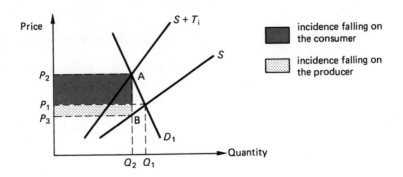

**Figure 3.4** An *ad valorem* indirect tax. Area $P_3P_2AB$ equals the total amount of tax revenue raised

### (g) Subsidies

- A subsidy (*Su*) is a discount on price given by the government.
- A subsidy can be specific or *ad valorem*.
- The effect on a supply curve is shown by deducting the amount of the subsidy from the supply curve.
- The more price-inelastic the demand for a good the greater the share of the subsidy going to the consumer.

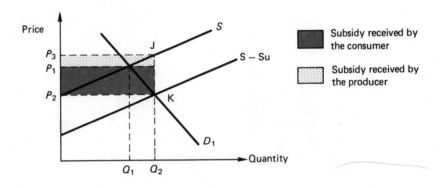

**Figure 3.5** A specific subsidy. Area $P_2P_3JK$ equals the total amount of subsidy paid

## 3.2 Data Response

### Worked Example 3.1

The following information refers to an imaginary market for corn. Farmers are assumed to plan next year's production on the basis of last year's price.

| Year | Price per tonne (£) | Amount bought and sold (tonnes) |
|------|---------------------|----------------------------------|
| 1900 | 150                 | 3000                             |
| 1991 | 200                 | 1000                             |
| 1992 | 125                 | 4000                             |
| 1993 | 162.5               | 2500                             |
| 1994 | 145                 | 3250                             |
| 1995 | 150                 | 3000                             |
| 1996 | 150                 | 3000                             |

(a) Describe the annual variations in the price of corn shown in the table.

**(4 marks)**

(b) Given that demand conditions are unchanged, how would you explain the annual variations in the price of corn shown in the table? **(8 marks)**

(c) What pricing policies for corn might a government adopt for the period shown?

**(8 marks)**

*Solution 3.1*

(a) Figure 1 indicates that the price of corn moves between £150 per tonne in years 1990 and 1996. The highest price of £200 is achieved in 1991, and the lowest of £125 in the following year. Note that the severity of the oscillation diminishes.

(b) Market prices are determined by the interaction of supply and demand. Market equilibrium occurs when there is a stable long-run market price from which there is no tendency to move. A change in any of the conditions of supply or demand would affect equilibrium by causing a shift in a supply or demand curve and, hence, a change in price.

Agricultural goods such as corn are particularly prone to unforeseen weather conditions which affect supply from one year to another. The fact that the price of corn is £150 for three separate years would tend to suggest that this is the long-run equilibrium price for corn. The initial change in

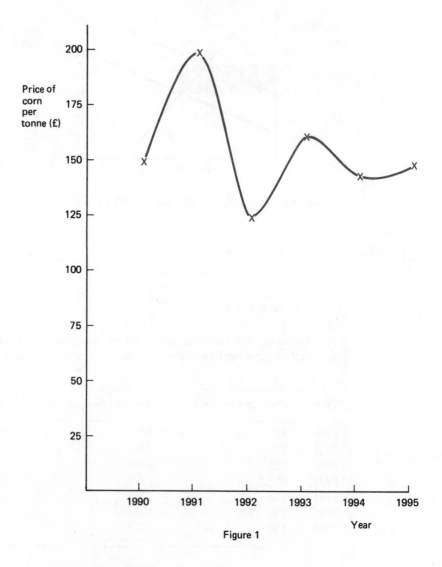

Figure 1

price in 1991 is likely to be the result of an unexpectedly poor harvest brought about by, say, frost damage. The resultant fall in supply shown in Figure 3 raises price to £200, with only 1000 tonnes bought and sold.

Figure 2 shows the path the market might follow in moving back to equilibrium. Long-run disequilibrium occurs between 1991 and 1995, because farmers are unable to accurately predict next year's price. In 1992, they make too much, and price falls to remove excess supply. In 1993, farmers make too little, and price rises to remove excess demand. By 1995, the amount producers want to sell at £150 equals the amount consumers want to buy, and price remains stable into 1996.

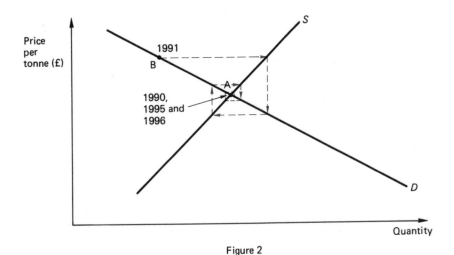

Figure 2

(c) Pricing policy refers to the government's ability to leave markets free to set their own price or to intervene to stabilise price. Price intervention in the corn market requires the government to keep a buffer stock. For instance, Figure 3 shows that the effect of the poor harvest of 1991 on price could be overcome by the government selling 2000 tonnes from stock at the prevailing price of £150. Such price intervention would avoid the subsequent 'cobweb' shown in Figure 2.

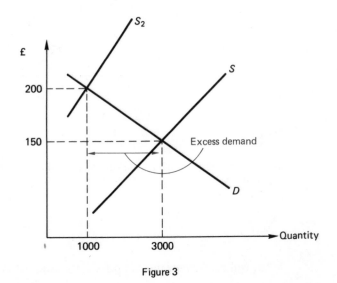

Figure 3

## 3.3   Objective Questions

**Example 3.2**

Other things being equal, a normal supply curve for corn slopes upwards from left to right because:
A   farmers charge more to cover a rise in the price of seed
B   farmers increase supply following increases in demand
C   farmers' profits increase as price increases
D   farmers are willing to produce more corn as price increases
E   farmers are given government subsidies to encourage production

**Example 3.3**

The supply of a good is represented by the equation $P = 10 + 0.8Q_s$, where $P$ refers to the price in pounds (£) and $Q_s$ is the quantity of the good sold. At what price will the producer sell 20 units?
A   £10          B   £16          C   £20          D   £26          E   £30

**Example 3.4**

A supply curve shifts to downwards to the right following:
A   an increase in customs duties          B   a decrease in specific subsidies
C   a decrease in VAT                       D   an increase in production costs
E   a decrease in the number of firms in the industry

*Examples 3.5–3.7 refer to the following diagram, which shows the supply of and demand for British-made lawnmowers. The market is initially in equilibrium at point A. After each question, indicate the new equilibrium position A, B, C, D or E.*

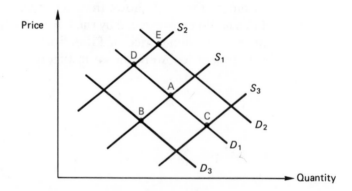

**Example 3.5**

What will be the new market price following the introduction of labour-saving technology?

**Example 3.6**

What will be the new market price if the price of imported mowers falls considerably?

**Example 3.7**

What will be the new market price if there is a successful advertising campaign for lawnmowers, while at the same time the government introduces an indirect tax on the sale of lawnmowers?

**Example 3.8**

The market demand for a good Y is given by the equation $Y = 80 - 10P$ and the market supply for good Y is given by the equation $Y = -40 + 20P$, where $P$ denotes the price of good Y. The equilibrium price for the good is

A  $2P$       B  $4P$       C  $10P$       D  $20P$       E  $40P$

**Example 3.9**

The burden of an expenditure tax falls entirely on the producer if the elasticity of demand is:

A  lower than the elasticity of supply       B  higher than the elasticity of supply
C  less than unity       D  greater than unity
E  infinite

**Example 3.10**

If a subsidy is given to a product whose demand is price-elastic but whose supply is price-inelastic:

A  producers keep the entire subsidy
B  consumers keep the entire subsidy
C  the subsidy is shared equally between consumers and producers
D  the bulk of the subsidy is kept by producers
E  the bulk of the subsidy is kept by consumers

*Select your answers to Examples 3.11–3.14 by means of the following code:*
*A if 1, 2 and 3 are all correct*
*B if 1 and 2 only are correct*
*C if 2 and 3 only are correct*
*D if 1 only is correct*

**Example 3.11**

Which of the following will cause the supply curve for apples to shift to the left?
1  a successful advertising campaign for pears
2  a reduction in EC subsidies to fruit growers
3  an increase in the total population consuming apples

**Example 3.12**

Good X and good Y are in competitive supply. Other things being equal, a decrease in the demand for good Y will:
1  increase the price of good X       2  increase the supply of good X
3  decrease the price of good X

**Example 3.13**

The government imposition of a maximum price below the equilibrium price in a competitive market will, in the short run, result in:
1   the development of a black market      2 excess demand
3   a decrease in quantity supplied


**Example 3.14**

The diagram indicates the conditions of demand and supply of wheat. If the government set a minimum price of $P_2$, this will:
1   cause an excess supply of wheat
2   make the market demand curve JKL
3   require the intervention buying of $Q_1 - Q_3$ wheat

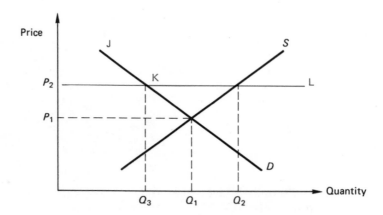

## 3.4  Essays


**Example 3.15**

Analyse the effect, in the short run only, on the price of coffee of (i) a severe frost; (ii) a fall in the rate of VAT; (iii) the introduction of rationing.

- You are not expected to have a detailed knowledge of the coffee industry.
- Apply your understanding of general supply and demand analysis.
- Make assumptions about the price elasticity of supply and demand for coffee and then draw flat or steep curves to match.

*Solution 3.15*

In a market economy the price of coffee is determined by the interaction of supply (the amount of a good which producers are willing and able to sell) and demand (the amount of a good which consumers are willing and able to buy).
  (i) In Figure 1, $S$ shows supply and $D$ demand at different prices. $P_1$ is the initial equilibrium market price (EMP) and $Q_1$ the initial amount of coffee bought and sold. The long time taken to grow coffee plants means that supply is price-inelastic. Demand is price-inelastic, because analysis has assumed that there are few substitutes for coffee. $S$ and $D$ are drawn assuming *ceteris paribus* (all other things being equal). A severe frost invalidates this assumption and I predict that there will be a decrease in the

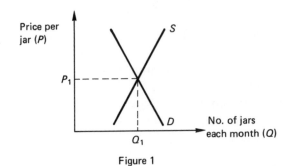

Figure 1

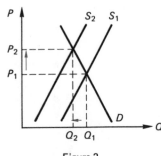

Figure 2

quantity of coffee supplied at all market prices, causing the supply curve in Figure 2 to shift to the left, to $S_2$. The decrease in supply causes a rise in price to $P_2$ and a contraction in demand.

The more severe the frost the greater the decrease in supply, and the greater the resulting increase in price. The more price-inelastic demand the greater the increase in price for a given fall in supply.

(ii) Vat is an *ad valorem* (according to value) indirect tax on the sale of goods and services. In Figure 3, the effect of VAT on coffee is found by adding the amount of the tax to the original supply curve, at each level of output. A fall in VAT rates reduces the amount of tax received at each level of output and the $S_1 + T_1$ curve shifts downwards to $S_1 + T_2$. The assumption of inelastic demand means a significant fall in price, to $P_2$.

(iii) Rationing usually occurs in response to a crisis such as war and is when the government intervenes in a market to fix the price and output of a good. In Figure 4, the government fixes the output of coffee at $Q_2$. Given that supply is now totally unresponsive to changes in price, $S_2$ is perfectly price-inelastic and price rises to $P_2$. Often rationing authorities consider high free market prices to be unfair to those on low incomes and unable to buy coffee. Instead, $Q_2$ coupons are issued to consumers, allowing them to buy a fixed amount of the good each month at, say, price $P_1$.

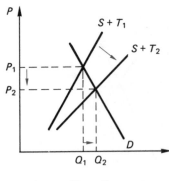

Figure 3

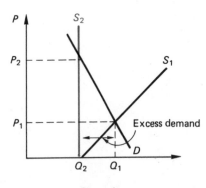

Figure 4

The final effect on the legal price is indeterminate. The government may decide to offer the good above, at or below the price prevailing before the introduction of rationing. However, the existence of excess demand at prices below $P_2$ encourages the development of an illegal black market, where price is likely to be higher than that set by the government.

**Example 3.16**

Why do the prices of some commodities fluctuate more than those of others?

(L 1987)

43

- Explain why unstable conditions of supply and demand result in price changes.
- Explain why price inelasticity amplifies the effect on price of changes in supply and demand.
- Introduce time lags and apply the cobweb theory.
- Make use of graphs and relevant examples.

*Solution 3.16*

Equilibrium is a situation of balance from which there is no tendency to change. Equilibrium prices change only if there has been a change in a condition of supply or demand. It follows that products where the conditions of supply and demand are inherently unstable are subject to greater price fluctuations than are those with constant supply and demand conditions.

For instance, goods where demand varies according to the time of year will display price instability. For example, the price of coal falls during the summer but rises in the winter. Similarly, a rise in income increases the demand for all normal goods. *Ceteris paribus*, the greater the increase in demand the greater the rise in price. Therefore, goods with a low income elasticity of demand usually possess great price stability. Goods with a low cross elasticity of demand with respect to all other goods have few substitutes or complements and are likely to show price stability. Similarly, products with few goods in joint or competitive supply are less likely to be subject to price changes.

Empirical (real-world) evidence suggests that agricultural goods have oscillating prices. Farm products are particularly prone to unforeseen events such as weather and disease. Figure 1 shows that as the weather changes, so does supply. The effect on price of each change in supply is exaggerated by inelastic demand. Agricultural products have a low price elasticity of demand (PED), because they are inexpensive, and consumers tend to buy much the same amount regardless of price.

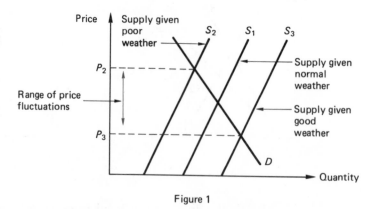

Figure 1

The cobweb theory explains why the price of some goods oscillates more than others. Assume that farmers expect to sell their next crop at the same market price as in the previous season. This means that this year's price has no effect on current production but instead determines next year's supply. In Figure 2, the initial price is $P_1$. A 'shock' to the system (e.g. an unexpected poor harvest) causes price to rise to $P_2$. Farmers expect price $P_2$ in the next time period and produce $Q_2$. However, consumers are only prepared to pay $P_3$ to buy up $Q_2$. Farmers then expect the next market price to be $P_3$ and so produce $Q_3$. Because supply is more inelastic than demand, the cobweb is *converging* and the long-run equilibrium price of $P_1$ is eventually restored. Had demand been more inelastic

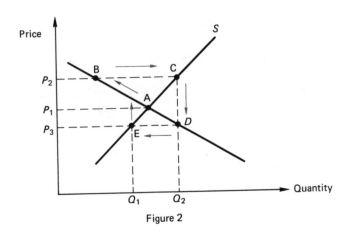

Figure 2

than supply, the resulting *divergent* cobweb would have caused even greater price variations over time.

In conclusion, it can be seen that the prices of some commodities fluctuate more than those of others, because of differences in the stability of the underlying conditions of supply and demand.

## 3.5  Solutions to Objective Questions

*Solution 3.2  Answer:* **D**

A supply curve slopes upwards from left to right, since higher prices induce producers to *extend* their supply. Other options are incorrect because:
**A** ⇒ when drawing a supply curve all variables are held constant except price. A rise in the price of seed shifts the supply curve to the left;
**B** ⇒ an increase in the demand for corn causes a rise in price and an extension in supply and not an increase in supply;
**C** ⇒ profitability cannot be assessed without further information about revenue;
**E** ⇒ a subsidy shifts the supply curve to the left.

*Solution 3.3  Answer:* **D**

The equation $P = 10 + 0.8Q_s$ simply means 'price equals 10 plus whatever quantity is being supplied multiplied by 0.8'. Therefore,

$$P = 10 + [0.8 \times 20] = 10 + 16 = 26$$

*Solution 3.4  Answer:* **C**

A decrease in VAT increases supply and shifts the supply curve to the right. All other options result in an increase in supply, which shifts the supply curve to the left.

*Solution 3.5  Answer:* **C**

The introduction of labour-saving technology reduces unit costs, increases supply and shifts the supply curve to the right, to $S_3$. The new equilibrium position is given by the intersection of $S_3$ and $D_1$ — i.e. point C.

*Solution 3.6   Answer:* **B**

A fall in the price of a substitute good for home-produced lawnmowers reduces demand and shifts the demand curve to $D_3$. The new equilibrium position is given by the intersection of $D_3$ and $S_1$ — i.e. point B.

*Solution 3.7   Answer:* **E**

A successful advertising campaign shifts the demand curve for lawnmowers to the right, to $D_2$. A tax on the sale of lawnmowers shifts the supply curve to the left, to $S_2$. The equilibrium position is point E.

*Solution 3.8   Answer:* **B**

In equilibrium, the two equations given in the question must equal each other. Remember when manipulating equations that whatever is done to one side must also be done to the other side of the equation. The market price is found by:

$$\text{quantity demanded} = \text{quantity supplied}$$

| | |
|---|---|
| *substituting* | $80 - 10P = -40 + 20P$ |
| *adding 10P* | $80 = -40 + 30P$ |
| *adding 40* | $120 = 30P$ |
| *dividing by 30* | $4 = P$ |

*Solution 3.9   Answer:* **E**

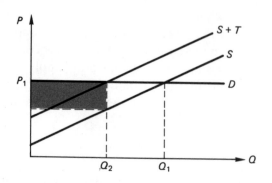

In general, price elasticity determines the slope of supply and demand curves (see Figures 4.2 and 4.3). The diagram shows that a demand curve of infinite price elasticity is horizontal. The shaded area is the amount of tax raised, and the incidence falls entirely on the producer.

*Solution 3.10   Answer:* **D**

It almost always helps to draw a diagram to illustrate details given in a question. $D_1$ represents a price-elastic demand curve and $S_1$ represents a price-inelastic supply curve. To show the effect of a subsidy, deduct an amount (say, $P_3 - P_2$) from the supply curve at all output levels and label the new curve $S_2$. The initial market price is $P_1$, with $Q_1$ bought and sold. The subsidy has increased supply and reduced the equilibrium price to $P_2$. While consumers pay only $P_2$, producers receive $P_3$ per unit sold. Because demand is price-elastic and supply is price-inelastic, the bulk of the subsidy (area A) goes to the producer.

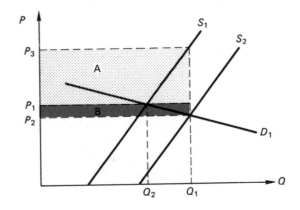

*Solution 3.11    Answer:* **B**

The following options are correct.
**1** ⇒ A successful advertising campaign for pears increases demand, raises the price of pears and increases the quantity of pears supplied. Some apple producers are now encouraged to replant their orchards with pears. The supply of apples falls, shifting the supply curve to the left.
**2** ⇒ Reduced subsidies cause a decrease in supply.
  **3** ⇒ Is incorrect because, in the short run, an increase in population increases demand and not supply.

*Solution 3.12    Answer:* **C**

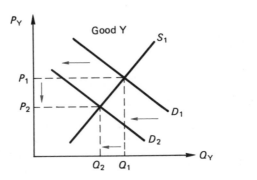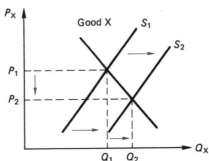

The left-hand diagram shows that a decrease in the demand for good Y reduces its price. Since good Y and good X are in competitive supply, a fall in the price of Y encourages producers to increase their supply of X. Option **2** is correct.
  The right-hand diagram shows that the increase in the supply of X reduces its price. Therefore, option **3** is correct and option **1** is incorrect.

*Solution 3.13    Answer:* **A**

All options are correct.
  **2** ⇒ In the diagram, the amount that consumers are willing to buy at the maximum price is found by projecting across to the demand curve and down, i.e. $Q_2$. A similar operation reveals that quantity supplied at the maximum price is only $Q_3$. There is an excess demand of $Q_2 - Q_3$.
  **1** ⇒ Intervention which results in excess demand tends to encourage the development of a black market.

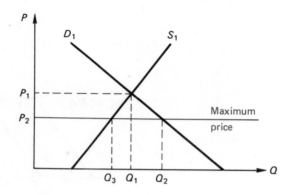

**3** $\Rightarrow$ At the initial market price, $Q_1$ is demanded. Price maintenance means that only $Q_3$ can be bought, and there has been a *contraction* in demand.

*Solution 3.14    Answer:* **B**

The following options are correct.
**1** $\Rightarrow$ At the minimum price producers want to sell more ($Q_2$) than consumers want to buy ($Q_3$).
**2** $\Rightarrow$ Above point K, the market demand curve is unaffected by government action. Beyond point K, the government is prepared to intervene and buy up any amount of wheat necessary to maintain the market price at $P_2$. The demand curve becomes perfectly elastic at K and extends to point L.

Option **3** is incorrect because the amount of unsold wheat to be bought and added to intervention stocks equals $Q_2 - Q_3$ and not $Q_1 - Q_3$.

# 4 Elasticity

## 4.1 Fact Sheet

### (a) Price Elasticity of Demand

*Price elasticity of demand* (P.E.D.) measures the responsiveness of demand to a given change in price. The P.E.D. coefficient (value) is calculated by use of either of the following equations:

$$\text{P.E.D.} = \frac{\text{percentage change in quantity demanded}}{\text{percentage change in price}} = \frac{P}{Q_D} \times \frac{\Delta Q_D}{\Delta P}$$

where $P$ is the initial price, $Q_D$ is the initial quantity demanded and $\Delta$ (delta) means 'the change in'.

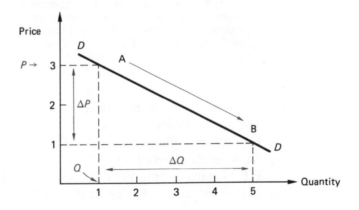

**Figure 4.1**   Calculating P.E.D.:

$$\text{P.E.D. between points A and B} = \frac{P}{Q_D} \times \frac{\Delta Q_D}{\Delta P}$$

$$= \frac{3}{1} \times \frac{4}{1} = 6$$

- The P.E.D. coefficient can be between zero and infinity ($\infty$).
- If P.E.D. is less than 1, demand is inelastic.
- If P.E.D. is greater than 1, demand is elastic.
- P.E.D. is usually treated as a positive number and any minus signs are ignored.

Figure 4.2 shows that the gradient (slope) of a demand curve generally reflects its P.E.D. However, great care should be taken when interpreting the gradient of a demand curve.

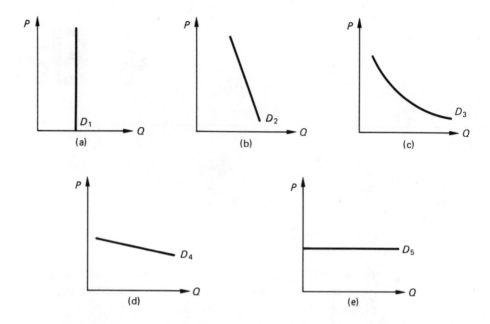

**Figure 4.2** Demand curves with different price elasticities. In (a) the demand curve is a vertical line; demand is perfectly inelastic; the P.E.D. coefficient is equal to 0; and a price rise means no decrease in $Q_D$. In (b) the demand curve is a steep line; demand is relatively inelastic; the P.E.D. coefficient is greater than 0 but less than 1; and a price rise means a smaller percentage decrease in $Q_D$. In (c) the demand curve is a rectangular hyperbola; demand is unitary elastic; the P.E.D. coefficient is equal to 1; and a price rise means an equal percentage decrease in $Q_D$. In (d) the demand curve is a shallow line; demand is relatively elastic; the P.E.D. coefficient is greater than 1 but less than ∞; and a price rise means a greater percentage decrease in $Q_D$. In (e) the demand curve is a horizontal line; demand is perfectly elastic; the P.E.D. coefficient is equal to ∞; and a price rise means consumers buying perfect substitutes

   (i) The slope of a demand curve is not *necessarily* a guide to price elasticity. The scale of each axis affects P.E.D.
  (ii) On a steep demand curve, P.E.D. at points near the *y*-axis can be elastic.
 (iii) On a flat demand curve, P.E.D. at points near the *x*-axis can be inelastic.
 (iv) P.E.D. falls as you move down a linear demand curve.
  (v) A demand curve shifting to the left becomes more elastic.

**Table 4.1** Factors influencing price elasticity of demand

| Factor | The demand for a good is relatively price-inelastic because: |
| --- | --- |
| Number of substitutes | if there are few substitutes for a good, consumers are unlikely to switch products |
| Consumer loyalty | if consumers are in the habit of buying a good, they are unwilling to use substitutes |
| Absolute price of the good | if a good is inexpensive, a large percentage change in price represents only a few pence |
| Proportion of income | if the good takes up only a small proportion of income, consumers will not react significantly |
| Number of complements | if the good has many complements, the product is needed if the other items are used |
| Consumer adjustment | if consumers are slow to react to a change in price, the amount bought is largely unaffected |

## (b) Price Elasticity of Supply

Price elasticity of supply (P.E.S.) measures the responsiveness of supply to a given change in price:

$$\text{P.E.S.} = \frac{\text{percentage change in quantity supplied}}{\text{percentage change in price}} = \frac{P}{Q_S} \times \frac{\Delta Q_S}{\Delta P}$$

- The P.E.S. coefficient can be between zero and infinity ($\infty$).
- If P.E.S. is less than 1, supply is inelastic.
- If P.E.S. is greater than 1, supply is elastic.

Figure 4.3 shows that the gradient of a supply curve generally reflects its P.E.S.

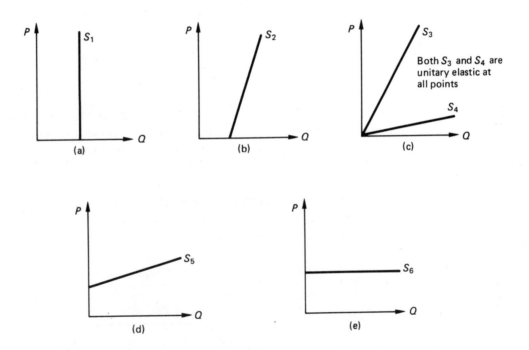

**Figure 4.3**  Supply curves with different price elasticities. In (a) supply is perfectly inelastic; the P.E.D. coefficient is equal to 0; and a price fall means no decrease in $Q_S$. In (b) supply is relatively inelastic; the P.E.D. coefficient is greater than 0 but less than 1; and a price fall means a smaller percentage decrease in $Q_S$. In (c) supply is unitary elastic; the P.E.D. coefficient is equal to 1; and a price fall means an equal percentage decrease in $Q_S$. In (d) supply is relatively elastic; the P.E.D. coefficient is greater than 1 but less than $\infty$; and a price fall means a greater percentage decrease in $Q_S$. In (e) supply is perfectly elastic; the P.E.D. coefficient is equal to $\infty$; and a price fall means that suppliers halt production

It is important to remember that for linear supply curves:

- P.E.S. is inelastic at all points when the supply curve intersects the $x$-axis first.
- P.E.S. is elastic at all points when the supply curve intersects the $y$-axis first.
- P.E.S. is unitary at all points when the supply curve intersects the origin.

**Table 4.2**  Factors influencing price elasticity of supply

| Factor | The supply for a good is relatively price-elastic because: |
|---|---|
| Time | in the long run, firms can adjust all factor inputs to change supply easily |
| Production time | if a good is manufactured quickly, supplies can be changed easily |
| Stocks | if a firm has a large amount of stocks, supplies can be changed easily |
| Capacity | if labour and capital are underused, supplies can be changed easily |
| Factor mobility | if resources can move in and out of the industry, supplies can be changed easily |

## (c) Income Elasticity of Demand

*Income elasticity of demand* (Y.E.D.) measures the responsiveness of demand to a given change in income:

$$\text{Y.E.D.} = \frac{\text{percentage change in quantity demanded}}{\text{percentage change in price}} = \frac{Y}{Q_D} \times \frac{\Delta Q_D}{\Delta Y}$$

- Since Y.E.D. can be negative, it is important to include minus signs.
- If Y.E.D. is negative, the product is an *inferior good*.
- If Y.E.D. is positive, the product is a *normal good*.
- If Y.E.D. is positive and greater than 1, the product is a *superior good*.

An *Engel curve* shows the amount of a good demanded at different levels of income. Figure 4.4 shows that the slope of an Engel curve reflects its Y.E.D.

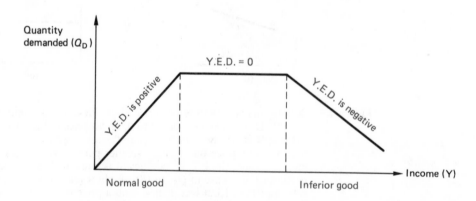

**Figure 4.4**  An Engel curve with different income elasticities

## (d) Cross Elasticity of Demand

- *Cross elasticity of demand* (X.E.D.) measures the responsiveness of demand for good A to a given change in the price of good B:

$$\text{X.E.D.} = \frac{\text{percentage change in the quantity of A demanded}}{\text{percentage change in the price of B}} = \frac{P_B}{Q_{DA}} \times \frac{\Delta Q_{DA}}{\Delta P_B}$$

- Since X.E.D. can be negative, it is important to include minus signs.
- If X.E.D. is positive, the two goods are in competitive demand — i.e. *substitutes*.
- If X.E.D. is negative, the two goods are in joint demand — i.e. *complements*.
- If X.E.D. is zero, the two products are unrelated — i.e. *independent goods*.

### (e) Price Elasticity of Demand and Revenue

The effect of a price change on revenue depends on the elasticity of demand. Figure 4.5 shows how a change in price can increase revenue.

- If P.E.D. is elastic, a fall in price increases revenue.
- If P.E.D. is inelastic, a rise in price increases revenue.
- If P.E.D. is unitary, a price change leaves revenue unchanged.

The relationship between P.E.D. and marginal revenue is analysed in Figure 6.5

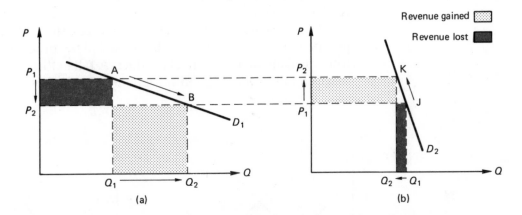

**Figure 4.5**   (a) Elastic demand and revenue. Since the price decrease results in a proportionately larger increase in quantity demanded, revenue rises. (b) Inelastic demand and revenue. Since the price increase results in a proportionately smaller decrease in quantity demanded, revenue rises

## 4.2  Data Response

**Worked Example 4.1**

Products X and Y are both produced in perfectly competitive product markets using unskilled labour obtained from a perfectly competitive labour market.

X has an income elasticity of demand = $-0.5$
Y has an income elasticity of demand of $0.5$

Firms produce either X or Y, and initially all firms within each industry are at a long-run equilibrium. Over the next year there occurs an increase of 20% in the average consumer disposable income.
(a) What term would you use to describe good X?                    **(1 mark)**
(b) Calculate how the change in income will affect the demand for each good.
                                                                   **(2 marks)**

53

(c) Describe, with the help of relevant diagrams, the changes which will occur over time in the above product and factor markets. **(14 marks)**

(d) Why might a problem occur if labour were occupationally immobile? **(3 marks)**

(SUJB June 1987)

*Solution 4.1*

(a) A good with a negative income elasticity of demand is known as an inferior good. An increase in income results in a fall in demand for this type of good.

(b) Income elasticity of demand (Y.E.D.) is calculated from the equation

$$Y.E.D. = \frac{\text{percentage change in quantity demanded}}{\text{percentage change in income}}$$

For good X, $-0.5 = ?/20 = -10\%$. Demand for X falls by 10%.
For good Y, $0.5 = ?/20 = +10\%$. Demand for Y rises by 10%.

(c) Answer (b) indicates that the demand for good X falls by 10% over one year. The effect on the product market for X is shown in Figure 1 and the effect on the labour market is given in Figure 2.

In Figure 1 the increase in income is used to buy less of the inferior good X. The demand curve shifts to the right. Note that the fall in quantity supplied is achieved by releasing resources such as labour to contract production. The demand for labour used in the production of X is derived from the demand for the final product. A fall in the demand for product X means a fall in the demand for labour. This is shown in Figure 3.

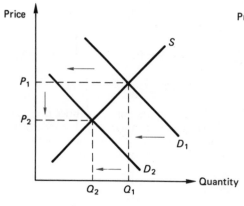

Figure 1: Good X

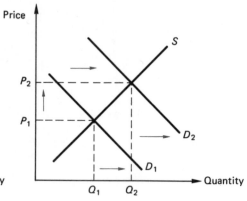

Figure 2: Good Y

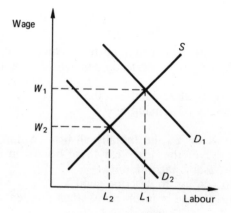

Figure 3: Labour used in X

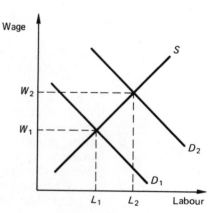

Figure 4: Labour used in Y

Figure 2 shows the increase in the demand for product Y following an increase in income. The demand curve for Y has shifted to the right. The resultant increase in quantity supplied is achieved by attracting additional resources such as labour into the industry. The increase in the demand for the final product raises the demand for labour used in the manufacture of Y, causing the demand curve for labour in Figure 4 to shift to the right.

Figure 3 shows a fall in wages in industry X. The increase in wages occurring in industry Y will attract redundant labour from X. The reallocation of resources has been achieved through a change in the relative price of products and labour between the two product and factor markets.

(d) The occupational immobility of labour refers to the inability of workers to move between jobs requiring different skills. For instance, a teacher does not necessarily possess the skills which would allow him to transfer to a plumbing occupation.

If labour is occupationally immobile between industries X and Y, workers no longer required in industry X will be unable to move across to industry Y, even though there has been an increase in relative pay. In the long run, workers once employed in making X may retrain for Y, thereby overcoming occupational immobility.

## 4.3  Objective Questions

**Example 4.2**

The following table shows a demand schedule for a particular good:

| Price (£) | 1 | 2 | 3 | 4 | 5 |
|---|---|---|---|---|---|
| Quantity demanded (lb) | 40 | 35 | 30 | 25 | 20 |

In which range does the price elasticity of demand (expressed as a positive number) lie for a rise in price from £3 to £4?
A   0.0–0.1     B   0.2–0.3     C   0.3–0.4     D   0.5–0.8
E   greater than or equal to 0.9

**Example 4.3**

If the demand curve for a normal good is linear, the price elasticity of demand for the good:
A   decreases as the amount bought increases
B   increases as the amount bought increases
C   is always less than 1
D   is always more than 1
E   is unity

**Example 4.4**

From the following diagram it can be inferred that the price elasticity of demand is:
A   the same at point A and point B
B   the same at point C and point B
C   more inelastic at point C than at point B
D   more inelastic at point A than at point B
E   the same for both demand curves at point B

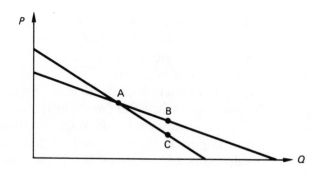

## Example 4.5

If market price falls by 5% following a rise in supply, and there is no change in the quantity bought, the demand curve is:

**A** kinked            **B** relatively elastic        **C** relatively inelastic
**D** completely elastic    **E** completely inelastic

## Example 4.6

Which one of the following graphs refers to a good which exhibits a negative income elasticity of demand at all levels of income?

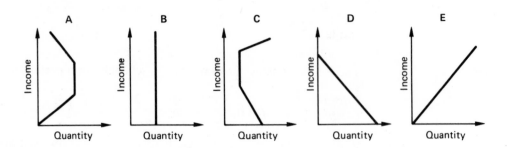

## Example 4.7

The following table gives an individual's demand for three goods at two different income levels:

| Income (£ 000) | 5 | 6 |
|---|---|---|
| Units of A | 10 | 15 |
| Units of B | 8 | 10 |
| Units of C | 10 | 11 |

It follows that the proportionate rise in income leads to:

**A** a proportionately equal increase in the quantity of A demanded
**B** a proportionately greater increase in the amount of A demanded
**C** a proportionately greater increase in the amount of C demanded
**D** a proportionately greater increase in the demand for good B than for good A
**E** a proportionately greater increase in the demand for good C than for good B

## Example 4.8

Which one of the following diagrams represents the relationship between two normal goods which are in joint demand?

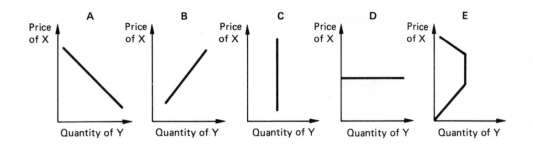

**Example 4.9**

If the price elasticity of demand for a good is 2, a decrease in price:
A  increases consumers' expenditure on the good
B  decreases consumers' expenditure on the good
C  does not change consumers' expenditure on the good
D  increases the profits of the firm
E  decreases the profits of the firm

**Example 4.10**

A cinema discontinues offering half-price mid-week tickets and instead charges full price. As a result, the cinema finds that its total revenue from mid-week sales falls. This shows that:
A  if weekend prices were reduced, total revenue would fall
B  the demand for mid-week tickets is more elastic than the demand for weekend tickets
C  the demand for mid-week tickets is more inelastic than the demand for weekend tickets
D  at these prices the demand for mid-week tickets is elastic
E  at these prices the demand for mid-week tickets is inelastic

*Select your answers to Examples 4.11–4.15 by means of the following code:*
A  *if 1, 2 and 3 are all correct*
B  *if 1 and 2 only are correct*
C  *if 2 and 3 only are correct*
D  *if 1 only is correct*

**Example 4.11**

If elasticity of demand is unitary:
1  the demand curve is a rectangular hyperbola
2  revenue remains unchanged as price changes
3  the good is a manufactured product

**Example 4.12**

The demand for a product is elastic with respect to price if:
1  it has several substitutes
2  its price is high in relation to income
3  it has few complements

**Example 4.13**

Price elasticity of supply will be smaller:
1  the longer the time period under consideration
2  the smaller the amount of stocks held by firms
3  the more immobile the factors of production used


**Example 4.14**

The diagram below shows the supply of beer. Elasticity of supply is:
1  greatest at L          2  equal at all points      3  unitary at point L

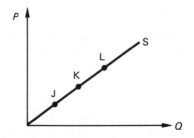


**Example 4.15**

If the cross elasticity of demand for good X with respect to good Y is zero, then X and Y are:
1  independent goods      2  substitute goods          3  in competitive demand


# 4.4  Essays


**Example 4.16**

Of what relevance is an understanding of each one of the three measures of elasticity of demand to the sales director of a firm of travel agents?

(C 1987)

- A detailed knowledge of the travel and tourism industry is not expected.
- Apply your general understanding of demand elasticity.
- Be careful to ensure that arguments are supported with worked examples relevant to a travel firm.
- Analyse each type of demand elasticity in separate paragraphs.


*Solution 4.16*

Elasticity of demand measures the responsiveness of demand to changes in other variables. There are three types of elasticity of demand. *Price elasticity of demand* (P.E.D.) measures the responsiveness of quantity demanded to a given change in price. The P.E.D. of a product will be of relevance to the sales director if he is contemplating a price change and needs to know the probable effect on revenue.

Figure 1 shows two possible demand curves for day coach trips. $D_1$ is relatively price-inelastic and $D_2$ is relatively price-elastic. At the initial price of £10, 100 trips are sold and the firm's total revenue (price × quantity) is £10 × 100 = £1000. A 'special offer' campaign where price is reduced by 20% affects revenue according to the P.E.D. for trips. Given $D_1$, total revenue becomes £8 × 110 = £880. Given $D_2$, total revenue is £8 × 150 = £1200. Therefore, the special offer only increases the revenue of the firm if P.E.D. is elastic.

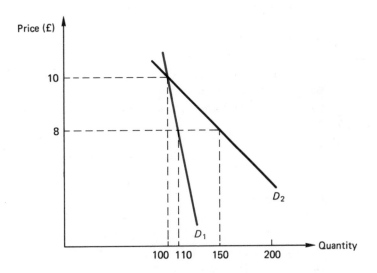

*Income elasticity of demand* (Y.E.D.) measures the responsiveness of demand to a given change in income. A knowledge of Y.E.D. allows the sales director to predict the likely pattern of future demand for travel as consumers' real income rises. For example, assume that the firm has to decide between increasing the number of day coach trips or introducing a new luxury tour service. If market research reveals that the Y.E.D. for day trips is negative, then demand will fall over time and the firm is operating in a declining market. If the survey finds that the Y.E.D. for luxury tours is positive and greater than 1, then demand will rise proportionately faster over time than income and the market is expanding.

*Cross elasticity of demand* (X.E.D.) measures the responsiveness of demand for one good to a given change in price of a second good. The X.E.D. value tells the firm which pair of products are substitutes (+X.E.D. coefficient), complements (−X.E.D. coefficient) or independent goods (X.E.D. = 0). The director can estimate the wider effects of discounting one holiday. Assume that the X.E.D. coefficient between holidays A and B is 2. The effect of a 10% reduction in the price of holiday A is calculated from the equation

$$\text{X.E.D.} = \frac{\text{\% change in quantity demanded of B}}{\text{\% change in price of A}}$$

The 20% fall in the quantity of B demanded may discourage the director from discounting the price of A.

X.E.D. also permits the firm to assess the effect of a *loss-leader* strategy, where the price of one good is heavily reduced in the hope that additional purchases of other products will compensate. Loss-leader campaigns are most effective when the X.E.D. of the product with respect to a large number of other goods sold by the firm is negative and less than 1, e.g. −4. The loss made on one item is made up by the profit from the sale of complements.

**Example 4.17**

What factors determine the elasticity of supply of any product (a) in the short run **(8)**, (b) in the long run? **(12)**

(SUJ 1987)

- Select a good whose elasticity of supply is affected by time.
- Avoid simply listing factors affecting elasticity of supply.
- Use your named product to illustrate why elasticity of supply varies between time periods.

*Solution 4.17*

*Price elasticity of supply* (P.E.S.) measures the responsiveness of quantity supplied to a given change in price. P.E.S. is calculated by comparing the proportionate change in price and quantity supplied by use of the equation

$$\text{P.E.S.} = \frac{\text{percentage change in quantity supplied}}{\text{percentage change in price}}$$

The short run is defined as the period of time in which a firm is unable to alter the amount of fixed factors such as capital used in production. Within a given time period, the elasticity of supply depends largely on the ability of a firm to vary output in response to price changes. If output is adjusted easily in response to price changes, then P.E.S. is elastic. Products whose output cannot be varied possess low P.E.S.

Therefore, analysis of the factors determining elasticity of supply requires a careful analysis of the factors determining the ability of a firm to vary output.

Consider the production of margarine. There are a number of reasons for believing that, in the short run, margarine output can be readily adjusted and the P.E.S. of margarine is elastic. For instance, margarine is a relatively simple manufactured good which requires little time for mass production. Output can be expanded rapidly by operating overtime or by working night shifts. Margarine can be refrigerated and stored for long periods. Stocks can then be used to effect changes in quantity supplied.

On the other hand, there are several factors which would make the short-run P.E.S. of margarine inelastic. The impact of diminishing returns and the difficulty of substituting one factor of production for another raises short-run unit costs and makes supply inelastic. If margarine factories are operating at or near full capacity, output cannot be expanded rapidly in response to a price rise. Again, if the labour used to operate machinery requires specialist training, it is also difficult to expand production rapidly.

The long run is defined as the period of time when the firm is able to vary the amount of any factor used in production. In the long run, P.E.S. is more elastic than in the short run, for a variety of reasons. In the long run, firms have an opportunity to overcome diminishing returns by adjusting the mix of labour and capital. The difficulties of factor immobility can be overcome through training.

Supply is elastic in the long run because firms have longer to plan their production decisions and more time to actually manufacture the good. For example, machinery used to produce similar products such as cheese spreads can be switched into or out of the production of margarine. The industry can adjust production capacity by installing or removing machines. If the firm decides on a very large adjustment in capacity, a new factory can be built or an existing plant can be closed down. Moreover, provided that there are no barriers to entry, new firms can enter the industry. Alternatively, existing firms can switch into the production of another good. It is also likely that supply will be affected by the development of new technologies which improve production techniques and increase P.E.S.

## 4.5 Solutions to Objective Questions

*Solution 4.2   Answer:* **D**

Price elasticity of demand (P.E.D.) is calculated here by using the equation

$$\text{P.E.D.} = \frac{P}{Q} \times \frac{\Delta Q}{\Delta P}$$

where $P$ is the initial price, $Q$ is the original quantity demanded, $\Delta Q$ is the change in quantity demanded and $\Delta P$ is the change in price. Substituting,

$$\text{P.E.D.} = \frac{3}{30} \times \frac{[30 - 25]}{[3 - 4]} = \frac{3}{30} \times \frac{5}{1} = \frac{15}{30} = 0.5$$

Note that the question states P.E.D. 'expressed as a positive number'. By convention, all negative signs are ignored when calculating P.E.D. The negative value from the rise in price $(-1)$ is treated as a positive.

*Solution 4.3   Answer:* **A**

A 'linear' demand curve is a straight line. The phrase 'a normal good' simply tells you that the demand curve in question slopes downwards from left to right.
   Consider the following diagram:

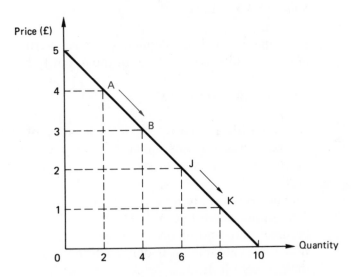

As you move down a demand curve, you are dividing a smaller percentage change in quantity demanded ($\%\Delta Q_D$) by a larger percentage change in price ($\%\Delta P$). For example:

$$\text{A to B} \quad \%\Delta Q_D = \frac{\text{change in } Q_D}{\text{original } Q_D} \times 100 = \frac{2}{2} \times 100 = 100\%$$

$$\%\Delta P = \frac{\text{change in } P}{\text{original } P} \times 100 = \frac{1}{3} \times 100 = 33.3\%$$

$$\therefore \text{ P.E.D.} \quad \text{A to B} = \frac{\%\Delta Q_D}{\%\Delta P} = \frac{100}{33.3} = 3 \text{ (i.e. P.E.D. is elastic)}$$

$$\text{J to K} \quad \%\Delta Q_D = \frac{2}{6} \times 100 = 33.3\%$$

$$\%\Delta P = \frac{1}{2} \times 100 = 50\%$$

$$\therefore \text{ P.E.D.} \quad \text{J to K} = \frac{33.3}{50} = 0.67$$

*Solution 4.4   Answer:* **C**

*In general*, the flatter a demand curve the more price-elastic is demand. Points B and C correspond to the same level of output. Since $D_1$ is flatter than $D_2$, C is more inelastic than B.

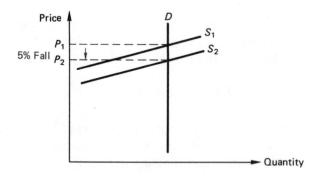

*Solution 4.5   Answer:* **E**

A completely inelastic demand curve is a vertical straight line. The 5% decrease in price results in no change in the quantity bought.

*Solution 4.6   Answer:* **D**

A good with a negative income elasticity of demand (Y.E.D.) is an inferior — i.e. as income rises, quantity demanded falls. Option **D** is correct. As you move up the *y*-axis, income rises but the quantity demanded continues to decline.

  Other options are incorrect because:

**A** ⇒ shows a positive Y.E.D. up to a certain level of income, then Y.E.D. becomes zero and finally negative;

**B** ⇒ the same amount is demanded no matter what the level of income — i.e. there is zero Y.E.D.;

**C** ⇒ shows a negative Y.E.D. up to a certain level of income, then Y.E.D. becomes zero and finally positive;

**E** ⇒ Y.E.D. is positive throughout.

*Solution 4.7   Answer:* **B**

The question requires the calculation of:
  (a) the percentage change in income;
  (b) the resulting percentage change in the amount of each good demanded.

The percentage (%) change ($\Delta$) in income ($Y$) is calculated by using the equation

$$\%\Delta Y = \frac{\Delta Y}{Y} \times 100 = \frac{\text{\pounds}5000 - \text{\pounds}6000}{\text{\pounds}5000} \times 100 = \frac{\text{\pounds}1000}{\text{\pounds}5000} \times 100 = 20\%$$

The percentage change in demand for each good equals the change in demand, divided by the original demand, times 100:

$$\%\Delta A = \frac{5}{10} \times 100 = 50\%; \quad \%\Delta B = \frac{2}{8} \times 100 = 25\%; \quad \%\Delta C = \frac{1}{10} \times 100 = 10\%$$

The 20% increase in income results in a proportionately greater increase in the quantity of A demanded of 50%.

*Solution 4.8   Answer:* **A**

Two goods in joint demand are complements. Complements have a negative cross elasticity of demand (X.E.D.). If the price of one good (e.g. electricity) rises, the demand for a complement (e.g. electric fires) falls. This type of relationship between price and demand is only shown in option **A**. Other options are incorrect because:
**B** $\Rightarrow$ shows positive X.E.D., which is possessed by substitutes;
**C** $\Rightarrow$ shows zero X.E.D., which occurs when goods are independent;
**D** and **E** $\Rightarrow$ do not represent any possible relationship.

*Solution 4.9   Answer:* **A**

If price elasticity of demand is 2, the good is relatively elastic. While consumers are now paying less for each unit bought, they are in fact buying proportionately more than before the price decrease. Other options are incorrect because:
**D** and **E** $\Rightarrow$ require information about revenue which is not supplied.

*Solution 4.10   Answer:* **D**

The effect of discontinuing half-price mid-week tickets is to increase price. If elasticity of demand for mid-week tickets is greater than 1 but less than infinity (i.e. elastic), then the increase in price brings about a greater percentage fall in sales. Total revenue falls.

*Solution 4.11   Answer:* **B**

The following options are correct:
**1** $\Rightarrow$ rectangular hyperbola demand curves possess unitary P.E.D. at all points;
**2** $\Rightarrow$ where P.E.D. is unitary, a given percentage change in price is followed by an equal but opposite percentage change in quantity demanded.
    Option **3** is incorrect, because manufactured goods do not necessarily possess unitary P.E.D.

*Solution 4.12   Answer:* **A**

All options are correct.
    **1** $\Rightarrow$ Demand is elastic if consumers can switch easily to substitutes following a price increase.
    **2** $\Rightarrow$ Consumers notice small percentage changes in the price of expensive goods. For instance, a 4% increase adds £400 to the price of an £8000 car.

**3** $\Rightarrow$ A product with few complements will not be needed for joint use with other goods.

*Solution 4.13   Answer:* **C**

**1** $\Rightarrow$ 'Price elasticity of supply will be smaller' means 'supply becomes more inelastic'. Option **1** is incorrect because firms can use more fixed factors in the long run to increase supply. The following options are correct:
**2** $\Rightarrow$ firms with few stocks are unable to increase quantity supplied, quickly;
**3** $\Rightarrow$ firms cannot increase quantity supplied, quickly, if they are unable to employ additional factors of production.

*Solution 4.14   Answer:* **C**

The following options are correct:
**2** $\Rightarrow$ a feature of any linear supply curve passing through the origin is that it possesses unitary price elasticity of supply (P.E.S.) at *all* points;
**3** $\Rightarrow$ P.E.S. equals 1 at point L (and points K and J).

*Solution 4.15   Answer:* **D**

The type of relationship between two goods is indicated by the cross elasticity of demand (X.E.D.) value. If X.E.D. equals zero, a change in the price of good X has no effect on the quantity of good Y demanded and the two goods are said to be independent of each other. Other options are incorrect because:
**2** and **3** $\Rightarrow$ substitute goods are in competitive demand and have a positive X.E.D.

# 5 Costs of Production

## 5.1 Fact Sheet

### (a) Short-run Product Curves

In the short run, firms can increase output by adding extra units of labour to a fixed amount of capital.

- The addition to output made by each extra worker is called *marginal product of labour* ($MP_L$).
- Output per worker is called *average product of labour* ($AP_L$).
- The concept of *returns* compares the percentage change in labour ($\%\Delta L$) with the resulting percentage change in output ($\%\Delta Q$).

**Table 5.1** Types of return

| Type of return | Description | Marginal product |
|---|---|---|
| Increasing returns | $\%\Delta L$ is smaller than the resulting $\%\Delta Q$ | is rising |
| Constant returns | $\%\Delta L$ is equal to the resulting $\%\Delta Q$ | is constant |
| Decreasing returns | $\%\Delta L$ is greater than the resulting $\%\Delta Q$ | is falling |

- The *law of diminishing returns* states that, as extra units of a variable factor are combined with a given amount of a fixed factor, the marginal product of the variable factor will eventually fall.
- If only diminishing returns are referred to, this is taken to mean diminishing marginal returns.

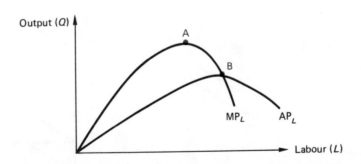

**Figure 5.1** Product curves: $AP = \Theta/L$; $MP = \Delta Q/\Delta L$. A is the point of diminishing returns; B is the point of diminishing average returns

## (b) Costs of Production

**Table 5.2** Types of cost

| Term | Symbol | Definition | Equation |
|------|--------|-----------|----------|
| Total cost | TC | The amount spent on producing a given output | TC = FC + VC |
| Variable costs | VC | Production expenses *dependent* on the level of output | VC = TC − FC |
| Fixed costs | FC | Production expenses *independent* of the level of output | FC = TC − VC |
| Average cost | AC | The amount spent on producing *each* unit | AC = TC ÷ $Q$ |
| Average variable cost | AVC | Unit variable costs *dependent* on the level of output | AVC = VC ÷ $Q$ |
| Average fixed cost | AFC | Unit fixed costs *independent* of the level of output | AFC = FC ÷ $Q$ |
| Marginal cost | MC | The amount spent on producing *one extra* unit | MC = $\Delta$TC ÷ $\Delta Q$ |

- Accountancy and economic definitions of costs are different.
- Economists use the concept of *opportunity cost* when calculating production costs.
- If resources are owned by the firm, the *imputed* (estimated) transfer earnings of the factor is included as a cost.

## (c) Short-run Cost Curves

There are two methods of illustrating short-run cost curves.

In Figure 5.2:
- MC curve rises given diminishing returns.
- AC curve rises if MC is greater than AC.
- MC is made up entirely of changes in VC.
- *Optimum* output is where AC is lowest (point A).

In Figure 5.3:
- TC curve rises if output increases.
- VC curve rises if output increases.
- FC stay constant as output increases.

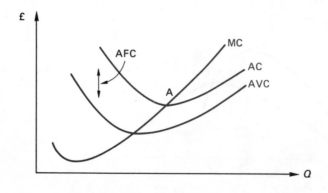

**Figure 5.2** Unit cost curves

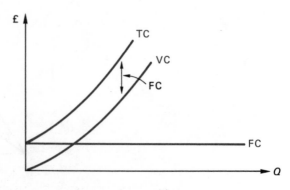

**Figure 5.3** Total cost curves

### (d) Economies of Scale

In the long run, the firm can increase output by varying all factors of production. *Economies of scale* (EOS) are reductions in long-run costs which occur from an increase in production.

- *Internal EOS* occur within the firm as output rises.
- *External EOS* occur outside the firm and are independent of the size of the individual firm.

**Table 5.3**  Types of internal economy of scale

| Types of internal EOS | Description |
| --- | --- |
| Specialisation | Large firms have more scope for the division of labour than have small firms |
| Indivisibilities | Some machines are of a minimum size which can only be kept fully occupied by large firms |
| Increased dimension | The cost of capital does not increase in proportion to the output of each machine |
| Principle of multiples | Large firms use a machine combination which eliminates bottlenecks caused by different machines working at different speeds |
| Linked processes | Bringing together different stages of production in one factory reduces costs |
| Managerial | Big firms can spread the cost of employing the best managers over a large level of output. Managerial costs do not increase in proportion with output |
| Financial | Large firms offer more security and pay a lower rate of interest on loans than do small firms. Large firms can raise capital cheaply through a rights issue |
| Commercial | Large firms buy raw materials and components in bulk and are therefore given a discount |
| Marketing | Transportation and advertising costs do not increase in proportion with output |
| Research and development | Large firms can spread the cost of improving products over a large level of output |

**Table 5.4**  Types of external economy of scale

| Types of external EOS | Description |
| --- | --- |
| Infrastructure | Proximity to a good transport and communications network |
| Ancillary firms | Local back-up firms supply specialist support services or components |
| Skilled local labour | An area may have trained workers looking for jobs |
| Education | An area may have colleges providing specialist training |

### (e) Diseconomies of Scale

*Diseconomies of scale* (DOS) are increases in long-run costs which occur from an increase in production.

(i) *Internal DOS* occur within the firm when increases in output raise long-run costs. They occur mainly because of managerial difficulties in oversized firms:
  (1) managers are unable to exercise effective control or co-ordination;
  (2) internal communications within the company are difficult;
  (3) workers feel isolated and out of touch with managers, and industrial relations decline.
(ii) *External DOS* occur outside the firm when the long-run costs of all local firms rise when:
  (1) local road congestion causes transportation delays;
  (2) local land and factories become scarce and rents rise;
  (3) labour shortages develop within the area and wages rise.

### (f) Long-run Cost Curves

- A *short-run average cost curve* (SAC) shows the unit cost associated with a given size of plant.
- A *long-run average cost curve* (LAC) shows the minimum unit cost of producing each level of output, allowing the size of plant to vary.
- A LAC curve is found by drawing a line tangential to each SAC curve.
- Each SAC curve shows the unit cost from plants of different size.
- The size of plant associated with $SAC_2$ is the smallest needed to minimise unit cost — i.e. *minimum efficient plant size* (MEPS).
- The slope of the LAC curve is determined by internal EOS.
- The position of the LAC curve is determined by external EOS.

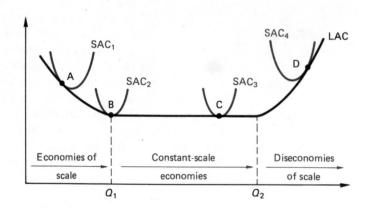

**Figure 5.4** Long-run average cost curve

The concept of *returns to scale* compares the percentage change in labour and capital ($\%\Delta L\&K$) with the resulting percentage change in output ($\%\Delta Q$). Table 5.4 explains the relationship between returns to scale and economies of scale.

**Table 5.5**  Returns to scale and scale economies

| Returns to scale | Description | Scale economies | Slope of LAC curve |
| --- | --- | --- | --- |
| Increasing returns to scale | $\%\Delta L\&K$ is smaller than the resulting $\%\Delta Q$ | Economies of scale | Falling |
| Constant returns to scale | $\%\Delta L\&K$ is equal to the resulting $\%\Delta Q$ | Constant | Horizontal |
| Decreasing returns to scale | $\%\Delta L\&K$ is greater than the resulting $\%\Delta Q$ | Diseconomies of scale | Rising |

## (g) Integration

*Integration* occurs when two firms combine. The new firm will probably enjoy significant economies of scale, and require fewer managers and workers.

- A *merger* is when the two firms agree to form a new company.
- A *takeover* is when one company buys a controlling interest in a second against the wishes of that company's directors.

There are three types of integration.

(i) *Horizontal*, between two companies at the same stage of production.
(ii) *Vertical*, between two companies at different stages of production, either:
    (1) forwards, with a firm further up the chain of production; or
    (2) backwards, with a firm lower down the chain of production.
(iii) *Lateral* (i.e. *diversification*), between companies making unrelated goods but with common inputs.
(iv) *Conglomerate* between companies making unrelated goods.

## 5.2 Data Response

### Worked Example 5.1

A profitable airline is considering the introduction of a new trans-Atlantic flight and is faced with the following costs per flight:

| | |
|---|---|
| Fuel charges | 10 000 |
| Depreciation | 700 |
| Insurance | 300 |
| Landing charges | 500 |
| Interest | 500 |
| Labour | 5 000 |
| Other fixed costs | 5 000 |

(a) From the above table distinguish between fixed and variable costs. Give reasons for your choice. **(4 marks)**
(b) (i) Given a maximum seating capacity of 300 persons per aircraft, what is the *minimum* price per seat that the airline must charge on this flight to avoid making a loss? **(5 marks)**
    (ii) If the above costs were representative of all flights, what price must the airline charge to remain in business in the long run? **(5 marks)**
(c) Discuss the factors that are likely to determine the *actual* price charged.
**(6 marks)**
(L Jan. 1987)

*Solution 5.1*

(a) *Fixed costs* are those costs of production independent of the level of number of flights undertaken. An allowance for depreciation has to be made whether or not an aeroplane flies. In a given time period, the amount of insurance paid, or interest owed on loans, does not change with the number of flights made. *Variable costs* are those costs dependent on the number of flights undertaken. Fuel charges, landing charges and labour costs are incurred after each flight. This assumes that labour is paid per flight and can be laid off at zero cost if no flights are made.

(b) (i) In the short run, a firm will continue to operate at a loss, provided that variable costs are covered. From the table, the total variable cost of each flight is £10 000 fuel charges, £500 landing charges and £5000 labour costs, making a total of £15 500. Assuming that all 300 seats are sold at £15 500 ÷ 300 = £51.67, then the operating loss is less than the total of fixed costs which would have to be met if the flight were cancelled. To avoid making a loss, all costs must be met. From the table, the total cost of each flight is £22 000. Dividing by seating capacity gives loss-avoiding price of £73.34.

(ii) A price of £73.34 would be sufficient to cover the costs specified in the table. However, this price may not be sufficient to reward the owners for the risk and responsibility of running the airline. Normal profit is considered to be a cost of production and may well have been included in the 'other fixed costs' category. If not, the airline may operate a 'cost-plus' pricing policy and add, say, 20% onto costs (£14.67), giving a flight price of £88.01.

It is also highly unlikely that the airline will be able to sell all 300 seats for every flight. The minimum price which must be charged is average cost ÷ average seating. For example, assume that 250 seats on average are sold for each flight. Minimum price becomes £22 000 ÷ 250 = £88.

(c) Airline flights are subject to international agreements between countries. These agreements are highly restrictive, and can specify the number of flights each week, the timing of flights and the prices which can be charged. Hence, the market for international flights is highly imperfect and essentially oligopolistic in nature. Evidence suggests that even where more than one transatlantic airline flies between two cities, companies operate as a cartel with price fixed above the likely market price. With each airline charging the same price, non-price competition and branding is used to differentiate products.

The actual price charged, then, is likely to be affected by the cost structure of each flight; the number of seats sold on average; and the degree of competition between airlines on the transatlantic route.

# 5.3 Objective Questions

**Example 5.2**

The addition to total output from the use of an extra unit of one factor is:
A  marginal cost          B  marginal product       C  average cost
D  average product        E  marginal product of labour

**Example 5.3**

In the following diagram, MP shows the marginal product of labour and AP shows the average product of labour, at each level of output. The law of diminishing returns begins to operate beyond output level:
A              B                C                D                E

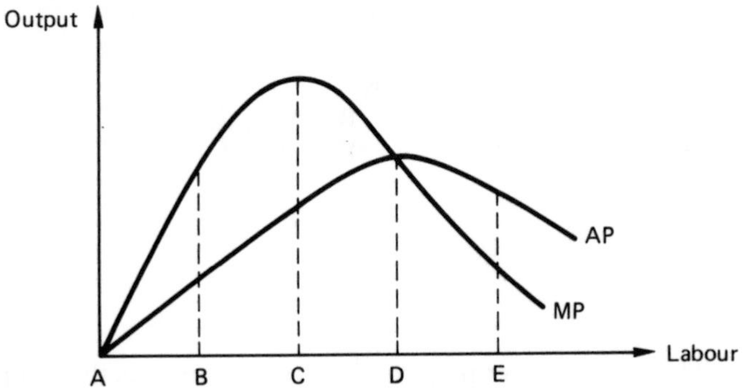
Output
AP
MP
Labour
A
B
C
D
E

*Examples 5.4–5.7 refer to the following table. Each question has a response* **A**, ***B***, ***C***, ***D*** *and* ***E***. *Each letter may be used once, more than once or not at all.*

The table shows the weekly output of a perfectly competitive firm.
Average revenue is £5.

| | | | | | |
|---|---|---|---|---|---|
| *Output (tonnes)* | 0 | 10 | 20 | 30 | 40 |
| *Total cost (£)* | 120 | 180 | 200 | 210 | 225 |

**A** 0 **B** 10 **C** 20 **D** 30 **E** 40

From the alternatives **A–E** above, select that which shows:

### Example 5.4

The level of output where average cost is highest.

### Example 5.5

The level of output where marginal cost is lowest.

### Example 5.6

The level of output where average variable costs are £4.

### Example 5.7

The level of output produced by the firm.

### Example 5.8

The diagram shows short-run per-unit cost curves for a firm:

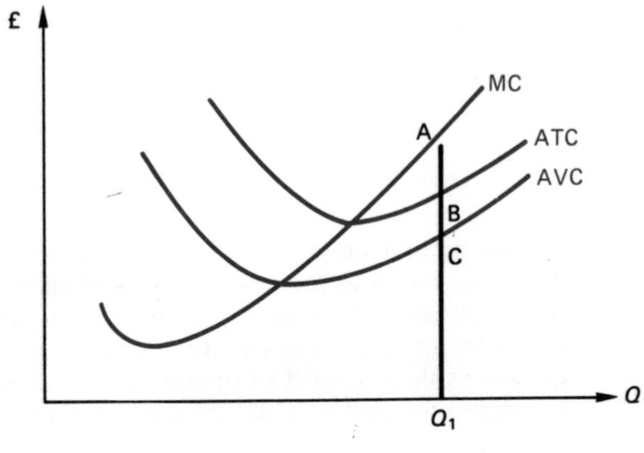
£
MC
ATC
AVC
A
B
C
Q
$Q_1$

Total fixed cost is given by:

**A**  A – B  **B**  A – C  **C**  (A – B) × $Q_1$
**D**  (B – C) × $Q_1$  **E**  (A – C) × $Q_1$

**Example 5.9**

The short-run total costs (TC) of an imperfectly competitive firm are given by the equation TC = £3000 + $5Q^2$, where $Q$ is the level of output. The fixed costs of the firm are:

**A**  0  **B**  $5Q^2$  **C**  £3000
**D**  £3000 × $Q^2$  **E**  £3000 + $5Q^2$

**Example 5.10**

If a firm's average variable cost curve is U-shaped, then, as output increases from zero, marginal cost must:
**A**  always increase
**B**  always decrease
**C**  be constant
**D**  initially decrease and then increase
**E**  initially increase and then decrease

**Example 5.11**

The diagram shows the total cost curve of a firm. It follows from the diagram that, as the level of output increases, marginal cost must:

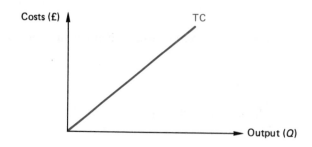

**A**  always increase
**B**  always decrease
**C**  remain constant
**D**  initially decrease and then increase
**E**  initially increase and then decrease

**Example 5.12**

The long-run average cost curve of a firm:
**A**  is tangential to the lowest points of short-run average cost curves
**B**  decreases continuously because of increasing returns to scale
**C**  shifts upwards following the opening of a local motorway
**D**  shows the unit cost of operating a given size of plant
**E**  shows the unit cost of operating different plant

## Example 5.13

A firm increases the amount of labour, raw materials and capital used in production by 25%. If output increases by 15%, the firm is subject to:
A   the law of diminishing returns
B   decreasing returns to capital
C   decreasing returns to labour
D   diseconomies of scale
E   decreasing marginal efficiency of capital

## Example 5.14

Horizontal integration occurs when a car manufacturer:
A   merges with a second car manufacturer
B   buys a chain of garages
C   merges with a steel firm
D   merges its accounts and sales departments
E   sells part of the company to a competitor

*Select your answers to Examples 5.15–5.17 by means of the following code*:
A   *if 1, 2 and 3 are all correct*
B   *if 1 and 2 only are correct*
C   *if 2 and 3 only are correct*
D   *if 1 only is correct*

## Example 5.15

Theory of the firm usually assumes that in the short run:
1   at least one factor is fixed
2   firms eventually experience diminishing returns
3   firms are perfectly competitive

## Example 5.16

In the short run, the variable cost of producing one extra unit is £220. Therefore:
1   marginal cost is £220
2   marginal fixed costs are zero
3   marginal variable costs are £220

## Example 5.17

An oil company acquires a chain of petrol stations. This is an example of:
1   external growth
2   forward vertical integration
3   a holding company

# 5.4   Essays

## Example 5.18

Explain the determination of the firm's average cost curve in (a) the short run and (b) the long run.

(AEB Nov. 1985)

- The question tests your understanding of returns and returns to scale.
- Make good use of accurate graphs.
- Use examples to develop important points.

*Solution 5.18*

A firm is that unit which organises the production of goods and services. Traditional neoclassical theory assumes that firms use only two factors to produce output: labour and capital. Furthermore, it assumes that firms can only increase output in the short run by adding extra units of labour to a fixed number of machines.

Marginal cost (MC) refers to the cost of producing an extra unit. Extra units are manufactured by employing additional workers. Assume that each worker receives the same wage. Initially, each extra worker is able to produce more than the previous worker, because, at first, marginal workers have easy access to a fixed number of machines and the division of labour principle can be applied. Since the firm is initially obtaining an increasing return for a constant outlay on wages, marginal costs are falling and the MC curve in Figure 1 slopes downwards. Beyond $Q_1$, the law of diminishing returns operates and the firm receives back a decreasing return for a constant outlay on wages. Workers experience delayed access to machines and the opportunities for the division of labour have been fully exploited.

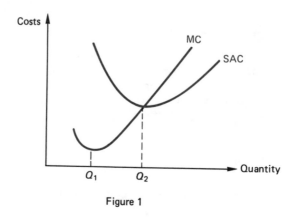

Figure 1

Average cost is the unit cost of producing a given level of output. The shape of the short-run average cost curve (SAC) in Figure 1 depends critically on the behaviour of marginal costs. SAC slopes downwards up to $Q_2$ because marginal cost is less than unit cost. Beyond $Q_2$, marginal cost exceeds average cost and the SAC curve begins to rise.

It has been established that the shape of the short-run average cost curve is determined by the shape of the marginal cost curve, which, in turn, is determined by the law of diminishing returns. The type of return experienced depends on the degree of access workers have to machines and on the scope for the division of labour.

In the short run, the firm is constrained to its current SAC curve. In the long run, the firm can increase plant (production unit) size and move to a new SAC curve. Increasing the amount of capital employed shifts the SAC curve to the right. The type of scale economy then experienced determines whether or not the new SAC curve also shifts upwards or downwards. SAC shifts downwards if the firm experiences economies of scale (Figure 2), upwards if diseconomies of scale begin to come into effect (Figure 3) and horizontally given constant scale economies (Figure 4).

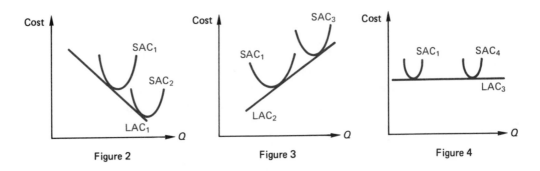

Figure 2                    Figure 3                    Figure 4

A long-run average cost curve (LAC) is the envelope of the firm's SAC curves. The shape of the LAC curve is determined by the type of internal scale economies experienced by the firm.

For example, the manufacture of cars offers significant potential technical economies of scale. Highly automated production lines populated with robot arms reduce LAC. As more cars are produced, the firm's greater requirement for raw materials such as steel allows it to negotiate substantial discounts with suppliers. Initially, the LAC curve of a car manufacturer slopes downwards as in Figure 2. However, beyond a certain level of output, LAC begins to rise as in Figure 3. Management becomes more difficult when the activities of the firm become more complex. Additional strata of middle managers (e.g. foremen) increase wages with no corresponding increase in output. Productivity may fall if workers feel alienated by impersonal mass production techniques.

In conclusion, it has been demonstrated that the firm's average cost curve is determined by the type of return experienced in the short run and the type of scale economy enjoyed in the long run.

**Example 5.19**

'Large firms have such overwhelming technical and financial advantages that the survival of the small business is surprising.' Discuss.

(SUJB 1986)

- The question tests your understanding of technical and financial economies of scale open to large firms.
- Describe the circumstances in which small firms thrive.
- Where possible, use real-world examples.

*Solution 5.19*

It is important to distinguish between large and small firms. The Bolton Committee Report (1971) suggests that small businesses are firms managed by the owner(s) and with a relatively small share of the market. Small manufacturing firms employ fewer than 200 people. Large firms are typically incorporated (limited companies), where ownership and management are separated. Large companies which exploit economies of scale enjoy a cost advantage over small firms in the same industry. In particular, large firms have access to the following technical and financial economies.

Technical economies occur in the production of a good. As the firm expands, there is greater scope for specialisation and the division of labour. For example, large factories can employ specialist skilled workers to do the same job all day with no time lost in changing tools or doing unfamiliar tasks. The indivisibility of certain types of capital means that many production processes including chemicals are impossible on a small scale. Mass production allows large firms to keep specialist capital fully utilised. Large firms can benefit by linking production processes that would otherwise be carried out in separate factories. For example, a large shift manufacturer can reduce transport costs by combining the weaving and cutting of cotton under the same roof. Economies of increased dimensions mean that doubling the size of the machine results in more than double an increase in output. The principle of multiples suggests that large firms can avoid the bottlenecks that occur when machines operate at different speeds, by installing a ratio of machines which keeps each fully utilised.

Financial economies allow large enterprises to raise capital on advantageous terms. Large firms are considered to be reliable and are therefore charged a low rate of interest. In particular, large firms have access to capital markets such as the Stock Exchange. Selling shares is a relatively inexpensive method of raising large sums of capital.

Despite the cost advantage to large firms of producing in bulk, small businesses continue to survive for a variety of reasons. Limited opportunities for economies of scale allow them to find niches in providing specialised products for small markets. For instance, in design where the product is specialised, is non-uniform and cannot be manufactured in bulk. Service industries such as hairdressing cannot easily achieve a large scale of operation, and therefore tend to be dominated by small firms. An irregular or limited demand for a product prevents mass production.

Small firms have the flexibility and low overheads needed to undertake 'one-off' projects — e.g. building construction. Often small firms survive by accepting subcontracted work from large companies. In industries such as printing, where fixed costs form only a small percentage of total costs, low set-up costs encourage the development of small firms. Where the market for a good is restricted and highly localised, small firms survive. For example, village shops.

In an attempt to stimulate the supply side of the economy, the government has introduced a number of schemes which help the survival of the small firm. For instance, the Enterprise Allowance pays a weekly sum to the unemployed while they are setting up their own firm. The Business Expansion Scheme gives relief against income tax to investors in unquoted companies.

## 5.5 Solutions to Objective Questions

*Solution 5.2   Answer:* **B**

Marginal product refers to the addition to total product following the employment of an extra unit of a variable factor.

**E** ⇒ Economists usually assume that capital is the fixed factor while labour is variable. However, since there is no reason why labour could not be the fixed factor instead of capital, option **E** is incorrect.

*Solution 5.3   Answer:* **C**

Unless otherwise stated, the law of diminishing returns refers to diminishing *marginal* returns. In the diagram the apex (top) of the marginal product curve shows the point of diminishing returns and this corresponds to output level C. Output beyond this point results in diminishing returns.

Solutions 5.4–5.7 make use of the following table.

| Output (tonnes) | 0 | 10 | 20 | 30 | 40 |
|---|---|---|---|---|---|
| Total cost (£) | 120 | 180 | 200 | 210 | 225 |
| Average cost | – | 18 | 10 | 7 | 5.6 |
| Marginal cost | – | 6 | 2 | 1 | 1.5 |
| Abnormal loss | −120 | −130 | −100 | −60 | −25 |

*Solution 5.4   Answer:* **B**

Dividing total cost by each level of output gives average cost. From the table, average cost is highest at output level 10.

A $\Rightarrow$ Note that there are no average costs involved in producing zero output.

*Solution 5.5   Answer:* **D**

Marginal cost is calculated by dividing the change in total cost involved in increasing output by the resulting change in output. For instance, the marginal cost of the thirtieth unit is the cost of making 30 tonnes (£210), less the cost of making 20 tonnes (£200), i.e. £10, divided by the increase in output of 10 tonnes (30 − 20). Marginal cost here is £1.

*Solution 5.6   Answer:* **C**

Fixed costs have to be paid out by the firm even if it produces zero output. There are no variable costs involved in producing nothing. However, the table indicates that the total cost of zero production is £120. Therefore, the firm's fixed costs must be £120.

Total cost minus fixed cost gives variable cost. The variable cost of producing 20 tonnes is £200 − £120 = £80.

Variable cost divided by the level of output gives average variable cost. The average variable cost of producing 20 tonnes is £80/20 = £4.

*Solution 5.7   Answer:* **E**

Figures 6.3 and 6.4 show how loss-making firms decide whether or not to carry on production. Multiplying each output level by average revenue (£5) gives total revenue. The abnormal loss column is found by subtracting total cost from total revenue, at each level of output.

A $\Rightarrow$ The loss of £25 from producing 40 tonnes is less than the fixed costs of £120 which would have had to be met even if the firm stopped production altogether.

*Solution 5.8   Answer:* **D**

Total fixed cost is found by multiplying average fixed cost by the level of output ($Q_1$). Average fixed cost is the difference between average total cost and average variable cost (B − C).

*Solution 5.9   Answer:* **C**

The equation TC = £3000 × $5Q^2$ means 'total cost is found by multiplying a fixed sum of £3000 by 5 times the particular level of output, squared'. Fixed costs are £3000. Variable costs are 5 times the particular level of output, squared.

*Solution 5.10   Answer:* **D**

Fixed costs are not affected by changes in output. Therefore, marginal cost (MC) determines changes in variable costs. Figure 5.2 shows a U-shaped average variable cost (AVC) curve. Note that the AVC curve slopes downwards, provided that MC is less than AVC. The MC curve intersects AVC at its lowest point. Once MC is above AVC, the AVC curve begins to rise.

*Solution 5.11   Answer:* **C**

A linear total cost curve means the cost of making each extra unit, marginal cost, remains the same.

*Solution 5.12   Answer:* **E**

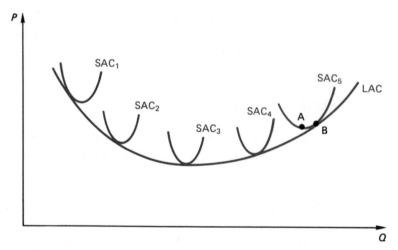

Other options are incorrect because:
A ⇒ while the long-run average cost (LAC) curve is tangential to each SAC, the point of tangency does *not* always occur at the lowest point of each SAC curve (for example, on $SAC_5$, A is the lowest point on the curve but B is the point of tangency);
B ⇒ the LAC curve of some firms slopes upwards because of decreasing returns to scale;
C ⇒ is an external economy of scale which would shift the LAC upwards;
D ⇒ each individual SAC shows the unit cost of operating a *given* size of plant.

*Solution 5.13   Answer:* **D**

Returns to scale compares the percentage change in *all* factors with the resulting change in output. Since a 25% increase in production results in a smaller percentage increase of only 15%, the firm is experiencing decreasing returns to scale. Decreasing returns to scale are the result of diseconomies of scale.
   A ⇒ The law of diminishing returns is a short-run concept where only one factor is varied, usually labour. The question specifies changes in more than one factor.

*Solution 5.14   Answer:* **A**

Horizontal integration occurs when two firms at the same stage of production merge. Other options are incorrect because:
**B** and **C** ⇒ are examples of vertical integration;
**D** ⇒ is an example of management reorganisation;
**E** ⇒ has nothing to do with integration.

*Solution 5.15   Answer:* **B**

Option **3** is incorrect because theory of the firm considers several types of market structure apart from perfect competition.

*Solution 5.16   Answer:* **A**

There are no fixed costs involved in increasing output. Therefore, in the short run, marginal cost and marginal variable costs are identical.

*Solution 5.17   Answer:* **B**

**1** ⇒ External growth occurs when a firm becomes larger through merger or takeover.
**3** ⇒ A holding company owns a subsidiary. Holding companies are not a necessary consequence of vertical integration.

# 6 Markets

## 6.1 Fact Sheet

### (a) Market Structure

- A *market* exists where buyers and sellers negotiate the exchange of a product.
- An *industry* is made up of firms producing similar products.
- *Market structure* refers to the number and type of firms in a particular industry.
- *Concentration ratios* measure the proportion of an industry's output or employment accounted for by, say, the five largest firms.

**Table 6.1** Market structure

| Market structure | No. of firms | Substitutes | Price Taker/ Maker | Barriers to entry | Abnormal profit ($\pi$) |
|---|---|---|---|---|---|
| Perfect competition | Many small | Many perfect | Taker | None | Only in the short run |
| Monopolistic competition | Many small | Many close | Maker | None | Only in the short run |
| Oligopoly | Several large | Few | Maker | Some | Possible in the long run |
| Pure monopoly | One large | None | Maker | Complete | Possible in the long run |

### (b) Revenue

- The money received from the sale of output is called *revenue*.

**Table 6.2** Types of revenue

| Term | Symbol | Definition | Equation |
|---|---|---|---|
| Total revenue | TR | The income received from the sale of a given output | $TR = AR \times Q$ |
| Average revenue | AR | The amount received from the sale of each unit | $AR = TR \div Q$ |
| Marginal revenue | MR | The amount received from selling one extra unit | $MR = \Delta TR \div \Delta Q$ |

## (c) Profit

**Table 6.3**  Types of profit

| Term | Symbol | Definition | TR − TC is |
|---|---|---|---|
| Normal profit | $\pi = 0$ | The minimum amount of profit the firm must receive to carry on producing (i.e. *transfer income*) | Zero |
| Abnormal profit | $\pi$ | Profits exceed the amount the firm must receive to carry on producing (i.e. *economic rent*) | Positive |
| Abnormal loss | $-\pi$ | Profits are below the amount the firm must receive to carry on producing (i.e. *subnormal profit*) | Negative |

- Accountancy and economic definitions of profit are different.
- Economists regard normal profit as a *cost* of production.
- Revenue minus production costs equals *abnormal profit* ($\pi$):

$$\pi = \text{TR} - \text{TC} = (\text{AR} - \text{AC}) \times Q$$

- Neoclassical theory assumes that firms aim to maximise profits. However, where ownership and control of a company are in separate hands, managers may have a different aim, such as sales maximisation.

## (d) Perfect Competition

- A *perfectly competitive industry* is made up of a large number of small firms, each selling homogeneous (identical) products to a large number of buyers.
- No individual customer receives preferential treatment.
- Each firm is a *price taker*; therefore, $\text{MR} = P$.
- There are no barriers to entry.
- Consumers and producers have perfect market knowledge.
- The *profit-maximising level of output* occurs where marginal cost (MC) rises to equal marginal revenue (MR) — i.e. where $\text{MR} = \text{MC}$.

In Figure 6.1, the representative firm has to decide whether or not to produce extra units. The firm compares the cost of the marginal unit (i.e. MC) with the revenue received from its sale (i.e. MR). An extra unit is only worth producing if MR exceeds MC. Since MC includes an amount of normal profit, the firm maximises its profits by increasing production up to and including $Q_1$.

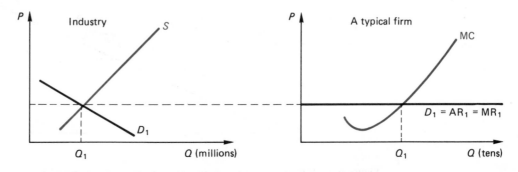

**Figure 6.1**  Profit maximisation in perfect competition

## (e) Supply Curves in Perfect Competition

In Figure 6.2, an increase in demand raises market price to $P_2$. In the short run, the firm earns an abnormal profit of $(P_2 - P_3) \times Q_2$. In the long run, the entry of new firms increases supply and the supply curve shifts to the right. Assuming constant scale economies, price falls back to $P_1$, where normal profits are restored.

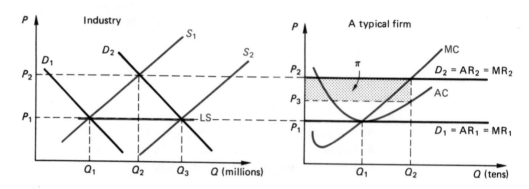

**Figure 6.2**  Long-run supply curve of a perfectly competitive firm

- The MC curve shows combinations of price and quantity supplied by a firm. Therefore, the MC curve is the supply curve of the firm.
- The addition of each firm's MC curve gives the industry's short-run supply curve.
- The long-run supply curve (LS) shows the amount of a good supplied by the industry at different prices, allowing the number of firms and size of plant to vary.

## (f) Abnormal Losses in Perfect Competition

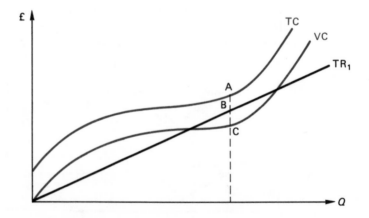

**Figure 6.3**  Revenue covers variable costs: losses are minimised by carrying on production because total revenue covers all variable costs and some (BC) of the fixed costs

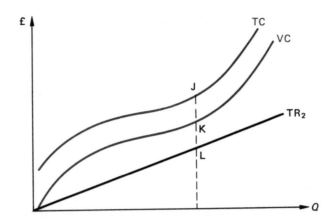

**Figure 6.4**  Variable costs exceed revenue: losses are minimised by ceasing production because total revenue fails to cover any variable costs and none of the fixed costs

- A loss-making firm carries on production in the short run, provided that variable costs are met.
- In the long run, some firms making abnormal losses leave the industry, supply decreases and price rises. The total revenue curve in Figures 6.3 and 6.4 would shift upwards until normal profits are restored.

## (g) Imperfect Competition

- An *imperfectly competitive industry* is made up of a firm or firms selling a differentiated (non-identical) product.
- The most extreme form of imperfect competition is pure monopoly.
- Monopolists are *price makers* and can set price *or* output for their own product.
- The more price-inelastic the firm's demand curve the greater its market power.

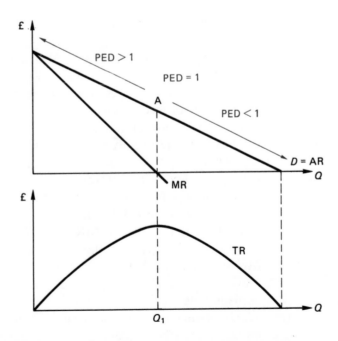

**Figure 6.5**  Revenue curves and price elasticity of demand (P.E.D.)

- The MR curve bisects the origin and the AR curve.
- To sell more output, the firm has to reduce price on the extra unit and *all* preceding units. Therefore, MR is always less than price.
- Up to $Q_1$, MR is positive, TR is rising and P.E.D is elastic.
- Beyond $Q_1$, MR is negative, TR is falling and P.E.D is inelastic.
- At A, P.E.D is unitary.
- Total revenue is maximised at $Q_1$.

### (h) Profit Maximisation in Imperfect Competition

- Monopolists do not automatically earn abnormal profits.
- The ability of monopolists to exclude competition allows them to earn abnormal profits in the long run.
- The intersection of the MC and MR curves give the profit-maximising level of output.
- In Figure 6.6, abnormal profits equals the area $(P_1 - P_2) \times Q_1$.
- In Figure 6.7, normal profits only are being earned.

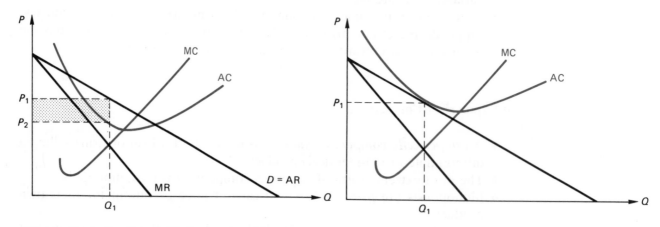

**Figure 6.6**  Abnormal profits in imperfect competition          **Figure 6.7**  Normal profit in imperfect competition

### (i) Alternative Pricing Strategies

(i) *Cost-plus* pricing occurs when a firm adds a given percentage mark-up to average cost. A loss can be made if sales fall short of estimates.

(ii) *Price discrimination* occurs when the same product is sold in different markets for different prices. A *discriminating monopoly* is only able to practise price discrimination if it:
   (1) has some monopoly power and is able to exclude competitors;
   (2) is able to prevent the resale of the product;
   (3) has markets with different price elasticity of demand for the product.
   The monopolist adds together $MR_1$, from market A and $MR_2$ from market B to find the MR curve for both markets $(MR_1 + MR_2)$. Output is fixed where the $MR_1 + MR_2$ curve intersects the MC curve at $Q_1$. $Q_1$ is then divided between the two markets by setting output where $MC = MR$ in each market. Note that $Q_A + Q_B = Q_1$. Price is $P_1$ in market A and $P_2$ in market B. Price is higher in the market where demand is less elastic.

(iii) *Market penetration* pricing occurs when a firm reduces price to increase *market share* (the percentage of an industry's sales accounted for by one firm).

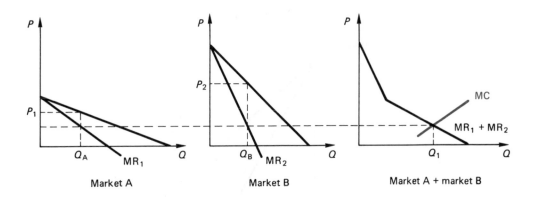

**Figure 6.8** Price discrimination in two markets

   (iv) *Limit pricing* occurs when a firm sets price just low enough to discourage possible new entrants.

   (v) *Predatory pricing* occurs when a firm reduces price in the short run so as to force competitors out of the industry.

   (vi) *Skimming pricing* occurs when a firm charges a high initial price where some consumers are prepared to pay more for a new product. Eventually price is lowered to extend demand.

### (j) Non-price Competition

*Oligopolies* tend to avoid price competition because competitors will match any price cuts. Firms wishing to increase sales are more likely to use non-price competition such as:

   (i) Advertising, where firms promote information about the company or a product. Advertising aims to:

      (1) increase demand for a product;

      (2) improve brand image and encourage consumer loyalty, thereby making demand more price-inelastic;

      (3) create separate markets for the same product so that price discrimination can take place — e.g. soap powders.

   (ii) Organising promotion campaigns (e.g. free offers).

   (iii) Providing improved after-sales service.

## 6.2   **Data Response**

**Worked Example 6.1**

A publishing firm has decided to publish a new hard-cover Economics textbook. The publisher incurs substantial fixed costs in the form of editing, type setting, proof reading and advertising. After these initial expenses there is additionally the costs of paper, printing, binding, etc., such costs being a constant amount per book produced. The author of the book negotiates a contract with the publishing firm whereby he is paid a percentage of the publisher's gross profits from the sale of the book. The publisher has exclusive rights to publish the book as enforced through copyright law. The relevant average revenue and marginal revenue curves as estimated by the publisher are indicated in the diagram on the next page.

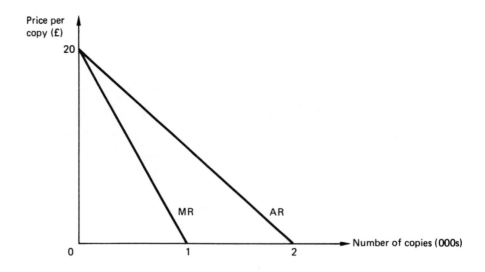

(a) Why are the average revenue and marginal revenue curves downward-sloping as indicated in the diagram?

**(4 marks)**

(b) Reproduce the diagram and draw in the general form of the publisher's marginal cost curve, average fixed cost curve and average total cost curve.

**(4 marks)**

(c) With reference to your diagram, explain in general terms the price the publisher will set for the book if he seeks to maximise profits.

**(4 marks)**

(d) Suppose the publisher is considering increasing his expenditure on advertising the book by a certain amount. Would this necessarily increase his profits?

**(4 marks)**

(e) Suppose that instead of a profit-sharing agreement the author had negotiated to receive royalty payments calculated as a percentage of the publisher's sales revenue. Explain why in this case there is likely to be a conflict of interest between the publisher, who is seeking to maximise profits, and the author as to the appropriate price for the book.

**(5 marks)**

(f) Why might it be profitable for the publisher, after a lapse of time, to publish a paperback edition at a lower price?

**(4 marks)**
(WJEC 1987)

*Solution 6.1*

(a) The average revenue curve is the consumers' demand curve for the book. The downward-sloping curve indicates that consumers are prepared to buy more copies of the book as price falls because of the substitution effect (the book is now relatively cheaper than substitutes) and the income effect (consumers can now afford to buy more copies of the text).

   The marginal revenue curve slopes downwards because the publisher is a price maker. In order to sell more copies, price must fall not only for extra copies sold, but also on all preceding books. Hence, marginal revenue is always less than price.

(b)

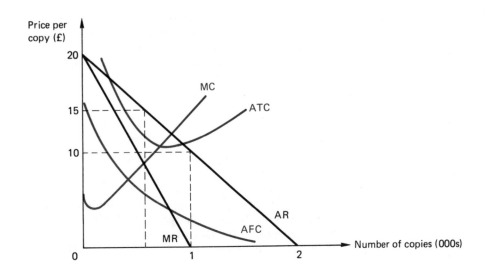

(c) The publisher will continue to print books up to the point where the cost of the extra unit (MC) equals revenue from the sale of the extra text (MR). This suggests a price of £15. (*Note that the actual price charged depends on where the candidate draws the actual MC curve.*)

(d) Advertising would increase cost of production and so diminish profits. However, successful advertising would increase demand and shift the demand curve to the right, thereby increasing sales. Hence, profits only increase if the net revenue from extra sales more than pays for the cost of the initial advertising.

(e) The profit-maximising publisher would set output where MC = MR and charge the corresponding price. In the diagram this is £15. However, the point of sales revenue maximisation occurs where MR intersects the *x*-axis, at 1000 copies. Up to this point, marginal revenue has been positive and revenue has increased with sales. The author would want to increase sales to 1000 by reducing price to £10.

(f) Publishing a paperback edition creates a second market for the same good and allows the publisher to act as a discriminating monopolist. The price elasticity of demand for the paperback edition is more elastic. However, by equalising the marginal revenue generated by each edition, the publisher earns a higher level of profit than would be the case if uniform prices were charged.

## 6.3 Objective Questions

### Example 6.2

Which of the following is the most likely characteristic of a perfectly competitive industry?

A some firms offer discounts to important customers

B firms are price takers

C price competition between firms

D some differentiation of products

E the presence of barriers to entry

**Example 6.3**

One difference between a firm operating in a perfectly competitive market and one operating in a monopolistically competitive market is that, for the latter only:
A  all firms produce an identical product
B  some producers have imperfect market knowledge
C  average revenue equals price
D  the number of producers is small
E  some producers advertise

**Example 6.4**

A tailor charges £100 per suit up to and including the fifth suit made. If more than 5 suits are ordered, the price charged for *all* suits falls to £80 per suit. What will be the marginal revenue to the tailor for the sixth suit?
A  £100          B  £80          C  £0          D  −£20          E  −£80

**Example 6.5**

The diagram shows a marginal revenue curve (MR). From the diagram it can be seen that as output increases from 0 to $Q$, total revenue is:
A  increasing                  B  decreasing                  C  at a maximum
D  at a minimum                E  zero

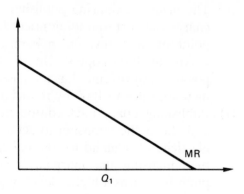

**Example 6.6**

The following table shows the cost and revenue conditions facing a firm. At what level of output would the firm be making maximum profit?

|   | Weekly output | Total cost | Total revenue |
|---|---|---|---|
| A | 1 | £60 | £24 |
| B | 2 | £110 | £56 |
| C | 3 | £150 | £94 |
| D | 4 | £180 | £154 |
| E | 5 | £200 | £274 |

*Examples 6.7–6.11 are based on the diagram below, which shows the total revenue (TR) and total cost (TC) curves of a firm.*

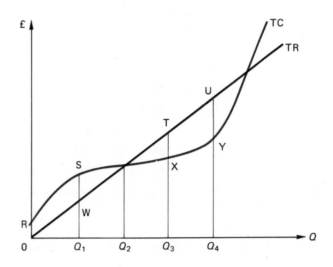

Which level of output   **A** 0   **B** $0Q_1$   **C** $0Q_2$   **D** $0Q_3$   **E** $0Q_4$   shows:

## Example 6.7

Where profits are maximised?

## Example 6.8

Where break-even occurs?

## Example 6.9

Where losses are maximised?

## Example 6.10

The firm's fixed costs:
**A**   are equal to 0R          **B**   are equal to WS          **C**   are equal to XT
**D**   are equal to YU          **E**   cannot be calculated from the diagram

## Example 6.11

Which market form is implied by the diagram?
**A**   perfect competition          **B**   monopolistic competition
**C**   oligopoly                         **D**   monopsony
**E**   monopoly

*Examples 6.12–6.14 are based on the diagram below, which shows the cost curves of a perfectly competitive firm.*

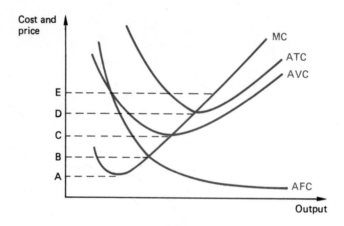

For each of Examples 6.12–6.14, select from the prices **A** to **E**:

### Example 6.12

The price which gives the firm the largest amount of profit.

### Example 6.13

The price at which the firm will earn normal profits.

### Example 6.14

The price below which the firm will cease production in the short run.

*Examples 6.15–6.17 are based on the following diagram, which illustrates the cost and revenue situation of a firm.*

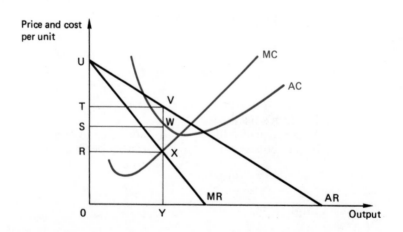

**A** 0RXY    **B** RSWX    **C** STVW    **D** UTV    **E** 0TVY

For each of Examples 6.15–6.17, select the appropriate area which shows:

90

**Example 6.15**

Abnormal profit.


**Example 6.16**

Consumer surplus.


**Example 6.17**

Total revenue.


**Example 6.18**

A profit maximising monopolist will increase output if:
A   marginal revenue is less than marginal cost
B   marginal revenue is positive
C   average costs fall
D   advertising costs rise
E   a profits tax is imposed


**Example 6.19**

A firm will continue production in the short term, provided that revenue covers:
A   indirect cost         B   total cost              C   average cost
D   fixed cost            E   variable cost


**Example 6.20**

Which of the following is a necessary condition for a monopolist to practise price discrimination?
A   different cost structures in each market
B   different price elasticities of demand in each market
C   consumers can buy in one market and resell in another
D   consumers can choose which market to buy in
E   consumers in each market have perfect market knowledge

*Select your answers to Examples 6.21–6.23 by means of the following code*:
A   *if 1, 2 and 3 are all correct*
B   *if 1 and 2 only are correct*
C   *if 2 and 3 only are correct*
D   *if 1 only is correct*


**Example 6.21**

In the long run, for each firm under conditions of perfect competition price equals:
1   average revenue         2   marginal revenue         3   marginal cost

### Example 6.22

Oligopolistic industries are usually characterised by:
**1** price stability     **2** non-price competition  **3** price takers

### Example 6.23

For a profit-maximising monopolist earning normal profit, price is equal to:
**1** marginal revenue     **2** average revenue     **3** average cost

## 6.4 Essays

### Example 6.24

Why are a firm's profits maximised when marginal cost equals marginal revenue? In what circumstances might a firm use criteria other than profit maximisation for determining the price of its products?

(AEB Nov. 1986)

- Demonstrate profit maximisation, assuming either perfect or imperfect competition.
- The second part of the question asks you why firms use non-profit maximising pricing strategies.

*Solution 6.24*

There are two types of profit in economics. Normal profit is the return sufficient to keep the firm in the industry. Normal profit is seen as a cost of production and is therefore included in the firm's cost curves. Any return above normal profit is called abnormal profit.

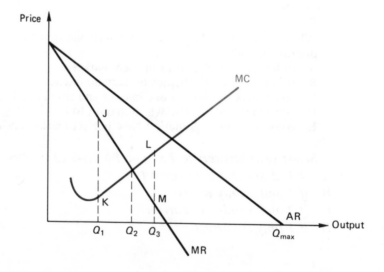

The diagram shows the short-run unit cost and revenue curves of an imperfectly competitive firm. Assume that the firm can produce any level of output between 0 and $Q_{max}$. The marginal cost curve, MC, tells the firm the cost of making the extra unit. The marginal revenue curve, MR, tells the firm the revenue received from the sale of the extra unit. At $Q_1$, the difference between MR and MC (J − K) is greatest. However, there is an incentive for the profit-maximising firm to increase output beyond this point. The revenue received from the sale of every additional unit up to $Q_2$ is greater than the cost of making that extra unit. Any firm which fixed output at $Q_1$ would be forgoing a profit on each of $Q_2 − Q_1$. A normal profit is made on the sale of the $Q_2$ unit. Above output level $Q_2$, a loss is made on the sale of each extra unit, because marginal cost exceeds marginal revenue. For example, at $Q_3$ a loss of L − M is made on the sale of that unit alone. Profits are therefore maximised when marginal cost equals marginal revenue.

Economic theory assumes that individuals and firms are 'rational', acting in a manner which maximises their own satisfaction. In the case of the firm, the maximisation of profits guarantees the largest possible income for the owners of a company. A profit-maximising pricing policy is likely to be used by sole traders and partnerships.

However, the emergence of limited companies means that ownership and control of the most important firms are now separated. In general, shareholders expect the firm to maximise profits and therefore set output where marginal cost equals marginal revenue. Managers may have different objectives.

New 'managerial' theories of the firm suggest that companies use pricing criteria which improve the welfare of managers. For example, salaries and 'fringe benefits' are more likely to be linked to sales than to profits. Bonuses may be paid for achieving sales targets. It follows that manager-controlled firms will try to maximise sales revenue rather than profit and fix output where average cost equals average revenue.

Managers may decide that setting a price which maximises the firm's rate of growth is in their own best interest. An expanding company increases managers' salary and status. Moreover, the resulting increase in the value of the company's shares is in the interest of the owners.

Large businesses are highly complex, with different departments responsible for specialised functions such as production, sales and finance. Each department has a different objective, so that the maximisation of one goal, profits, is inappropriate. Instead, satisficing occurs where each department is set minimum acceptable levels of performance — for example, asking the sales department to achieve a given market share.

The firm may feel that the cost of collecting information about marginal cost and revenue is too high and therefore managers use a cost-plus pricing strategy. The firm fixes output and then estimates unit cost. Adding a profit margin to average cost gives the final selling price.

Nationalised industries aim to operate in the public interest. Profit maximisation results in an inefficient allocation of resources. Instead, state-owned firms adopt a marginal cost pricing strategy and increase output to the point where, including externalities, marginal cost equals price.

**Example 6.25**

Explain the differences between oligopoly and monopolistic competition. Why do some firms tend towards oligopoly and some towards monopolistic competition?
(NISEC 1987)

*Solution 6.25*

Monopolistic competition and oligopoly are types of market structure and differ in the following respects.

(a) *Type of product* Monopolistically competitive firms produce a good which is only slightly different from that of all other sellers. Buyers can therefore tell the difference between the output of different firms. The output of oligopolies can be homogeneous (identical) or differentiated.

(b) *Number and size of sellers* In monopolistic competition, there are a large number of small producers selling to a large number of buyers. In oligopolistic industries, there are a small number of large producers also selling to a large number of buyers.

(c) *Barriers to entry* In monopolistic competition, new firms are free to start up in the industry. In oligopoly industries, entry is more restricted.

(d) *Interdependence* The large number of firms in monopolistic competition means that the actions of one firm have little effect on competitors. In oligopoly, there are only a few sellers and the actions of one firm have a significant effect on competitors.

(e) *Price and output decisions* The independence of monopolistically competitive firms means that pricing policy is influenced only by cost and revenue considerations. Interdependence means that oligopoly pricing strategies take into account the likely response of other firms. For instance, the Sweezey model argues that if an oligopolistic firm increases its price, other firms will not raise theirs and customers are lost. Reducing price has no effect on market share, because other firms will follow suit. Oligopolies therefore exhibit price rigidity.

(f) *Profits* Figure 1 shows a representative firm in monopolistic competition. Abnormal profits attract new firms into the industry, reducing market share and thereby reducing demand for the individual firm. In Figure 2, the demand curve shifts to the left until price equals average cost. Monopolistically competitive firms only earn normal profits in the long run. The ability of oligopolies to exclude competition allows them to continue earning abnormal profits in the long run.

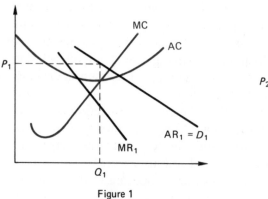

Figure 1

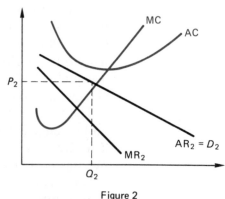

Figure 2

There are two main reasons why some firms are oligopolies and some are in monopolistic competition.

*Economies of scale* (EOS) influence market structure. Where EOS are available, those firms which are able to increase their plant size acquire a cost advantage over smaller competitors. Small firms are uncompetitive, and the industry becomes oligopolistic or monopolistic. In industries offering no scope for scale economies, firms are unable to reduce unit costs by increasing their size. Such industries tend to be monopolistically or perfectly competitive.

*Brand image* influences market structure. Industries where the consumer can be convinced that the products of a few large companies are superior to the output of smaller firms will tend to be oligopolistic. Advertising is used to increase demand, and to create the impression of differences between the firm's product and those of its competitors. Consequently, UK advertising is dominated by oligopolies trying to increase consumer loyalty to their product. Industries where the consumer cannot be easily persuaded that the output of one firm is distinctly different from the product of others will tend to be monopolistically competitive.

## 6.5  Solutions to Objective Questions

### Solution 6.2   Answer: B

A *price taker* is a firm which is unable to change market price by varying its own output. For instance, if a small perfectly competitive firm were to ask more for its produce than the current market price, consumers would buy a perfect substitute from a competitor. Since the firm is able to sell *all* its output at the going market price, there is no reason why it should sell any of its output for less.

$A \Rightarrow$ In perfect competition, no one buyer is sufficiently large to be able to negotiate a discount on purchases.

$C \Rightarrow$ The firm can sell all its output at the equilibrium market price and does not need to cut its prices to increase market share.

$D \Rightarrow$ *Differentiated products* means that consumers are able to tell the difference between the output of one firm and another. A condition of perfect competition is that the produce of each firm is identical.

$E \Rightarrow$ A condition of perfect competition is that firms are free to leave or enter the industry at will.

### Solution 6.3   Answer: E

Unlike a firm in perfect competition, monopolistically competitive firms produce a slightly different product from others in the industry. Therefore, firms benefit from advertising because: (i) it increases demand for the product and (ii) it improves the brand image of the good so that demand becomes more price-inelastic.

$B \Rightarrow$ The amount of information which firms have about the market does not explain the difference between perfect and monopolistic competition.

$C \Rightarrow$ Average revenue equals price in *all* market structures.

$D \Rightarrow$ There are a large number of producers in both perfect and monopolistic competition.

### Solution 6.4   Answer: D

The marginal revenue (MR) of the sixth suit is found by dividing the change in ($\Delta$) total revenue (TR) by the change in output ($Q$) — that is, MR = $\Delta$TR $\div \Delta Q$. Total revenue is calculated by multiplying price ($P$) by output — that is, TR = $P \times Q$.

TR from the sale of 5 units = £100 × 5 = £500
TR from the sale of 6 units = £ 80 × 6 = £480
$\therefore$ MR = (£500 − £480) ÷ (5 − 6) = −£20

*Solution 6.5   Answer:* **A**

The relationship between total revenue and marginal revenue is explained in Figure 6.5. Since $Q_1$ is to the left of the point where the marginal revenue curve intersects the x-axis, total revenue is rising.

*Solution 6.6   Answer:* **E**

The firm will maximise profits by fixing output at the level where the difference between total revenue and total cost is greatest and positive — i.e. at output level 5.

|   | Weekly output | Total cost | Total revenue | Profit |
|---|---|---|---|---|
| A | 1 | £60 | £24 | −£36 |
| B | 2 | £110 | £56 | −£54 |
| C | 3 | £150 | £94 | £56 |
| D | 4 | £180 | £154 | £26 |
| E | 5 | £200 | £274 | £74 |

*Solution 6.7   Answer:* **E**

Profits will be maximised at the output level where the vertical distance between the total revenue and total cost curves is greatest and positive.

   **D** $\Rightarrow$ By producing $Q_3$, the firm is making a profit of XT but this is not as much as the profit of YU gained from producing $Q_4$.

*Solution 6.8   Answer:* **C**

*Break-even* refers to the situation where total revenue equals total cost.

*Solution 6.9   Answer:* **B**

Losses will be maximised at the output level where the vertical distance between the total revenue and total cost curves is greatest and negative.

*Solution 6.10   Answer:* **A**

Even when output is zero, the firm still incurs fixed costs for such items as rent and insurance. The amount of fixed costs is given by the intersection of the total cost curve with the y-axis.

*Solution 6.11   Answer:* **A**

A linear total revenue curve implies that price remains constant as output increases. Perfectly competitive firms are *price takers* and sell extra units at a constant market price. Firms in imperfect competition are *price makers* and are able to change market price. However, in order to increase output, price must be reduced not only for the extra unit, but also on all preceding units as well. Eventually, marginal revenue becomes negative and the total revenue curve begins to slope downwards. See Figure 6.5.

*Solution 6.12    Answer:* **E**

The answers to Examples 6.12–6.14 depend on your ability to derive revenue curves from the information given. Remember that since the firm is in a perfectly competitive market, marginal revenue will be constant and equal to price. Hence, projecting a horizontal line across from a given price gives the firm's demand ($D$), average revenue (AR) and marginal revenue (MR) curves at that price. For example, at price **E** (assuming profit maximisation) the firm produces $Q_1$ and makes an abnormal profit equal to the shaded area in the following diagram:

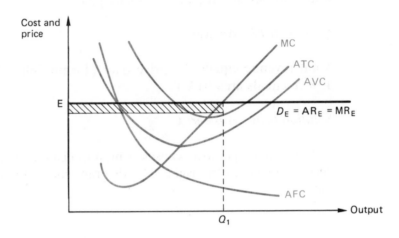

*Solution 6.13    Answer:* **D**

Normal profits occur when average revenue equals average total cost (ATC). Note that ATC and average cost (AC) mean the same thing. Only at price **D** does ATC = AR.

*Solution 6.14    Answer:* **C**

A loss-making firm has two choices: (i) cease production and incur fixed costs; (ii) carry on production and incur abnormal losses. At prices below **C**, the firm

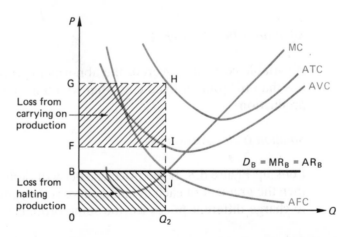

minimises losses by stopping production for the current time period and paying out fixed costs. For example, at price **B** in the diagram, the loss the firm makes from halting production equals AFC × $Q$ = J × $Q_2$ — that is, area 0BJ$Q_2$. The abnormal loss from production (ATC − AR) × $Q$ = (H − I) × $Q_2$ — that is, area FGHI.

*Solution 6.15   Answer:* **C**

When using per unit cost and revenue curves, abnormal profit ($\pi$) is the difference between average revenue (AR) and average cost (AC), multiplied by the level of output ($Q$). In the diagram for Examples 6.15–6.17, AR = V, AC = W and $Q$ = Y. (V – W) $\times$ $Q$ equals area STVW.

*Solution 6.16   Answer:* **D**

Consumer surplus is the difference between the maximum price consumers are willing to pay and the price actually paid.

*Solution 6.17   Answer:* **E**

Total revenue equals the price paid (T) multiplied by the quantity sold (Y). T $\times$ Y equals area 0TVY.

*Solution 6.18   Answer:* **C**

A fall in average costs causes a monopolist's average cost and marginal cost curves to shift to the right. The diagram shows the effect of a fall in costs on output.

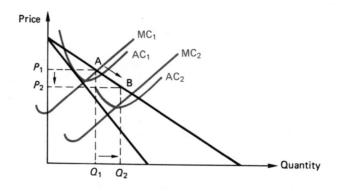

*Solution 6.19   Answer:* **E**

If variable costs are covered, the abnormal loss from continuing manufacture is less than the total of fixed costs that would have to be paid out if the firm halted production.

*Solution 6.20   Answer:* **B**

Look up Figure 6.8. If the price elasticity of demand in each market is identical, then the gradient of each demand curve is the same and the monopolist is unable to charge different prices for the same product.

*Solution 6.21   Answer:* **A**

Referring back to Figure 6.2, the perfectly competitive firm and industry are in long-run equilibrium at price $P_1$. At $P_1$, price equals average revenue, marginal revenue and marginal cost.

*Solution 6.22    Answer:* **B**

An oligopolistic industry is dominated by a few large firms, and where there are some barriers to entry. For example, the car industry. The following options are correct.

**1** and **2** ⇒ Oligopolistic firms are interdependent. For example, if one firm reduces prices to increase market share, other firms follow, thereby undermining the effectiveness of *price competition*. Hence, oligopoly industries tend to show stable prices. Non-price competition such as special offers is used to increase sales.

**3** ⇒ is incorrect because oligopolies are large enough to influence the price at which their product is sold.

*Solution 6.23    Answer:* **C**

Looking back at Figure 6.7, the monopolist produces $Q_1$ and sells each unit for $P_1$.

**1** ⇒ is incorrect because marginal revenue is always less than price in imperfect competition.

**2** ⇒ is correct because average revenue and price are always the same.

**3** ⇒ is correct because normal profit requires that average cost and average revenue — hence, price — are the same.

# 7 Regional Economics

## 7.1 Fact Sheet

### (a) Influences on Industrial Location

A profit-maximising firm expands on the location which minimises unit costs. The firm takes account of:
  (i) *Natural advantages*, including:
      (1) an area's proximity to raw materials;
      (2) the physical features of the area;
      (3) the climate of an area.
 (ii) *Acquired advantages* from other firms having located in the area. The resulting external economies of scale are described in Table 5.4.
(iii) Government regulations and financial incentives.

- *Weight-losing* industries use bulky raw materials to produce a compact finished product, and tend to locate near the major source of raw materials.
- *Weight-gaining* industries use compact raw materials to produce a bulky finished product, and tend to locate near the major market for the good.
- A *footloose* industry gains no cost advantage from any one site.
- Improved transport and power networks (e.g. motorways and the national grid) have made many industries footloose.
- *Industrial inertia* occurs when external economies of scale cause a firm to remain in its original location even after natural advantages have disappeared.

### (b) Localisation of Industry in the UK

**Table 7.1** Structure of UK industry by region

| Standard regions | Major industries |
| --- | --- |
| North | Traditional heavy industry concentrated around Tyneside and Teeside |
| North-west | Heavy engineering; cotton; clothing; glass; chemicals; vehicles |
| Yorkshire and Humberside | Iron and steel; textiles and clothing; coal; fishing |
| East Midlands | Diverse industry, but specialises in hosiery, footwear and clothing |
| West Midlands | Mechanical and electrical engineering; vehicles; iron and steel; Potteries |
| South-west | Agriculture and food processing; tourism; aerospace; tobacco |
| East Anglia | Agriculture and food processing; footwear; tourism |
| South-east | Financial and commercial centre; technological and light engineering |
| Wales | Coal, iron and steel in South Wales; agriculture; light engineering |
| Scotland | North Sea oil; agriculture; coal; shipbuilding; tourism |
| Northern Ireland | Shipbuilding; textiles |

### (c) Deindustrialisation

*Deindustrialisation* refers to a continuing reduction in the share of manufacturing in national output. Deindustrialisation may cause:

  (i) unemployment if there is no corresponding increase in service industry employment;

  (ii) economic decline in regions with a high concentration of manufacturing industries;

  (iii) a reduction in the rate of economic growth;

  (iv) a deterioration in the balance of payments if the import of manufactures increases, while the export of goods falls.

### (d) Regional Problem

The *regional problem* refers to an uneven spread of living standards and employment levels between different areas of the UK. A region may be in relative decline because:

  (i) factory closures result in a *regional multiplier effect*;

  (ii) *net migration* from the area reduces:

  (1) the local demand for products;

  (2) the local supply of skilled labour;

  (iii) local authorities have insufficient income to provide an adequate infra-structure and services;

  (iv) a contracting industrial base reduces the external economies of scale of an area.

### (e) Regional Policy

- Sufficiently low wages and rents attract the movement of new firms to declining regions. However, market forces are unable to remove the regional problem if labour and capital are immobile, or if firms prefer to locate in prosperous areas.
- Government regional policy aims to reduce high levels of regional unemployment and to reduce congestion in prosperous areas.
- Regional policy instruments include:

  (i) offering financial incentives to firms locating in:

  (1) *Development Areas*,

  (2) *Intermediate Areas*

  (note that Regional Development Grants were abandoned as a policy instrument in 1988);

  (ii) issuing only a limited number of *Industrial Development Certificates* (IDCs) to firms wanting to expand in non-development areas (note that IDCs were abandoned as a policy instrument in 1981);

  (iii) increasing public spending in declining regions.

- Government measures have been mainly geared to moving jobs to workers rather than workers to jobs.
- The European Regional Development Fund is used to give financial assistance to declining regions.

### (f) Urban Problem

Since 1945, there has been a significant movement in employment and population from conurbations to rural areas because:
  (i) there is little urban land for expansion;
  (ii) urban rents, rates and wages are high;
  (iii) more industries have become footloose.

  • The most serious decline has occurred in inner-city areas. The population has a high proportion of semi-skilled, low-income and ethnic minorities who cannot afford to move elsewhere.


### (g) Urban Policy

Government urban policy instruments include:
  (i) restricting the growth of urban areas through *green-belt* legislation;
  (ii) encouraging firms to locate in derelict inner-city *enterprise zones* by offering rate and tax rebates, and exemption from many planning restrictions;
  (iii) encouraging investment in declining areas by allowing *Freeports*, where goods can be processed for re-exportation without incurring customs duties;
  (iv) establishing *Urban Development Corporations* (UDCs) to buy up and improve derelict land with the involvement of local private sector firms.


### (h) Multinationals

A *multinational corporation* (MNC) is a company which produces over 25% of its product outside its parent country (country of origin).

  • The largest MNCs have turnovers in excess of the GNP of most countries, and account for the bulk of world trade in manufactures.
  • MNCs reduce unit costs by locating different production processes in different countries.

**Table 7.2** Multinationals

| Advantages of MNCs for the host country | Disadvantages of MNCs for the host country |
| --- | --- |
| MNCs provide domestic employment opportunities | MNCs may force local firms in competition out of business |
| Investment improves the current balance of payments | Returned profits worsens future balance of payments |
| Investment increases the domestic growth rate | MNCs may exploit monopsony (sole buyer) power in wage negotiations |
| Imports replaced by home-produced MNC-made goods | MNCs may deplete local natural resources too quickly |
| Technology and production techniques are transferred | *Transfer pricing* may be used to minimise tax payments |

## 7.2 Data Response

'What has emerged is that until the mid-1960s concentrations of declining industries, including coal, textiles and shipbuilding, were chiefly to blame for job losses in depressed areas. But since then the causes of decline have been very different.

The main problem, it now seems, is that regions such as Scotland and the North are being dragged down by their big cities. In other parts of these regions employment trends are not nearly as bad. Throughout Britain a massive shift of jobs from cities to smaller towns and rural areas is occurring on a scale which swamps most other trends in industrial location.'

Source: S. Fothergill and G. Gudgin, *The Guardian*, 1982

(a) Explain how the changed pattern of industrial location may have been the result of:
    (i) more capital intensive production methods **(4 marks)**
    (ii) market forces affecting industrial location **(8 marks)**
(b) What are the implications of the described change for government investment in social capital? **(4 marks)**
(c) Discuss the use of Enterprise Zones as a response to the observed trend.
    **(4 marks)**

*Solution 7.1*

(a) The changed pattern of industrial location specified in the passage is the 'massive shift of jobs from cities to smaller towns and rural areas' — that is, the switch of production and employment from cities to small town/country locations.

  (i) Capital-intensive production processes such as chemical manufacture involve the extensive use of large plant and machinery. Capital-intensive processes are likely to occupy large sites which may either be too expensive or simply not available in city areas. It is cheaper to locate at green-field sites in a rural area or on the outskirts of an urban area.

One reason for locating in a city is to utilise the large supply of local labour. Capital-intensive processes place less emphasis on the need for large amounts of labour, and can therefore consider rural or town locations.

  (ii) In a market economy each good has its own product and factor market where the interaction of supply and demand set price. Changes in relative price between two markets act as an incentive to producers and consumers to adjust their behaviour. As city areas become relatively more expensive, firms are increasingly attracted to smaller town and rural areas. For example, if the percentage increase in inner-city rent and rates exceeds that of rural areas, firms will tend to move out of cities. Labour costs may be relatively cheaper in rural as opposed to city areas. Increased traffic congestion in city areas causes external diseconomies of scale, and the resulting increase in costs encourages firms to relocate close to efficient transport networks offered by motorways such as the M25.

(b) Social capital refers to infrastructure usually provided by the state for use by the general community. Examples of social capital include schools and hospitals. The observed trend for employment to move out of city to small town/rural areas poses a number of problems. Schools and hospitals in urban areas will be faced with falling demand, while the growing rural population require additional facilities. Hence, the government is unlikely to invest in new social capital in city areas in decline but will instead locate new schools and hospitals in new towns. At the same time, the decline of inner-city areas increases the need of local residents for improved social capital.

(c) Enterprise zones are located in the more derelict parts of inner-city areas and offer firms a number of privileges. Companies setting up in enterprise zones are exempt from local authority rates and development land tax; receive substantial tax allowances; and are free from a number of planning regulations. Such financial incentives will attract firms. However, it is likely that such firms would probably have located in an urban area in any case. Companies whose prime requirement is for access to motorways or proximity to ancillary firms, or who need large amounts of land, usually find the financial incentives offered insufficient.

## 7.3  Objective Questions

### Example 7.2

Industrial inertia occurs when:
A  labour is geographically immobile
B  the share of manufacturing in national output declines
C  firms fail to exploit economies of scale
D  industry gains no cost advantage from any one site
E  the initial reasons for location have disappeared

### Example 7.3

Weight-gaining industries tend to locate:
A  close to the source of raw materials
B  close to major markets
C  close to important transport networks
D  in development areas
E  in relatively prosperous areas

### Example 7.4

Which one of the following industries is *least* dispersed throughout the UK?
A  wholesaling       B  agriculture       C  tourism
D  car manufacturing   E  construction

### Example 7.5

Multinational corporations are firms which:
A  export and import goods
B  form cartels to set minimum prices
C  have shareholders in many countries
D  produce goods in more than one country
E  invest overseas

*Select your answers to Examples 7.6–7.8 by means of the following code*:
A   *if 1, 2 and 3 are all correct*
B   *if 1 and 2 only are correct*
C   *if 2 and 3 only are correct*
D   *if 1 only is correct*

**Example 7.6**

External economies of scale are available:
1   to new firms locating in an area
2   where firms are geographically close to each other
3   only to firms large enough to manufacture in bulk

**Example 7.7**

The regional problem occurs:
1   following net migration between geographical areas of a country
2   if resources are geographically immobile
3   if living standards vary between geographical areas of a country

**Example 7.8**

A host country which allows a multinational to undertake direct foreign investment generally benefits from:
1   a technology transfer
2   increased exports of manufactured goods
3   an increase in gross national product at factor cost

# 7.4   Essays

**Example 7.9**

Consider the view that, since 1945, the location of industry has been largely determined by regional policy.

(NISEC 1986)

- Avoid simply describing the theory of location and the regional problem.
- Explain how post-war government industrial policy has affected industrial location decisions.
- Consider the likely impact of other factors on location.

*Solution 7.9*

The UK is divided into eleven standard economic regions. The 'core' area of the South-east has experienced far greater growth than the other 'periphery' regions. Governments consider the resultant income and employment disparities so great that they constitute a regional problem requiring a regional policy. In theory, market forces should eliminate regional disparities over time. The low wages and rents of depressed areas influence location decisions and attract new firms. However, capital and labour can be geographically immobile.

To offset these market imperfections, a number of controls and incentives have operated since 1945 to influence the location decisions of firms. *Industrial Development Certificates* (IDCs) were only granted to firms expanding in specified regions until 1988. *Regional Development Grants* offered assistance to firms locating in designated Development Areas.

Firms, then, have to compare the cost advantage of sites in development and non-development areas. Companies take into account the natural advantages of an area, including the physical features and climate of a region. The acquired advantages of an area, such as the transport network, labour force and proximity to markets, are also important factors.

However, it is difficult to isolate the impact of government regional policy on location decisions since 1945. Detailed regional statistics have only recently become available, and the areas actually qualifying for assistance have been changed frequently. Let us consider the evidence.

New firms may ignore offers of assistance and be reluctant to locate in declining regions because the younger members of the local workforce have moved to areas of high employment. The negative regional multiplier reduces the size of the market, thereby reducing the area's external economies of scale. Firms which suffer industrial inertia expand on their current site, and their location decision is unaffected by regional policy.

The effect of IDCs is uncertain. There is no guarantee that a firm denied an IDC to expand in a prosperous area will automatically locate in a Development Area. Multinationals could simply build their new factory overseas. In terms of general depression, no region is willing to accept restrictions on development, and for this reason IDCs have been suspended since 1981.

Firms where government financial incentives make up a large proportion of location costs are most likely to take account of regional policy. For example, capital-intensive firms such as ICI have been attracted into assisted areas. Multinational enterprises considering direct foreign investment in UK green-field sites have accepted grants and located in Development Areas. The Nissan plant at Washington, Tyne and Wear, is an example. However, other multi-nationals have emphasised different location factors, such as proximity to markets and transport networks, in their location decision. Honda have sited their engine plant in Swindon without any government assistance.

Microtechnology is a footloose industry where no one site offers a cost advantage. Transport costs are only a small proportion of total costs. Despite the allowances on offer elsewhere, many 'sunrise' information technology firms decide to locate along the M4 corridor between London and Bristol. However, government assistance has helped to create in Scotland's Glens a high concentration of silicon chip firms.

In conclusion, it has been demonstrated that the financial assistance given by post-war regional policy is an important but not overriding consideration in the location decision of the firm. Direct controls such as IDCs have had no impact since 1981.


**Example 7.10**

How would you explain the economic decline of inner-city areas in the United Kingdom? Suggest possible remedies and discuss their economic implications.
(AEB June 1987)

- Inner-city decline has been targeted as a key economic issue by the third Thatcher administration. Make sure you include examples of recent government policies and their effects.

*Solution 7.10*

The decline in inner-city areas can be measured in terms of falling output, increased unemployment and below-average income levels. Two major factors have contributed to this trend: (a) the movement of labour-intensive firms away from inner areas and (b) the flight of well-paid employees to outer-urban and rural areas.

One reason for the migration of inner-urban firms is the introduction of modern production techniques, which have increased the demand for floor space. Green-belt restrictions and the active use of Industrial Development Certificates in the 1960s and 1970s made it difficult for firms seeking expansion to locate in inner-city areas. Footloose firms faced with high rents and the availability of Regional Development Grants in Development Areas have left some inner-city areas. In the service sector, many companies have relocated their offices, with a subsequent loss of inner-city office jobs. The continuous flight of firms generates a negative inner-city multiplier effect, causing even further decline. The negative multiplier effect is shown in the diagram.

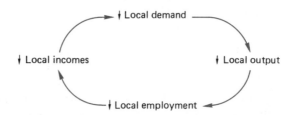

The type of external economy of scale available in inner-city areas has changed. Transport economies from locating weight-gaining industries close to the market have been eroded by diseconomies caused by traffic congestion. Inner-city decline leaves local authorities with insufficient income to maintain an adequate social infrastructure.

Demographic trends are also to account for the decline of inner-city areas. Many workers have used increased real incomes to move to suburban and rural areas where improved communications allow them to commute to work. Many of the jobs left to inner-city residents are low-skilled low-income ones. As a result, average earnings in outer areas rise while inner-city earnings decline. The resultant negative local multiplier effect further reduces income output and employment in inner cities.

Inner-city decline can only be arrested by government intervention. One possible remedy is to offer firms incentives to locate in inner cities. Since 1981, a number of Enterprise Zones in the most derelict inner-urban areas have been established, which give firms tax allowances and exemption from rates and certain planning regulations. Special agencies for urban renewal (Urban Development Corporations) have been given resources to acquire land, improve social and industrial infrastructure, and involve private-sector firms. Urban Development Grants are available which encourage investment in inner-city areas which would not otherwise have taken place.

Incentive schemes which are successful in generating new investment have a spin-off multiplier effect. Local businesses experience an increase in the demand for their products. Yet there is no guarantee that the employment created by new investment will automatically reduce unemployment in inner-city areas. New jobs may be filled by workers from other areas. Moreover, incentives can have the effect of simply *diverting* investment from one region to another. Increased employment in inner-urban areas would have taken place elsewhere.

Government intervention can lead to a misallocation of resources. Siting production in inappropriate inner-urban areas is justified on the basis of the resulting social benefits. However, these must be weighed against the costs of not producing at the least-cost site.

## 7.5 Solutions to Objective Questions

*Solution 7.2   Answer:* **E**

Once the natural advantages of a site have disappeared, the firm may still find it cheaper to expand at its current location. This is because it is expensive to move plant to a new site. Hence, steel plants are found in areas where the local supply of coal has long been exhausted.

**B** ⇒ Refers to deindustrialisation.
**D** ⇒ Refers to footloose industries.

*Solution 7.3   Answer:* **B**

See Section 7.1(a).

*Solution 7.4   Answer:* **D**

Some industries are footloose and widely dispersed throughout the UK because there is no cost advantage from one site. Other industries are concentrated in particular regions of the UK. See Table 7.1.

Each region of the UK has different *factor endowments* — that is, different natural resources, labour force, transport network, etc. Regional specialisation occurs when each area uses its particular factor endowment to concentrate in the manufacture of certain goods and services.

**A, B, C, E** ⇒ are examples of dispersed industries.

*Solution 7.5   Answer:* **D**

A multinational is a company which produces over 25% of its product overseas.

**A** ⇒ Any firm may import and export goods.
**B** ⇒ A *cartel* is a group of producers who act together to fix price or output.
**C** ⇒ Companies which produce in only one country may have shareholders from many different countries.
**E** ⇒ While multinationals often undertake foreign investment, so do private individuals, governments, etc.

*Solution 7.6   Answer:* **B**

**1** ⇒ Is correct because external economies of scale (EOS) are reductions in unit cost as a result of an increase in the size of the entire industry. These are equally available to existing firms and new firms in the area.

**3** ⇒ Refers to internal EOS and is therefore incorrect.

*Solution 7.7   Answer:* **C**

**1** ⇒ Is not correct, because net migration may occur as a result of uneven living standards between regions but it does not cause the regional problem. The other options are correct.

**2** $\Rightarrow$ If resources were geographically mobile, lower rents, wages, etc., in depressed areas would attract an inflow of resources from prosperous areas until living standards between different regions were equal.

**3** $\Rightarrow$ Defines the regional problem.

*Solution 7.8   Answer:* **B**

**1** $\Rightarrow$ Multinationals based in developed countries can introduce modern production techniques and technologies to less-developed host countries.

**2** $\Rightarrow$ Once the multinational is established, goods produced in the host country can be exported.

**3** $\Rightarrow$ Is not correct, because profits made by the overseas branch of the multinational company will be returned to the parent country. The resultant negative property income from abroad reduces the gross national product of the host country.

# 8 Income and Wealth

## 8.1 Fact Sheet

### (a) Factor Incomes

The demand for all factors of production (inputs) is a *derived demand* — i.e. the demand for factors of production depends on the demand for the products they produce. In return for providing their services, land, labour, capital and entrepreneurs receive factor incomes.

### (b) Profit

- *Profit* is the reward for bearing uninsurable risks associated with production. The types of profit are explained in Table 6.3. Note that profit is uncertain and may even be negative. Profit has the following functions:
  - (i) rewards those who bear uncertain risks;
  - (ii) encourages invention and innovation;
  - (iii) indicates efficiency;
  - (iv) encourages firms to switch resources from loss-making to profit-making operations;
  - (v) provides a source for the purchase of investment goods.

### (c) Economic Rent

- *Rent* is the payment for the use of all natural resources.
- *Economic rent* has a wider meaning — i.e. a surplus paid to any factor of production over its supply price.
- *Transfer earnings* is the minimum payment needed to keep the factor in its present occupation. This can also be defined as the payment which can be earned in the factor's next-best-paid occupation:

  present earnings        less   transfer earnings        = economic rent.
  (lawyer's pay £20 000)   less   (teacher's pay £15 000)  = £5000

- *Quasi-rent* is short-term economic rent arising from a temporary inelasticity of supply.
- *Pure economic rent* is the reward to any factor that is in completely inelastic supply.
- The proportion of a factor's earnings made up of economic rent increases as supply becomes more inelastic.

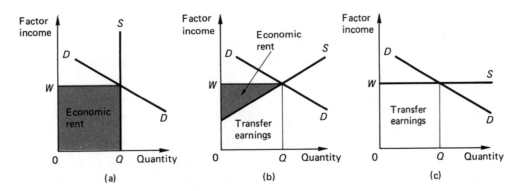

**Figure 8.1** Economic rent and elasticity of supply: (a) perfectly inelastic supply; (b) elastic supply; (c) perfectly elastic supply

## (d) Interest

- *Interest* is the reward for forgoing liquidity, and is an amount paid to a lender over and above the original sum borrowed.
- *The Loanable Funds (Classical) Theory* states that the rate of interest is determined by the demand for loanable funds (investment) and the supply of loanable funds (savings).
- *Keynesian theory* states that the rate of interest is determined by the demand for and supply of money. For simplification, the supply of money is presumed to be largely government-determined and to be perfectly interest-inelastic. Keynes identified three motives for demanding money (*liquidity preference*) — that is, for holding wealth in the form of money:
  - (i) The *transactions motive* is the desire to keep money to make everyday purchases.
  - (ii) The *precautionary motive* is the desire to hold money to meet unexpected expenses.
  - (iii) The *speculative motive* is the desire to hold idle balances to take advantage of changes in the price of bonds.
- In Figure 8.2, the *liquidity trap* occurs after point A, when the rate of interest is so low (and the price of bonds is so high) that everyone anticipates a future fall in the price of bonds. If the money supply increases, people will hold all the extra money for fear of making a capital loss from holding bonds. Hence, the demand for money becomes perfectly interest-elastic.

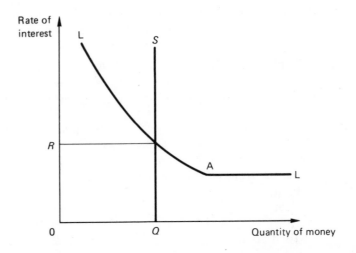

**Figure 8.2** Determination of the rate of interest

111

### (e) Wages

*Wages* are a payment made to labour. A number of factors help determine wage rates:

(i) The *marginal productivity theory* suggests that any factor of production will receive a payment equal to the value of its marginal product:

$$\text{wage rate} = \text{marginal physical product} \times \text{marginal revenue}$$

(ii) Government action in the form of incomes policies, arbitration and conciliation, and as an employer.

(iii) Trade unions (see Section 9.1).

### (f) Wage Differentials

*Wage differentials* are the differences in wages between workers in different occupations, age groups, etc. Wage differentials arise through:

(i) occupational immobility due to non-monetary advantages and disadvantages of jobs;

(ii) occupational immobility because of age, physical factors, mechanical skills and qualifications;

(iii) geographical immobility due to family ties, housing shortages, etc.;

(iv) economic rent arising from high demand for special talents;

(v) differences in the strengths of trade unions and professional organisations;

(vi) social convention and public opinion influencing wages claims and settlements.

Workers will be in a stronger position to gain wage rises if demand for labour is inelastic. The elasticity of demand for a factor will depend on:

• the degree of substitution between factors;
• the elasticity of demand for the product produced;
• the proportion of the factor's costs in total costs.

### (g) Income Distribution

• *Income* is a flow of earnings. The *functional distribution of income* is the distribution of income between factors of production.

**Table 8.1** The functional distribution of income in the UK, 1986

| Source (factor of production) | Share of total earnings | |
|---|---|---|
| | *(£m)* | % |
| Income from employment | 209 445 | 63.8 |
| Income from self-employment | 34 340 | 10.5 |
| Profit | 59 072 | 18.0 |
| Rent | 24 497 | 6.8 |
| Other | 3 026 | 0.9 |
| Total domestic income | 328 380 | 100.0 |

Source: Adapted from CSO *Annual Abstract of Statistics* (1988)

- The *size distribution of income* is concerned with the proportion of income received by different proportions of the population. The degree of income inequality can be represented by *Lorenz curves* and *Gini coefficients*.

  In the case of a Lorenz curve, the degree of inequality can be assessed by the extent to which the curve showing a country's distribution deviates from the 45° line.

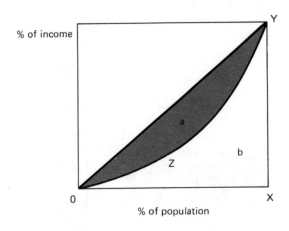

**Figure 8.3**    The Lorenz curve. 0Y = complete equality; 0XY = complete inequality, with the last person having all the income; 0ZY = degree of inequality

The Gini coefficient is the ratio between the area between a Lorenz curve and the 45° line and the area below the 45° line:

$$\frac{\text{area } a}{\text{area } a + b} \times \frac{100}{1}$$

The Gini coefficient has a range from 0 (complete equality) to 1 (complete inequality).

## (h) Wealth Distribution

- *Wealth* is a stock of all those assets capable of earning an income.
- Wealth can be *human* (e.g. skills, qualifications) or *material* (e.g. time deposits, shares, property).
- Inheritances, capital gains, pensions and savings are the major sources of wealth.

**Table 8.2**    Distribution of wealth in the UK in 1985

| % of wealth owned by | Marketable wealth (%) | Marketable wealth plus occupational and state pension rights (%) |
| --- | --- | --- |
| Most wealthy 1% | 20 | 11 |
| Most wealthy 5% | 40 | 25 |
| Most wealthy 10% | 54 | 36 |
| Most wealthy 25% | 76 | 57–60 |
| Most wealthy 50% | 93 | 81–85 |

Source: *Social Trends 1988* (CSO)

- Note that wealth is more unequally distributed than income in the UK.
- The 1988 UK budget reduced the highest rate of income tax to 40%. This is likely to make the distribution of income and wealth more uneven over time.

## 8.2 Data Response

**Worked Example 8.1**

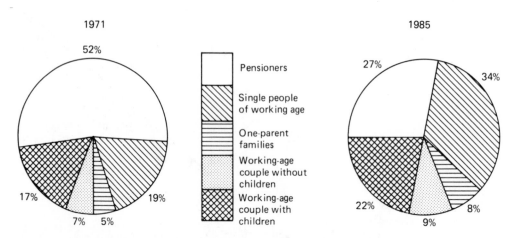

Lowest quintile group of income by family type. Source: *Social Trends 1988*

The lowest quintile group is the 20% of families receiving the lowest net income in the country. The figures are adjusted for differences in the size and composition of the families. During the period shown, there was an increase in the actual number of pensioners and the proportion of pensioners in the total population. There was also a significant rise in unemployment and an increase in the number and proportion of one-parent families in the population. Most of the poor in the UK are either unemployed, retired or single parents, with the main causes of poverty being old age, sickness, unemployment (and in relation to these the level of benefits), failure to claim benefits and low wages.

(a) What is meant by the highest quintile group of income?      **(1 mark)**

(b) Describe the changes in the lowest quintile group between 1971 and 1985.

**(4 marks)**

(c) If during the period 'there was an increase in the actual number of pensioners and the proportion of pensioners in the total population', why did the proportion of pensioners in the lowest quintile group fall?      **(4 marks)**

(d) In what sense is the lowest quintile group of income a measure of relative rather than absolute poverty?      **(3 marks)**

(e) One solution some economists advance to reduce poverty is the introduction of a national minimum wage. Which of the categories shown in the lowest quintile group might this benefit?      **(4 marks)**

(f) What other measures could be taken to reduce poverty?      **(3 marks)**

*Solution 8.1*

(a) The highest quintile group is the 20% of families receiving the highest net income in the country.

(b) The most significant changes were a fall in the proportion of pensioners in the lowest quintile from just over a half (52%) in 1971 to just over a quarter in 1985 (27%) and a rise in the proportion of single people from 19% to 34%. There were also increases in the proportion of working-age couples with children (17% to 22%), working-age couples without children (7% to 9%) and one-parent families (5% to 8%). So, while the

114

proportion of the pensioners category fell, the proportion of all the other categories rose.

(c) A fall in the number of pensioners can be rejected as a possible explanation. The change in the proportion of pensioners in the lowest 20% of income receivers must have been the result of other categories becoming worse off in relation to them and thereby moving down into the lowest quintile. One main cause of the relative decline in the position of the other categories identified in the information provided is a rise in unemployment in the period shown. There were also more single parents in the total population.

(d) The lowest quintile group of income compares the income of one group of the population with other groups and not against an absolute standard. The lowest quintile group are poorer than other members of the community. However, to determine whether they are experiencing absolute poverty, it would be necessary to identify what is a level of living standards necessary for human health and existence. Those living below this level could be said to be experiencing absolute poverty.

(e) Single people of working age, one-parent families, and working-age couples with and without children would benefit if they are in employment initially receiving less than the national minimum wage and if they remain in employment after its introduction. Pensioners and the unemployed would not benefit directly.

(f) Among other suggested measures to reduce poverty are:
   (1) increasing benefits and pensions;
   (2) increasing tax thresholds and lowering the standard rate of taxation;
   (3) retraining, training and education;
   (4) increasing employment by increasing demand and/or incentives.

# 8.3 Objective Questions

### Example 8.2

Which of the following does not describe the economist's definition of profit?
A   a reward which may be positive or negative
B   a reward for bearing uninsurable risks
C   a return to enterprise
D   a contractual payment fixed in advance
E   a return which is uncertain in amount

### Example 8.3

Normal profit is:
A   the level of profit made by the average firm in the industry
B   the positive difference between total revenue and total cost
C   the level of profit necessary to keep the firm in the industry
D   quasi-economic rent earned under conditions of perfect competition
E   the level of profit earned when MC = MR

## Example 8.4

The diagram below shows a firm producing under conditions of monopoly.
OYBZ contains:

**A** abnormal profit?     **B** abnormal loss?     **C** normal profit?

**D** economic rent?     **E** quasi-economic rent?

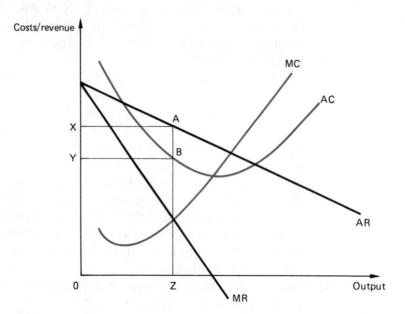

## Example 8.5

An acre of land in a Development Area could receive a yearly rental of £5000 in its least remunerative occupation. It is currently earning £7600 in its present use. Which of the following statements is correct?

**A** economic rent is £5000     **B** transfer earnings are £2600

**C** economic rent is £7600     **D** economic rent is £2600

**E** economic rent cannot be determined from the information given

## Example 8.6

A factor of production's earnings will consist entirely of economic rent if:

**A** supply is perfectly inelastic and demand is elastic

**B** supply is perfectly elastic and demand is elastic

**C** demand is perfectly inelastic and supply is elastic

**D** demand is perfectly elastic and supply is elastic

**E** demand is perfectly inelastic and supply is perfectly elastic

*Examples 8.7 and 8.8 are based on the diagram opposite, which shows the demand for and supply of word processors.*

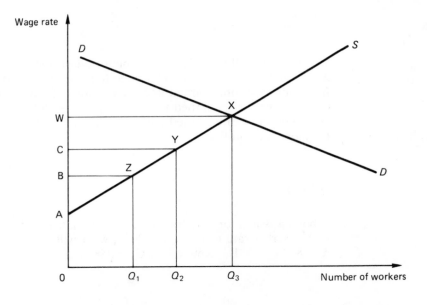

## Example 8.7

If $0Q_3$ workers are employed, what are the total transfer earnings received by the labour force?

**A** $0AXQ_3$    **B** AWX    **C** BWX    **D** $0WXQ_3$    **E** CWXY

## Example 8.8

The economic rent earned by word processor operator $Q_2$ is shown by the distance:

**A** BC    **B** BW    **C** CW    **D** ZY    **E** YX

## Example 8.9

The table shows how many people would be willing to work for a firm at different weekly wage rates.

| Wage rate (£s per week) | Number of people |
|---|---|
| 115 | 20 |
| 120 | 45 |
| 125 | 70 |
| 130 | 120 |
| 135 | 240 |
| 140 | 320 |

If the firm pays a wage of £135 and employs 240 people, what is the total economic rent earned by the workers?

**A** £330    **B** £600    **C** £1275    **D** £1600    **E** £4800

## Example 8.10

Which of the following is an example of quasi-rent?
A normal profits earned under conditions of perfect competition
B abnormal profits earned under conditions of perfect competition
C abnormal losses earned under conditions of perfect competition
D abnormal profits earned under conditions of oligopoly
E monopoly profits

## Example 8.11

A bond is issued for £970 for which the government will pay £1200 in one year's time. If the market rate of interest is 20%, what will be the market price of this bond?
A £818  B £960  C £1000  D £1012  E £1149

## Example 8.12

If the market rate of interest is 12%, what will a bond paying £18 interest sell for now?
A £82  B £88  C £112  D £150  E £168

## Example 8.13

According to Keynesian analysis, interest rates are likely to rise when there is:
A an increase in liquidity preference
B an increase in the money supply
C an increase in the price of bonds
D a decrease in national income
E a decrease in the price level

## Example 8.14

The liquidity trap is said to occur when:
A a change in the rate of interest has no effect on the price of bonds
B a change in the price of bonds has no effect on the rate of interest
C increases in public-sector borrowing crowd out private investment
D demand for money becomes perfectly inelastic at high rates of interest as people expect the rate of interest to fall in the future
E demand for money becomes perfectly elastic as people expect the rate of interest to rise in the future

## Example 8.15

|                  | Year 1 | Year 2 |
|------------------|--------|--------|
| Hourly wage rate | £3     | £5.50  |
| Price index      | 120    | 150    |

The table above shows that between years 1 and 2 the hourly wage rate in real terms changed by approximately:
A 126%  B 83%  C 47%  D $33\frac{1}{3}$%  E 17%

**Example 8.16**

Which of the following would result in an increase in demand for bank clerks?
A   the widespread introduction of an electronic funds transfer point of sales system (EFTPOS)
B   the reduction in the cost of automated teller machines
C   an increase in bank clerks' wages
D   an increase in building society deposits
E   an increase in the number of cheques bank customers write

**Example 8.17**

A firm operating under conditions of perfect competition in both the labour and product markets is faced with the following output schedule:

| Number of workers | Total output |
|---|---|
| 1 | 500 |
| 2 | 560 |
| 3 | 640 |
| 4 | 740 |
| 5 | 810 |
| 6 | 850 |

The price of the product is £4 and the wage rate is £280. How many workers should the firm employ to maximise profits?
A   2          B   3          C   4          D   5          E   6

**Example 8.18**

Demand for a factor of production will be more elastic:
A   the greater the ease with which the factor input can be substituted by other inputs
B   the greater the level of employment of factors in the economy
C   the less elastic the demand for the final product
D   the lower the proportion of the cost of the factor in the total cost of production

*Select your answers to Examples 8.19–8.23 by means of the following code:*

A   *if 1, 2 and 3 are all correct*
B   *if 1 and 2 only are correct*
C   *if 2 and 3 only are correct*
D   *if 1 only is correct*

**Example 8.19**

Which of the following is/are a tax on wealth?
1   capital transfer tax
2   capital gains tax
3   corporation tax

119

**Example 8.20**

Economic rent can be described as:
1 a surplus earned by a factor of production in excess of its supply price
2 the difference between a factor's present earnings and its transfer earnings
3 equivalent to the factor's opportunity cost

**Example 8.21**

A first division football player earns £2000 per week. His next best paid occupation would be as an economics teacher earning £205 per week. From this information it can be concluded that:
1 his economic rent is £2000 per week
2 his transfer earnings are £205 per week
3 his economic rent exceeds his transfer earnings

**Example 8.22**

Which of the following would cause the liquidity preference curve to shift to the left?
1 a rise in interest rates
2 a fall in the general price level
3 a fall in national income

**Example 8.23**

Wage drift can arise due to:
1 wage negotiations at the factory level
2 occupational wage differentials increasing
3 wages rising more rapidly than prices

# 8.4  Essays

**Example 8.24**

Discuss the arguments for and against the establishment of a national minimum wage.
(AEB June 1986)

- Explain how minimum wage legislation works.
- Concentrate on a minimum wage set above the existing level.
- Discuss the impact on wages and poverty.
- Discuss the impact on employment.

*Solution 8.24*

The effects of introducing a national minimum wage will depend mainly on the level at which it is set and how workers and employers respond. The main motive is likely to be to reduce poverty, while the main argument against the introduction of a minimum wage is that it may result in a rise in unemployment.

If a minimum wage is set below the existing level, then there will be little or no effect. For instance, if an employer is paying a wage rate of £110 and legislation is introduced stating that workers have to be paid at least £100, it is unlikely that there will be a change in the wage paid to existing workers. However, there is a possibility, particularly during times of high unemployment, that new workers may be recruited at lower wages, although existing workers are likely to resist any cut in money wages.

However, it is more likely that the minimum wage will be set above the existing wage level in some industries. The introduction of a national minimum wage is sometimes urged as a measure to reduce income inequality and, in particular, poverty. A national minimum wage can be imposed to raise the wage level of the lowest-paid and possibly reduce the number of people who decide not to work, although there are vacancies, because the wages they would receive are below the benefits they are currently receiving.

Another argument for setting a minimum wage is to protect workers in industries dominated by monopsonists. In the case of a monopsonist, the marginal cost of hiring additional (labour (MCL) will be greater than the average cost of labour (wage per employee). Figure 1 shows that the employer initially equates the marginal cost of labour with his/her demand for labour ($D_L$) and employs $0L_1$ amount of labour at a wage of $W_1$. The establishment of a government minimum wage of $W_2$ (where $D_L$ equals the average cost of labour) raises both the wage rate and employment.

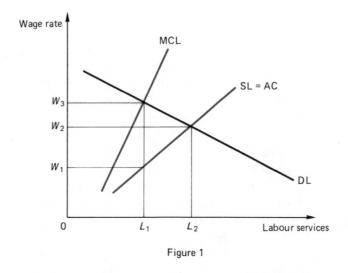

Figure 1

However, in most industries a minimum wage set above the equilibrium level, while raising wages, is likely to result, at least in the short term, in the supply of workers exceeding the demand for workers and a fall in employment. Figure 2

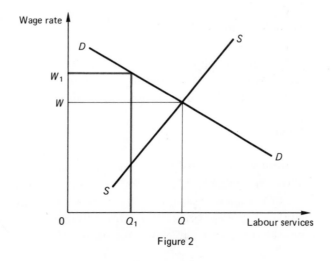

Figure 2

121

shows the minimum wage ($W_2$) being set above the equilibrium wage ($W_1$). This causes a fall in employment from $0L_1$ to $0L_2$.

The groups of workers who are most likely to be made redundant or who are less likely to be taken on include the elderly, the disabled and the less skilled workers. These may be the very groups that the implementation of a national minimum wage may be designed to help. Raising the wage rate will also increase the cost of training workers, which may result in higher unemployment among school leavers and in the longer term may lead to a shortage of skilled workers.

The extent to which unemployment will occur in different industries will depend on a number of factors. These include the profitability of the industry, the proportion of total costs accounted for by wages, the type of market structure and the elasticity of demand for the product.

Another influence will be the extent to which labour can be substituted. As labour becomes more expensive, there may be some substitution of capital for labour. The extent to which this occurs will depend on the nature of the product being produced, the relative productivities and prices of the factors.

Monetarists believe that a government-imposed national minimum wage will interfere with free market forces and thereby reduce the efficiency of the labour market. This could result in a decrease in aggregate supply and a fall in output and employment.

However, some Keynesians argue that if a national minimum wage is imposed, then demand for most industries' products will rise. So, although costs will rise, the level of employment may remain constant or possibly rise.

Nevertheless, the response of workers to the policy may result in a further rise in production costs, inflation and unemployment. Workers may press for wage rises to restore their wage differentials. If successful and if productivity does not rise, this will increase costs of production and possibly cost push inflation. Rising prices may reduce domestic competitiveness and, hence, domestic employment. If unsuccessful, the narrowing of wage differentials may reduce labour mobility and result in a shortage of skilled workers.

The effectiveness of a national minimum wage in reducing poverty may be offset by a number of factors. Employers may try to circumvent the legislation by reclassifying jobs (e.g. from full-time to part-time and taking on more part-time workers and fewer full-time workers). Also, there may be a large number of poor people who will not be helped by the legislation, including those past retirement age, the unemployed and some single parents.

### Example 8.25

What is economic rent and why do some economists argue that taxes should be imposed on economic rent?

- Define economic rent and give examples.
- Explain the main determinants of economic rent.
- Discuss the effect on resource allocation of a tax on economic rent.

*Solution 8.25*

Economic rent can be earned by any factor of production. It is a surplus paid above the income needed to keep that factor in its present occupation.

For instance, a football player earning £2500 a week may have as his next best paid occupation bricklaying, for a wage of £150 a week. So the football player will be receiving an economic rent of £2350 and the opportunity cost of his present job will be the £150 (transfer earnings) he is forgoing as a result of being a professional sportsman. Similarly, an area of land which is used for industrial purposes may receive a rent of £1000 per week, whereas, if it were to be used for residential purposes, it might receive a rent of £800. So the land will be receiving an economic rent of £200. If a piece of machinery has no alternative use, then all of its earnings will be economic rent.

Indeed, one of the main determinants of the economic rent a factor receives is that factor's elasticity of supply. If supply is perfectly inelastic, then all of the factor's earnings will constitute economic rent, whereas, if the supply is perfectly elastic, no economic rent will be received and all of the earnings will represent transfer earnings. In practice, for most factors supply will be neither perfectly elastic nor perfectly inelastic. Figure 1 shows that in a case where supply is relatively elastic some of the payment received will represent economic rent, while the rest will represent transfer earnings.

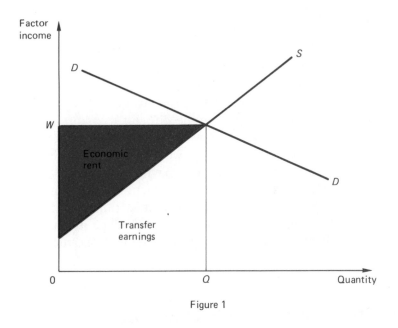

Figure 1

It is sometimes suggested that a tax should be placed on economic rent, as it is a surplus. If some but not all of this surplus is taken by the government in tax, then the factors are unlikely to transfer to other uses. For instance, if a model is being paid £4000 per week when her next best paid occupation is as a shop assistant earning £110 per week, then taxing her economic rent of £3880 at 90% is unlikely to result in her giving up her modelling job.

Monopoly profits are a form of economic rent, and a tax on monopoly profits (provided that it is less than 100%) will not result in a change in the output or pricing policy of the monopolist. Figure 2 shows the total revenue and total cost curves of a monopolist. Prior to the imposition of a tax, maximum profits are earned at $0Q$ output. The imposition of a tax causes the total cost curve to shift from $TC_1$ to $TC_2$, but the maximum profit output remains at $0Q$. Some economists argue that at least part of monopoly profits should be taxed away on grounds of equity.

The economic rent on land can also be taxed without affecting the allocation of resources. If all land, irrespective of use, is taxed at the same rate, the relative profitability of different uses will be unaffected. As supply will be unaffected, prices will not change and the burden of the tax will fall entirely on landlords. In addition, some economists argue that the economic rent earned on land should

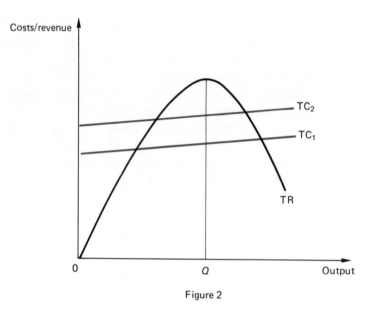

Costs/revenue

TC₂

TC₁

TR

0

Q

Output

Figure 2

be taxed, because a high return from land may result partially from public spending on the infrastructure.

However, in practice it is not always easy to identify economic rent, particularly as it may be difficult to ascertain what a factor's transfer earnings are. For instance, few workers, at any particular time, will know with certainty what employment they would be able to gain if they left their present jobs.

So economic rent is a payment in excess of transfer earnings which may be earned by any factor of production which is not in perfectly elastic supply. It has been suggested that economic rent could be taxed without affecting the allocation of resources, but in practice it can be difficult to isolate that part of a factor's payment which represents economic rent.

## 8.5 Solutions to Objective Questions

*Solution 8.2   Answer:* **D**

When an entrepreneur undertakes production, he will not know in advance how much profit will be earned, since he will not be certain what demand and costs will be in the future. Whereas workers will usually know what wages they will be paid before they start working, lenders what interest they will be paid and owners of land what rent they will receive, an entrepreneur will not have a contract setting out what profit will be earned.

**A, B, C, E** ⇒ All apply to profit.

*Solution 8.3   Answer:* **C**

Normal profit is the supply price of entrepreneurship — i.e. the minimum which needs to be paid to the entrepreneur for him to supply his services and keep his firm in the industry. This can also be referred to as transfer earnings.

**B, D** ⇒ Refer to abnormal profits.

**E** ⇒ A firm which produces where MC = MR is producing at the equilibrium output, and this may be where normal profits are earned. However, it may also be where abnormal profits or abnormal losses are earned.

*Solution 8.4   Answer:* **C**

0YBZ represents the cost of producing 0Z quantity. Normal profits are included in costs of production. So costs of production include the return to all the factors of production — i.e. wages, interest, rent and normal profit. In this case, the firm is producing where total revenue is greater than total cost and, hence, it is earning more than normal profits. The area of abnormal profits is shown by YXAB.

*Solution 8.5   Answer:* **E**

If an acre of land can earn £5000 in its least remunerative occupation, the word 'least' implies that the land has more than two uses. Economic rent is a surplus above what can be earned in its next best paid occupation — i.e. above transfer earnings. In this case, it is not known what can be earned in the next best paid occupation — just what can be earned in the least most profitable use. So it is not possible to calculate economic rent or transfer earnings.

*Solution 8.6   Answer:* **A**

If supply is perfectly inelastic, then the factor would continue to supply the same quantity of its service irrespective of the financial reward received. So, even if no reward was paid, the factor would continue to provide the service. Hence, any money paid is a surplus above what is needed to keep the factor in its present use.

*Solution 8.7   Answer:* **A**

Transfer earnings is the minimum which must be paid to keep a factor in its present occupation. It is shown by the area below the supply curve.

   **B** $\Rightarrow$ AWX represents economic rent.

   **D** $\Rightarrow$ 0WXQ$_3$ represents total earnings, consisting of both economic rent and transfer earnings.

*Solution 8.8   Answer:* **C**

Economic rent is a surplus paid to a factor above that needed to keep it in its present occupation. The diagram shows that word processor operator $Q_2$ would have been prepared to work for a wage of 0C. In fact, he is paid 0W. So his economic rent is the wage rate paid − transfer earnings — i.e. 0W − 0C = CW.

*Solution 8.9   Answer:* **C**

Some of the 240 people employed at a wage of £135 would have been willing to work for less. It is important to remember that, e.g., when 70 people are employed, this number includes 20 people who would have worked for £115 (and so are enjoying £20 economic rent each), 25 who would have worked for £120 (£15 economic rent each) and 25 who would have worked for £125 (£10 economic rent each). When 240 people are employed at a wage rate of £135, the total economic rent earned is:

| Number of people $\times$ | Economic rent per worker (£) $=$ | Total economic rent (£) |
|---|---|---|
| 20 | 20 | 400 |
| 25 | 15 | 375 |
| 25 | 10 | 250 |
| 50 | 5 | 250 |
| 120 | 0 | 0 |
| | | 1275 |

*Solution 8.10   Answer:* **B**

Quasi-rent is short-term economic rent. In the long term, it is usually competed away by an increase in the supply of the factor concerned.

Abnormal profits are a surplus over what is necessary to keep the firm in the industry. In perfect competition, these would last only in the short term, since, in the longer term, new firms will be attracted into the industry, which will lower price and return output to the normal profit level.

**A** $\Rightarrow$ Normal profits represent transfer earnings.

**D, E** $\Rightarrow$ Firms under conditions of oligopoly and monopoly may produce where AR > AC in the long term, and so, in these cases, abnormal (monopoly) profits may be regarded as economic rent.

*Solution 8.11   Answer:* **C**

The price of a bond will usually move to the point where the interest paid on it is equivalent to the market rate of interest. In this case, if the price of the bond was initially £970 and the bond is to be redeemed at £1200, £230 interest will be earned — i.e.

$$\frac{230}{970} \times \frac{100}{1} = 23.7\%$$

As this is above the market rate of interest, the price of the bond will be bid up until the interest paid is 20% of £1200:

$$\frac{1200}{1} \times \frac{100}{120} = £1000$$

Thus, someone who pays £1000 for the bond now will receive 20% interest on it.

*Solution 8.12   Answer:* **D**

If the market rate of interest is 12%, a bond paying £18 interest will sell for a figure which will mean that £18 is 12% of it:

$$\frac{18}{?} \times \frac{100}{1} = 12\% = 18 \times 100 = 12 \times ?$$

$$\frac{18 \times 100}{12} = ? = 150$$

The bond will sell for £150, earning £18 interest — i.e. 12% interest.

*Solution 8.13   Answer:* **A**

An increase in liquidity preference will mean a shift of the liquidity preference curve to the right. As people want more money, they will sell bonds, causing the price of bonds to fall and the rate of interest to rise.

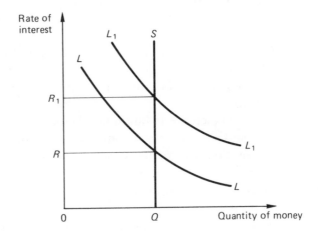

**B** ⇒ An increase in the money supply means that people are going to have higher money balances, so they are likely to buy bonds, causing the price of bonds to rise and the rate of interest to fall.

**C** ⇒ The price of bonds and the rate of interest move in an inverse direction.

**D, E** ⇒ A decrease in NY and a decrease in the price level would both tend to cause a decrease in the transactions demand for money. This would cause the liquidity preference curve to shift to the left and the rate of interest to fall.


*Solution 8.14   Answer:* **E**

Keynes believed that, at a low interest rate, demand for money could become perfectly elastic. If the rate of interest is very low (and, hence, the price of bonds is very high), everyone might expect that the price of bonds will fall and the rate of interest will rise in the future. They will hold any increase in the money supply, since they will not want to buy bonds now for fear of making a capital loss if and when their price falls.


*Solution 8.15   Answer:* **C**

To calculate rises in real income, it is first necessary to remove the effects of price changes by use of a price deflator. In this case, money wages have risen to £5.50 when the price index has increased from 120 to 150. Thus, in year 2 the real wage has changed to:

$$\frac{5.50}{1} \times \frac{\text{price index in base year}}{\text{price index in current year}} = \frac{5.50}{1} \times \frac{120}{150} = £4.40$$

So, in real terms, the wage has risen by £1.40, which, in percentage terms, is

$$\frac{1.40}{3.00} \times \frac{100}{1} = 47\%$$

*Solution 8.16   Answer:* **E**

One of the main functions of bank clerks is processing cheques. If there is an increase in the use of cheques, then more bank clerks may be employed to deal with these.

**A** ⇒ EFTPOS is a system whereby money can be transferred from one account to another electronically and without the use of cheques. EFTPOS is likely to result in a fall in banks' demand for labour and a rise in their demand for capital.

**B** ⇒ A reduction in the cost of automated teller machines is likely to result in a spread of their use and a reduction in demand for bank clerks.

**C** ⇒ *Ceteris paribus* an increase in wages is likely to cause a fall in demand for the factor.

**D** ⇒ An increase in building society deposits will tend to be accompanied by a fall in bank deposits as customers switch from one institution to another. If this is the case, demand for bank clerks will fall.

*Solution 8.17   Answer:* **D**

In theory, a firm will employ the number of workers where the wage rate equals the marginal revenue product of labour. To calculate MRP, it is necessary to work out marginal product (change in total output as a result of employing one more worker) and multiply it by MR (which, under conditions of perfect competition, equals price). So, in this case:

| Number of workers | Total output | Marginal product | × | Marginal revenue (£) | = | MRP (£) |
|---|---|---|---|---|---|---|
| 1 | 500 | | | | | |
| 2 | 560 | 60 | | 4 | | 240 |
| 3 | 640 | 80 | | 4 | | 320 |
| 4 | 740 | 100 | | 4 | | 400 |
| 5 | 810 | 70 | | 4 | | 280 |
| 6 | 850 | 40 | | 4 | | 160 |

Thus, the wage rate of £280 equals MRP when 5 workers are employed.

*Solution 8.18   Answer:* **A**

Demand for a factor of production will be elastic when a rise in the price of the factor causes a greater percentage fall in demand for the factor. If a factor can be easily substituted by another factor, then, if it rises in cost, the employer will switch to using more of the other factors.

**B, C, D** ⇒ In each case, demand will be inelastic and a rise in price of the factor would cause a smaller percentage fall in demand for the factor.

*Solution 8.19   Answer:* **D**

Capital transfer tax is a tax on gifts made during a person's life and on his or her death (inheritance). It is currently the only form of wealth tax in the UK.

**2** ⇒ Capital gains tax is a tax on the *income* received when certain capital assets are sold at a higher price than their purchase price.

**3** ⇒ Corporation tax is a tax on company profits, which are a form of income.

*Solution 8.20    Answer:* **B**

Economic rent is a surplus earned over and above the factor's transfer earnings.
   **3** ⇒ A factor's opportunity cost is equivalent to transfer earnings.

*Solution 8.21    Answer:* **C**

The first division football player's present wage is £2000 a week and the wage of his next best paid occupation is £205 per week. Thus, his economic rent is present earnings − transfer earnings — i.e. £2000 − £205 = £1795. His transfer earnings are £205, since, if he was paid less than this as a football player, he would switch to being a teacher. Thus, his economic rent of £1795 does exceed his transfer earnings of £205.

*Solution 8.22    Answer:* **C**

A shift to the left of the liquidity preference curve would be caused by a decrease in demand for money. A fall in the general price level and a fall in NY would result in a decrease in the transactions demand for money.
   **1** ⇒ A rise in interest rates will cause a contraction in demand for money — i.e. a movement along the same liquidity curve.

*Solution 8.23    Answer:* **D**

Wage drift arises when the wages workers actually receive exceed the nationally agreed rates. This can occur as a result of local agreements made at the factory level.

# 9 Labour Economics

## 9.1 Fact Sheet

### (a) Population Structure

*Demography* is the study of population statistics. Population size is a *stock value* (an amount at a given moment in time). Population size is affected by inflows (births and immigration) and outflows (deaths and emigration) over time.

- The *birth rate* is the number of live births per thousand of the population in a year.
- The *death rate* is the number of deaths per thousand of the population in a year.
- The *natural change* in population is the difference between the number of births and deaths in a year.
- *Net migration* is the difference between immigration and emigration in a year.

Figure 9.1 divides the population into two sections.

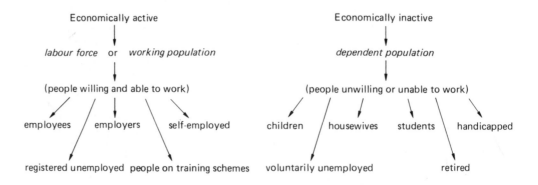

**Figure 9.1** Economic activity and inactivity

- The *activity* (or *participation*) *rate* is the percentage of the population of working age in the labour force.
- An *ageing population* occurs when the average age per person is rising.
- *Malthus* argued that since population has a tendency to grow geometrically (i.e. as the series 1, 2, 4, 8, 16), while the good supply rises arithmetically (i.e. as the series 1, 2, 3, 4, 5), economies may eventually operate at a subsistence level. Unless people raise small families, famine, war and disease would be the only checks on population growth.
- Agricultural innovations, international trade and a low birth rate have enabled the UK to avoid Malthus's prediction.

- *Optimum population* occurs when productivity (output per person) is highest.
- *Population pyramids* show the age and sex distribution of a country at a particular moment in time

### (b) Supply of Labour

The total supply of labour depends on:
  (i) the size and age of the population;
  (ii) the activity rate;
  (iii) social acceptance of women working;
  (iv) wage levels;
  (v) the level of income tax and of unemployment benefit;
  (vi) the length of the working week and of holidays.
  (vii) industrial relations record

### (c) Offer Curve of Labour

- The work indifference curves in Figure 9.2(a) show combinations of hours worked and income received which yield equal total satisfaction to the worker. They slope upwards because work is usually a *disutility* (i.e. gives negative satisfaction).
- As the worker moves to an indifference curve further to the left, a higher level of satisfaction is enjoyed.

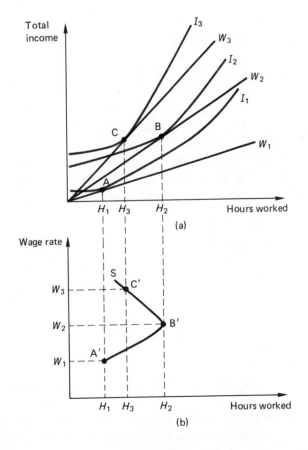

**Figure 9.2**  (a) Income–leisure trade-off; (b) offer curve of labour

131

- The wage rate line $W_1$ corresponds to a given hourly rate of pay. Multiplying the wage rate by the number of hours worked gives total wages. An increase in the hourly rates of pay pivots the wage rate line upwards, about the origin.
- Figure 9.2(b) shows that workers may eventually work fewer hours following an increase in wage rates, and the offer curve of labour, $S$, begins to slope backwards.

### (d) Occupational Distribution of Labour

Table 9.1 suggests that there has been a relative decline in the share of agricultural and manufacturing employment in total employment. The service sector of the economy has expanded.

**Table 9.1** Distribution of employment in the UK

|                   | 1964 | 1984 |
|-------------------|------|------|
| Primary sector    | 5%   | 3%   |
| Secondary sector  | 47%  | 32%  |
| Tertiary sector   | 48%  | 65%  |

### (e) Labour Mobility

There are three types of labour mobility:
  (i) Workers moving between jobs requiring different skills have *occupational mobility*, and this depends on:
   (1) the willingness and ability of an individual to retrain;
   (2) employment barriers to entry (e.g. *closed shops*).
  (ii) Workers moving between jobs requiring the same skills have *industrial mobility*. Workers in declining industries tend to be industrially immobile.
  (iii) Workers moving between different regions have *geographical mobility*, and this depends on:
   (1) regional variations in house prices;
   (2) the availability of rented accommodation;
   (3) existing family and social ties.

### (f) Trade Unions

A trade union is an organisation which represents groups of employees.

- *Collective bargaining* occurs when the union discusses pay and working conditions on behalf of its members with groups of employers. Figures 9.3 and 9.4 show how a trade union can increase wage rates.

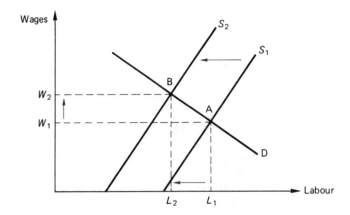

**Figure 9.3** Decreasing the supply of labour. Unions restrict the supply of labour by imposing a closed shop; insisting on long apprenticeship periods; insisting on high qualifications. Therefore, the number of workers employed falls

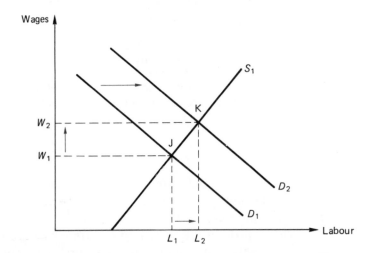

**Figure 9.4** Increasing the demand for labour. Unions increase the demand for labour by overmanning agreements; increasing productivity; supporting an advertising campaign. Therefore, the number of workers employed rises

## 9.2 Data Response

### Worked Example 9.1

One of the most likely changes in the budget is a cut in the top rate of income tax from 60 pence in the pound which Mr Lawson will justify on the grounds of incentives. There are two economic effects when tax rates are cut. The first, the so-called 'income effect'. You feel richer. You do not need to work so hard in order to earn what you need to buy your food, clothes and holiday on the beach. Tax cuts allow you to earn more for the same effort as before, so they make you lazier. They are a disincentive to effort.

The second opposite effect is the 'incentive' effect. Your top rate of tax comes down from 60 pence to, say, 45 pence. You will in future keep 55 pence of every pound you earn instead of 40 pence. You have a greater incentive than before to earn more money if you can.

How important is the laziness-inducing effect compared with the effort-inducing incentive effect? Economic research suggests that for most people one effect just about cancels out the other, so that on balance tax cuts have no effect on effort. A study commissioned by the Treasury at great expense from

133

Professor C. V. Brown of Sterling University even discovered that most people cannot increase their earnings. Their jobs are such that they are not paid more for extra work.

However, most economists think that the argument is more finely balanced for higher rate payers. In the main they can work harder. Because rates are so much higher — 60 per cent against 36 per cent for the basic rate payer (once National Insurance contributions are included) — the disincentive effect is likely to be more powerful than the income effect. The rate of tax on each extra pound is what economists call the marginal rate. It is not the same as the average rate of income tax, yet average rate is what determines your income. You can face a marginal rate of 40% but because a long band of your income is taxed at the base rate with a further slice tax free in the form of personal allowances, and a further slice tax free because of mortgage tax relief, your average rate may only be a quarter. The marginal rate determines incentives but the average rate determines income.

Source: 'Lawson Can Soak the Prosperous by Bringing Down Their Taxes',
C Huhne, *The Guardian*, 24 February 1988

(a) What is the difference between marginal and average rates of taxation?
**(2 marks)**
(b) What evidence is there in the passage for believing that the current system of income tax is progressive? **(4 marks)**
(c) Give three reasons why some workers will not work longer hours following a cut in the top rate of taxation. **(6 marks)**
(d) Use the passage to advise the Chancellor on how a future budget might cut tax rates but increase overall tax revenues. **(13 marks)**


*Solution 9.1*

(a) The marginal rate of taxation refers to the amount of each extra pound of income paid in tax. The average rate of tax refers to the proportion of total income paid in tax.

(b) A progressive system of taxation is where the proportion of income taken by the government in tax rises, as income rises. The passage notes that low-income earners pay no tax because of tax-free personal allowances. It also observes that at the time there were two different rates of taxation: a standard rate of 36%, including the effect of National Insurance contributions, and a higher rate of 60p in the pound paid only by top earners. It follows that high earners pay a greater proportion of their income in tax than do low earners.

(c) A large number of people are unaffected by changes in the top rate of tax because their pay does not bring them into the highest tax bracket. Others are unable to vary the amount of work done for more pay, because they are salaried and take-home pay is independent of the number of hours worked each individual month. Some workers may decide to work fewer hours and take home the same amount of pay following a cut in the top rate of tax.

(c) A cut in marginal rates of tax has two opposite effects. On the one hand, it acts as an incentive to work, because households are able to retain a greater proportion of their earnings to spend on goods and services of their own choice. They may be encouraged to work harder and earn more, with the effect that the absolute amount paid to the government actually rises. For example, a higher-rate payer earning £2000 in the highest tax bracket of 60p in the pound, pays £1200 in tax. A cut in the top rate to, say, 40p may encourage him to work extra hours, so that earnings eligible for tax at the highest rate rise to, say, £5000, and £2000 is now paid in tax. The Exchequer receives an additional £800.

This argument overlooks the possibility that there may be an opposite income effect whereby workers use the increase in take-home pay brought about by tax cuts to buy more leisure time. Tax receipts from workers who maintain a constant income by adjusting the number of hours worked falls following a cut in marginal rates of taxation. Using the above example, the higher-rate payer earning £2000 takes home £800 at the 60% rate. Once the rate falls to 40%, he need only work long enough to earn £1335 to maintain a disposable income of £800. Treasury receipts fall to £534.

Moreover, the passage indicates that salaried workers have no choice as to the number of hours worked. Tax receipts from those salaried workers earning sufficient to fall into the highest-rate group would fall.

# 9.3   Objective Questions

**Example 9.2**

An increase in population at the same time as a decrease in the birth rate can occur following:
A   positive net migration and a fall in the fertility rate
B   positive net migration and a rise in the fertility rate
C   positive net migration and a fall in the death rate
D   zero net migration and a rise in the fertility rate
E   zero net migration and a fall in infant mortality

**Example 9.3**

Optimum population occurs when, with current resources:
A   productivity is rising
B   productivity is constant
C   productivity is highest
D   labour is fully utilised
E   the largest population possible is supported

**Example 9.4**

An ageing population will be most likely to result in:
A   an increase in the dependent population
B   an increase in labour mobility
C   a reduction in unemployment
D   a reduction in transfer payments
E   a constant pattern of consumption

*Examples 9.5–9.8 refer to the following diagrams, which show the age distribution of the population in four countries.*

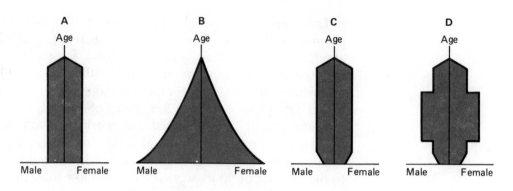

Which diagram (**A**, **B**, **C** or **D**) most accurately depicts:

### Example 9.5

A developing economy?

### Example 9.6

A developed economy with a constant birth rate?

### Example 9.7

An economy with a migrant population?

### Example 9.8

An economy with an increasing birth rate?

### Example 9.9

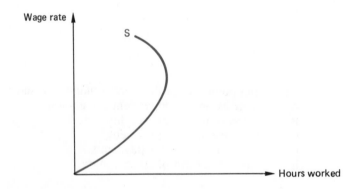

The diagram shows the offer curve (*S*) for labour. The offer curve shows that the number of hours worked eventually:
A increases as wage rates rise
B decreases as wage rates rise
C increases as the demand for labour increases
D decreases as the demand for labour increases
E is unresponsive to changes in wage rates

**Example 9.10**

In the short run, a trade union is most likely to increase wage rates in an industry without reducing the number employed by:
A  imposing a closed shop
B  insisting on long apprenticeship periods
C  negotiating overmanning agreements
D  imposing an overtime ban
E  insisting that only their members do certain jobs

*For Examples 9.11–9.13, use the diagram below, where $D_1D_1$ is the original demand curve for bricklayers and $S_1S_1$ is the original supply curve.*

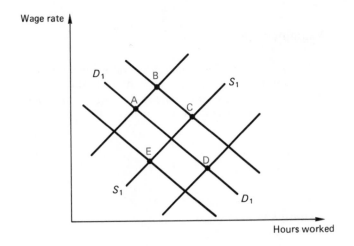

After each question indicate the new equilibrium position **A, B, C, D** or **E** following:

**Example 9.11**

An increase in the productivity of bricklayers, *ceteris paribus*.

**Example 9.12**

A reduction in the apprenticeship period for bricklayers from 4 years to 3.

**Example 9.13**

The introduction of a closed shop and a large fall in interest rates.

*Select your answers to Examples 9.14–9.16 by means of the following code:*
A  *if 1, 2 and 3 are all correct*
B  *if 1 and 2 only are correct*
C  *if 2 and 3 only are correct*
D  *if 1 only is correct*

**Example 9.14**

The working population includes:
1 the self-employed
2 employers
3 registered unemployed

**Example 9.15**

The immobility of labour is likely to be reduced by:
1 legislation restricting closed shops
2 the abolition of rent controls
3 compulsory retraining schemes for the unemployed

**Example 9.16**

If the supply of labour increases following an decrease in marginal rates of income tax:
1 workers value income more than leisure
2 the supply curve of labour does *not* slope backwards or vertically
3 the supply curve of labour has shifted to the right

# 9.4 Essays

**Example 9.17**

'The size of a nation's population is not as important as its age, sex and geographical distribution'. Discuss.

(AEB June 1986)

- This is an open question, with a number of possible answers.
- Establish criteria for judging the relative importance of population size and population characteristics.
- Discuss the relative *economic* importance of the stated population features.

*Solution 9.17*

Economists can compare the importance of population size and population characteristics in terms of their relative contribution to the production of goods and services.

In theory, population size is a major determinant of total product. Output depends on the quantity of inputs. All other things being equal, a larger population allows a country to produce more goods and services. The United States of America is able to use a large population to produce the highest GDP of any nation in the world. Yet countries with larger populations exist. Surely India should produce more than the USA? One reason why it does not lies in the different age distribution of the populations. Developing countries such as India tend to have a larger proportion of unproductive young people in the population than do developed nations such as the USA. Here size of population is not as important as the age composition of that population.

Population size must be assessed in relation to the quantity and quality of a country's resources.

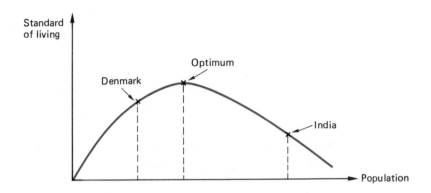

The diagram illustrates the relationship between the size of population and standards of living. India has over 140 times the population of Denmark but a far lower standard of living. This is because the population of Denmark combines with available resources to achieve almost the greatest output per person possible. Denmark is close to its optimum population. On the other hand, India is overpopulated in the sense that a reduction in population size would probably increase output per head and raise living standards. It follows that population size alone is relatively unimportant in determining a country's average living standard. A small population has not hindered the economic development of New Zealand or Austria. More important are the abilities and characteristics of all resources, including population.

For instance, less developed countries (LDCs) have a low average age, with 50% of the population under the age of 15. The rapid increase in the size of the population means that, even when output is rising, output per person can be falling. On the other hand, developed countries (DCs) have a high average age, with less than 25% of the population under 15. A relatively stable population means that increases in output usually cause productivity to increase as well.

The age structure of a population also affects the pattern of production. Countries with a high proportion of young dependants (e.g. Kenya) need to concentrate production on youth-related products such as education. Countries with an ageing population (e.g. France) have different considerations. An increasing proportion of old people requires the increased production of related products such as hospitals. Also, there is no direct relationship between the population size of a country and the mobility of labour. Mobility depends on age structure. Countries where average age is rising experience increasing labour immobility. Hence, it is age distribution and not the size of population which determines the pattern of employment and output.

Sex distribution has a similar effect in helping to determine the nature of economic activity. Developing countries such as Brazil have a larger number of men of working age than women. Nations with large numbers of migrant males aged 20–45 are likely to have a dynamic and flexible workforce. High rates of economic growth are probable.

In part, the uneven geographical distribution of population is caused by the inhospitable physical features and climate of some regions. However, geographical distribution affects and reflects the pattern of a nation's production. Less-developed economies with a large labour-intensive agricultural sector have an even geographical distribution of people. The industrialisation of developed countries has led to a concentration of populations in urban areas. For example, 80% of the UK population live in urban areas, and conurbations house a third of the population in only 3% of the land area.

In conclusion, it has been shown that the qualitative factors of age, sex and geographical distribution of a nation's population have a greater impact on economic systems than the actual size of that country's population.

**Example 9.18**

It has been suggested that the incentive to work in the UK will be increased by (a) a reduction in social security payments and (b) a reduction in the higher rates of taxation. Explain and evaluate the reasoning underlying these views.

(JMB 1986)

- Reductions in social security benefits increase net wage rates and are therefore an incentive to work.
- However, workers can use wage increases to 'buy' more leisure.
- The income–leisure trade-off depends on the income and substitution effects of wage increases.
- Indifference curves can be used to illustrate this trade-off.

*Solution 9.18*

Workers on low incomes are eligible to receive social security benefits, such as income support. The 'poverty trap' occurs when a low-paid worker gains little or nothing by working overtime once tax and lost benefits have been taken into account. A reduction in social security payments reduces the income of low-paid workers, who may then decide to make up lost benefits by working longer hours.

The 'unemployment trap' occurs when there is no substantial difference between income in or out of work. Studies suggest that low-paid workers with families of two earn only 15% more by working than when receiving unemployment benefit. Another indicator of the unemployment trap is the *replacement ratio* (RR), which measures the ratio between income in and out of work. The RR for a long-term unemployed family of two adults and two children is below 75%. Reducing unemployment benefit reduces the RR and so acts as an incentive to look for work.

A reduction in the higher rates of income tax makes overtime more attractive to high-income workers. Labour still has to decide between working extra hours for more money or enjoying more leisure time. The income–leisure trade-off can be analysed by using indifference curves. Look at Figure 1.

The work indifference curves $I_1$, $I_2$ and $I_3$ show combinations of hours worked and income received which yield equal total satisfaction to the worker. They slope upwards because work is usually a *disutility* and gives negative satisfaction.

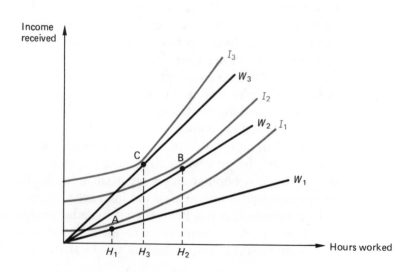

As the worker moves to an indifference curve further to the left, the higher the level of satisfaction enjoyed. The line $W_1$ shows the amount of income earned from working various hours at a given wage rate.

Assume that the worker is at point A. A reduction in benefits or tax rates increases net wage rates and pivots the wage rate line upwards, to $W_2$. The resultant 'income effect' means that a worker can use an increase in wages to buy more leisure time. The 'substitution effect' means that leisure is now relatively dearer, since more income is now sacrificed for each extra hour of leisure. Benefit or tax cuts which increase wage rates from $W_1$ to $W_2$ increase the incentive to work, because the substitution effect is stronger than the income effect. The worker moves from point A to point B. However, an increase from $W_2$ to $W_3$ reduces the incentive to work, because the income effect outweighs the substitution effect and extra income is used to buy more leisure time. The worker moves from point B to point C.

In conclusion, a reduction in social security benefits and rates of taxation acts as an incentive to work only if the substitution effect of the resultant increase in net wages is stronger than the income effect.

# 9.5 Solutions to Objective Questions

*Solution 9.2 Answer:* **A**

*Positive net migration* occurs when the number of people permanently entering a country is greater than the number leaving. Fertility rates affect birth rates.

**C** $\Rightarrow$ Positive net migration increases the size of the population, but the fall in the death rate has no direct effect upon the birth rate.

*Solution 9.3 Answer:* **C**

*Optimum population* occurs when *productivity* (output per person) from a given amount of resources is highest.

*Solution 9.4 Answer:* **A**

An ageing population is likely to cause an increase in the number of retired people. People who have retired are economically inactive and are classified as dependants.

*Solution 9.5 Answer:* **B**

Developing countries tend to have a high birth rate and a high death rate. As a result, the base of a population pyramid is broad, while the top is narrow.

*Solution 9.6 Answer:* **A**

Developed countries tend to have both a low birth rate and a low death rate. Consequently, the upper regions of a population pyramid are almost as broad as the base. The vertical slope of the pyramid indicates a constant birth rate.

**C** and **D** $\Rightarrow$ Also show developed countries, but the V-shaped base of the pyramid suggests that the birth rate is falling.

*Solution 9.7   Answer:* **D**

A *migrant population* consists of people, mainly of working age, who have settled in a country. As a result, there is a bulge in the mid-range of a population pyramid.

*Solution 9.8   Answer:* **B**

**B** is the only diagram where the base is the broadest part of the population pyramid. With an increasing birth rate, the sides of a population pyramid slope outwards as in Figure **B** in Example 9.5. It follows that there are more births now than there have been in the past.

*Solution 9.9   Answer:* **B**

Refer back to Figure 9.2. An increase in the wage rate results in a movement up the offer curve of labour. Eventually, the curve slopes backwards and the number of hours worked falls.

*Solution 9.10   Answer:* **C**

An overmanning agreement results in more workers being used for a job than is necessary. In the short run, employers are forced to increase their demand for labour. The wage rate of all workers in the industry rises. See Figure 9.4. In the long run, a loss of competitiveness may cause the firm to close down, with a resulting increase in unemployment.

*Solution 9.11   Answer:* **C**

An increase in productivity raises the marginal revenue product of bricklayers, which, in turn, increases the demand for their labour. The demand curve for bricklayers shifts to the right.

*Solution 9.12   Answer:* **D**

A reduction in the apprenticeship period means that all those bricklayers in their fourth year of training are now available for work, thus increasing supply.

*Solution 9.13   Answer:* **B**

The introduction of a closed shop means that all bricklayers must now belong to a recognised union. The resultant fall in supply shifts the supply curve to the left. The large fall in interest rates increases aggregate demand, and reduces the cost of mortgages. A consequent increase in the demand for houses increases the derived demand for workers, such as bricklayers, involved in construction.

*Solution 9.14   Answer:* **A**

See Figure 9.1.

*Solution 9.15    Answer:* **A**

1 ⇒ The industrial mobility of non-union workers is improved.
2 ⇒ The resultant increase in the supply of rented accommodation increases the geographical mobility of labour.
3 ⇒ Retraining increases the occupational mobility of labour.

*Solution 9.16    Answer:* **B**

A fall in the marginal rate of income tax increases wage rates. If the supply of labour increases following an increase in wages, workers value income more than forgone leisure, and the supply curve for labour slopes upwards.

3 ⇒ Is incorrect because an increase in wage rates results in a movement along the supply curve.

# 10 Welfare Economics

## 10.1  Fact Sheet

### (a) Optimal Resource Allocation

Economic systems have to choose between alternative allocations (uses) of land, labour and capital. Welfare economics provides a framework for deciding on the optimal (best) use of scarce resources. A particular resource allocation is assessed by using:

(i) *Efficiency criteria* (rules) first developed by *Pareto*, whereby the economy should have:

   (1) *Technical* or *productive efficiency*. This occurs when resources are fully employed and all firms are producing at minimum average cost. It is then impossible to increase the output of any one good without reducing the output of some other good.

   (2) *Consumption* or *allocative efficiency*. This occurs when it is impossible to redistribute products to increase the welfare of any one consumer without reducing the welfare of some other consumer.

(ii) *Equity (fairness) criteria*, which judge the 'desirability' of a particular resource allocation.

- Using Pareto criteria, a reallocation of resources is desirable only if someone gains *and no one loses*.
- A *Pareto optimal* allocation of resources exists when no one can be made better off without someone else being made worse off, following a reorganisation of production or distribution.
- Pareto efficiency criteria cannot be used in resource decisions where someone gains *and someone loses*, as this requires the use of equity criteria.
- Equity judgements can be made by using the *Kaldor–Hicks test*. A change in production or distribution is desirable only if those who gain can compensate those who lose, and still be better off. Note that compensation does not necessarily take place.

### (b) Social Costs and Social Benefits

Analysis of a resource allocation requires an accurate valuation of the true costs and benefits involved in economic activity, including externalities. *Externalities* are the spill-over effects of production or consumption, for which no compensation is paid.

(i) Externalities can be *positive* (e.g. beekeepers indirectly provide a source of pollination to market gardeners).

$$\text{Social benefit} = \frac{\text{private benefit}}{\text{(benefit to the individual)}} + \frac{\text{positive externalities}}{\text{(benefits to third parties)}}$$

(ii) Externalities can be *negative* (e.g. pollution from a power station may damage the health of local residents).

$$\text{Social cost} = \frac{\text{private cost}}{\text{(cost to the individual)}} + \frac{\text{negative externalities}}{\text{(costs to third parties)}}$$

Figures 10.1 and 10.2 show the effect of externalities on social cost and social benefits.

*Private marginal cost* (PMC) is the cost incurred by the firm in producing each extra unit of good X.

*External marginal cost* (EMC) is the amount that consumers are prepared to pay to avoid the negative externalities associated with extra units of X.

*Social marginal cost* (SMC) is the full opportunity cost of producing each extra unit of X.

*Private marginal benefit* (PMB) is the utility gained by the individual from the consumption of each extra unit of good X.

*External marginal benefit* (EMB) is the benefit to third parties from the consumption of each extra unit of X.

*Social marginal benefit* (SMB) is the full value placed by society on the consumption of each extra unit of X.

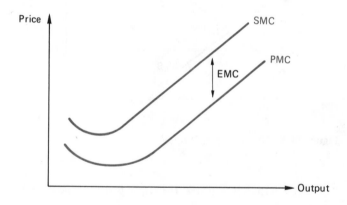

**Figure 10.1**  Social marginal cost

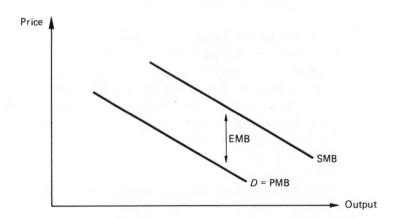

**Figure 10.2**  Social marginal benefit

145

### (c) Market Failure through Externalities

- An *efficient allocation of resources* occurs in a market where the opportunity cost of the extra unit (SMC) equals the value placed by society on its consumption (SMB) — i.e. where SMC = SMB.
- *Market failure* occurs when the price mechanism results in an inefficient allocation of resources.

Figures 10.3 and 10.4 show market failure caused by negative and positive externalities.

In Figure 10.3, $Q_1$ is the socially efficient level of output where SMC = SMB. $Q_2$ is supplied by the industry. The resulting *over*production results in a *welfare loss triangle* of ABC.

In Figure 10.4, $Q_1$ is the socially efficient level of output where SMC = SMB. Only $Q_2$ is supplied by the industry. The resulting *under*production results in a *welfare loss triangle* of JKL.

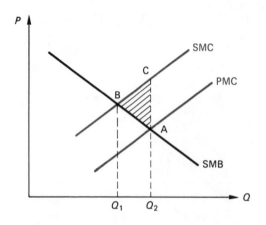

**Figure 10.3**  Negative externalities

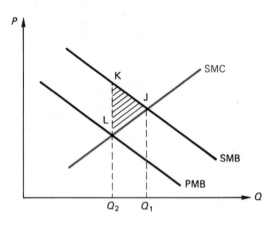

**Figure 10.4**  Positive externalities

### (d) Market Failure through Public Goods

A *public good* is a product such as defence which is:
  (i) *non-rival* — i.e. an individual's consumption of a public good does not reduce its benefit to others;
 (ii) *non-excludable* — i.e. once a public good is provided, others cannot be stopped from consuming it.

- The non-excludability of a public good encourages some consumers to avoid payment and become *free riders*.
- A *merit good* is a product, such as education, which consumers may undervalue but which the government believes is 'good' for consumers. Unlike public goods, merit goods can be bought and sold.
- *Market failure* occurs because profit-maximising firms underproduce public and merit goods.

### (e) Market Failure through Imperfect Competition

Assuming no externalities, marginal cost (MC) equals social marginal cost (SMC), and price (P) accurately measures social marginal benefit (SMB). Figure

146

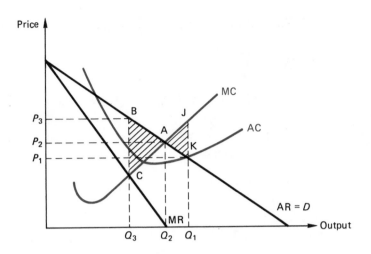

**Figure 10.5** Alternative pricing policies in imperfect competition

10.5 and Table 10.1 indicate that, unless a firm sets output where the cost of making the last unit equals its price (*marginal cost pricing*), market failure results.

- *Nationalised industries* generally use a marginal cost pricing policy. Following *privatisation* the same firm will underproduce if it uses a profit-maximisation pricing policy.

**Table 10.1** Consequences of pricing policies

| Pricing policy | Condition | | Price | Output | Result | Welfare loss |
|---|---|---|---|---|---|---|
| Average cost | $P$ | $= AC$ | $P_1$ | $Q_1$ | Overproduction | Triangle AJK |
| Profit maximisation | $MC = MR$ | | $P_3$ | $Q_3$ | Underproduction | Triangle ABC |
| Marginal cost | $P$ | $= MC$ | $P_2$ | $Q_2$ | Efficient production | None |

#### (f) Cost–Benefit Analysis

*Cost–benefit analysis* (CBA) is a method of assessing the social costs and benefits of an investment project. This involves comparing the private costs and negative externalities of a scheme with its private benefits and positive externalities, using money as a measure of value. Problems involved in CBA occur because:

(i) Externalities are difficult to measure:
   (1) negative externalities are valued by calculating how much consumers would pay to avoid any inconvenience caused by the scheme;
   (2) positive externalities are valued by estimating the change in consumer surplus of individuals affected by the project.
(ii) Future costs and benefits are difficult to measure. The *present value* (PV) of future *net social benefits* (social benefits less social costs) is found by *discounting*. For example, £500 lent for 2 years earning 10% interest per annum is worth:

£500 (loan) + £50 interest (in year 1) + £55 interest (in year 2) = £605 (total)

Therefore, the PV of £605 in 2 years' time, discounted at 10% per annum, is £500.

- The PV of an investment project is calculated by using the equation:

$$PV = \sum \frac{[NSB_n]}{[1 + r]^n}$$

where NSB is net social benefit, $r$ is the rate of social discount and $n$ is the life of the project.
- A scheme is worth undertaking only if the present value of net social benefits is positive.

## 10.2  Data Response

**Worked Example 10.1**

The firm represented in the diagram below is nationalised and follows a marginal cost pricing policy.

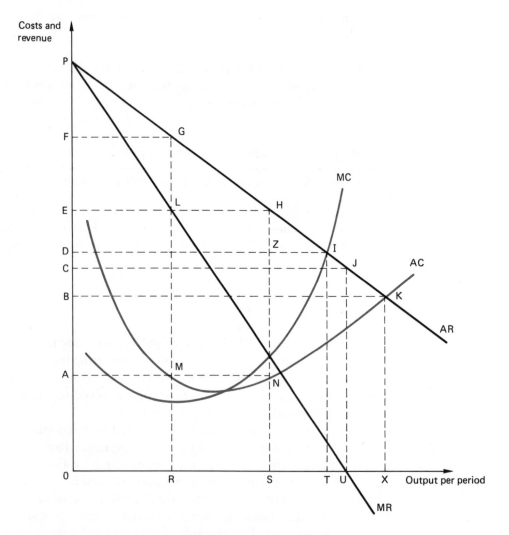

(a) With specific reference to the above diagram comment on the relationship between price elasticity of demand and marginal revenue.                    **(3 marks)**
(b) What price would a nationalised industry charge and what output would it produce if pursuing a marginal cost pricing policy?                    **(1 mark)**
(c) State the change in price that would occur if the firm were to adopt an average cost pricing policy.                    **(2 marks)**

(d) (i) What is meant by 'consumer surplus'? **(2 marks)**

(ii) Assume: (1) the firm is now privatised and, instead of following a policy of marginal cost pricing, it follows a policy of profit maximisation;

(2) cost conditions are unchanged and the firm charges the same price to all consumers.

What.is the change in consumer surplus? **(3 marks)**

(e) Subsequently, if this firm were to pursue a policy of price discrimination, explain with the aid of a diagram how profits could be increased. **(4 marks)**

(f) Examine the circumstances in which a nationalised firm following a marginal cost pricing policy would incur a loss. Use a diagram to illustrate your answer.

**(5 marks)**

(L June 1987)

*Solution 10.1*

(a) Up to output level U, marginal revenue is positive; therefore, the sale of extra units increases total revenue. Yet, as the firm moves down the demand (AR) curve, more is being sold but at a *lower* price. Since marginal revenue is positive, the given fall in price must give rise to a proportionately greater increase in quantity demanded. It follows that, up to output level U, demand is price-elastic. Beyond U, marginal revenue is negative and demand is price-inelastic.

(b) A firm following a marginal cost pricing policy sets output where MC = P. Output is T and price is D.

(c) A firm following an average cost pricing policy sets output where AC = P. Output is X and price is B. Price falls from D to B.

(d) (i) Consumer surplus is the difference between the price consumers pay and the price they would be prepared to pay rather than go without the product.

(ii) The initial area of consumer surplus lies below the demand (AR) curve but above the line DI. The new area of consumer surplus is PBK. Therefore, the change in consumer surplus is DBKI.

(e) Price discrimination occurs when a firm charges different prices in different markets for the same product. See Figure 6.8.

(f) A nationalised firm following a marginal cost pricing policy always incurs a loss if, at the corresponding level of output, costs are greater than revenue. In the diagram below the total cost of producing $Q_1$, $A \times Q_1$, is greater than the revenue of $B \times Q_1$ received from its sale.

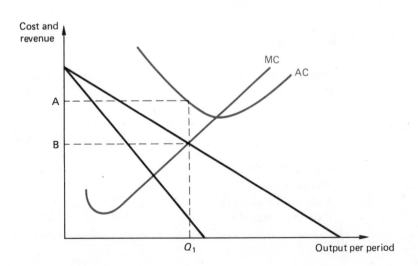

149

## 10.3  Objective Questions

**Example 10.2**

Productive efficiency in an economy is achieved in the long run when:
A   all resources are fully employed
B   the rate of economic growth is maximised
C   all firms are producing goods at minimum unit cost
D   firms can only supply more of one good by making less of another
E   all firms are maximising profits

**Example 10.3**

Demerit goods are products that:
A   are supplied by the government
B   create positive externalities
C   involve no external costs in production or consumption
D   can only be bought in a black market
E   are likely to be overconsumed in a market economy

**Example 10.4**

According to the Pareto criterion, a reallocation of resources that increases almost everyone's welfare:
A   represents an increase in social welfare
B   represents a decrease in social welfare
C   represents no change in social welfare
D   requires an accurate valuation of spillover effects
E   cannot be assessed

**Example 10.5**

Market failure occurs when there is an imperfectly competitive market because:
A   all firms are profit maximisers
B   marginal cost exceeds marginal revenue
C   price exceeds marginal cost
D   firms overproduce merit goods
E   firms underproduce demerit goods

**Example 10.6**

The following data refer to a cost–benefit analysis of three possible investment projects.

|                       | Project J | Project K | Project L |
|-----------------------|-----------|-----------|-----------|
| Private benefits (£)  | 125       | 140       | 50        |
| Private costs (£)     | 115       | 150       | 90        |
| External benefits (£) | 75        | 50        | 200       |
| External costs (£)    | 100       | 10        | 150       |

It can be deduced that economic welfare would be improved by undertaking:
A   project J only        B   project K only        C   project L only
D   both projects J and K   E   both projects K and L


**Example 10.7**

The government decides to fit filters which reduce the amount of sulphur dioxide discharged into the atmosphere by power stations. To maximise net social benefit, the government should fit extra filters up to the point where:
A   total social benefit is maximised
B   marginal social benefit is maximised
C   total social benefit minus total social cost is zero
D   marginal social benefit minus marginal social cost is zero
E   marginal social benefit is zero


**Example 10.8**

The private costs of a firm do not equal its social costs. All other things being equal, which one of the following government actions improves welfare?
A   tax the firm if social costs are more than its private costs
B   tax the firm if social costs are less than its private costs
C   subsidise the firm if social costs are more than its private costs
D   close the firm down if social benefits minus social costs are positive
E   do nothing


**Example 10.9**

The data below refer to a chemical factory which creates a spill-over effect in the form of river pollution.

| Output (units) | 1 | 2 | 3 | 4 | 5 | 6 | 7 |
|---|---|---|---|---|---|---|---|
| Average revenue (£) | 14 | 12 | 10 | 8 | 6 | 4 | 2 |
| Marginal private cost (£) | 2 | 4 | 6 | 8 | 10 | 12 | 14 |
| Marginal external cost (£) | 2 | 3 | 4 | 5 | 6 | 7 | 8 |

Assuming no external benefits, the socially efficient level of output is:
A   2        B   3        C   4        D   5        E   6


**Example 10.10**

Which one of the following comes closest to being a public good?
A   council houses        B   medical care        C   education
D   flood control         E   postal services


**Example 10.11**

Cost–benefit analysis does *not* allow the economist to:
A   calculate the national budget
B   calculate the full opportunity costs of spending
C   calculate the social effects of investment decisions
D   evaluate private-sector investment schemes
E   assess the purchase of new factory equipment

*Examples 10.12–10.15 are based on the following diagram, which shows the cost and revenue curves of a nationalised industry.*

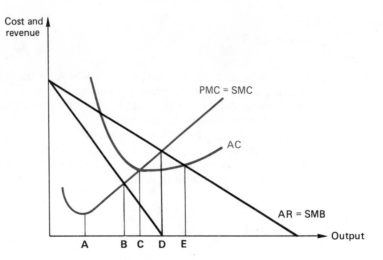

For each of Examples 10.12–10.15 select from the range of output **A–E** the level which is the result of:

### Example 10.12

A marginal cost pricing policy

### Example 10.13

A break-even pricing policy

### Example 10.14

A policy to maximise the difference between revenue and cost

### Example 10.15

A policy to maximise economic welfare

*Select your answers to Examples 10.16–10.19 by means of the following code:*
**A**   *if 1, 2 and 3 are all correct*
**B**   *if 1 and 2 only are correct*
**C**   *if 2 and 3 only are correct*
**D**   *if 1 only is correct*

### Example 10.16

A positive externality likely to result from the introduction of subsidised inter-city train service is (are):
1   reduced traffic congestion on inter-city motorways
2   reduced traffic congestion on city ring roads
3   a fall in the number of road accidents

**Example 10.17**

The following diagram illustrates the cost and revenue curves of a firm:

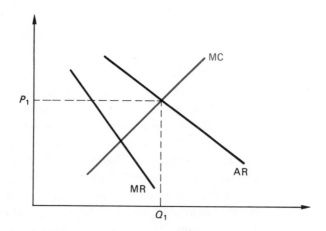

It can be deduced that the firm:
1 is imperfectly competitive
2 is using marginal cost pricing
3 has taken full account of externalities

**Example 10.18**

A pure public good is a product:
1 for which it is impossible to charge consumers directly
2 which is *not* available in a free market economy
3 which has zero opportunity cost in consumption

**Example 10.19**

Which of the following may prevent a market economy from establishing an optimal allocation of resources?
1 third party costs or benefits
2 the existence of monopolies
3 the price mechanism

# 10.4 Essays

**Example 10.20**

Suppose certain chemical firms discharge waste products into rivers and lakes.
(a) Explain why such discharges may constitute what is termed an 'externality'.
(5)
(b) Explain the argument which asserts that, from a social point of view, the level of chemical production may be excessive. (10)
(c) Consider whether government policy could lead to a socially more efficient level of chemical production. (10)
(WJEC 1987)

● This question focuses on a particular example of market failure through negative externalities.

- Use social cost and benefit curves to illustrate the welfare loss of over-producing chemicals which cause negative externalities.
- Be careful to concentrate analysis on the specific example of a chemical firm.

*Solution 10.20*

(a) An externality occurs whenever the production or consumption decision of an individual or firm directly affects others other than through market prices. That is, an externality is a spill-over effect from economic activity which affects third parties but for which no compensation is paid. The discharge of waste products into rivers and lakes is an example of a negative externality. The private cost to the firm of waste disposal is the cost of transportation. Society at large has to bear, without compensation by the firm, the external costs which arise from the resulting destruction of the environment, reduced leisure facilities and other inconveniences.

(b) The diagram illustrates the amount of welfare loss from the over-production of chemicals.

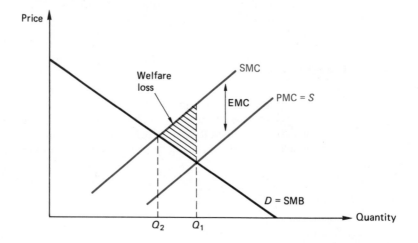

Assuming no positive externalities, the demand curve, $D$, shows the money value placed by society on the consumption of each *extra* unit of chemicals — that is, social marginal benefit (SMB).

Assuming perfect competition, the industry's supply curve, $S$, is the addition of each firm's marginal cost curve. The private costs of producing each extra unit of chemicals is given by the private marginal cost curve (PMC). In a market economy, profit-maximising chemical firms ignore the wider social costs of their activity. Any one company which incurred the cost of treating its waste product would become uncompetitive and unable to match the price of rivals. The interaction of supply and demand results in quantity $Q_1$ being produced.

In the diagram, external marginal cost, EMC, is the amount consumers would be prepared to pay to avoid the pollution associated with the manufacture of extra units of chemicals. Adding EMC to PMC gives the social marginal cost, SMC, of producing extra units of chemicals. The socially efficient level of output occurs at $Q_2$. Profit-maximising firms produce $Q_1$. Chemical production at levels above $Q_2$ is excessive, because social cost exceeds social benefit. Total loss from overproduction is given by the triangle ABC.

(c) The government can achieve a socially more efficient level of chemical production by imposing a specific tax equal to EMC at each level of output. Firms include the amount of the tax as a private cost and reduce their level of activity to the desired level of $Q_2$. However, a socially efficient level of output is achieved only if the government is accurate in calculating the monetary cost to society of pollution.

Alternatively, the government could introduce legislation banning the discharge of waste products into the environment. Firms would then have to include waste treatment as a private cost. However, the PMC of chemicals, including treatment, may now exceed SMC, excluding treatment. Legislation would only then achieve a socially efficient level of production if combined with a subsidy to chemical firms.

Finally, the government may consider a policy of banning chemical production altogether. This would result in a loss of welfare equal to triangle AJK. Even after taking into account the pollution chemicals cause, consumers still value extra units up to $Q_2$, more than the social cost of manufacture. Government policy would be more successful if a quota restricting output to $Q_2$ were introduced.

**Example 10.21**

'Public sector investment decisions present greater difficulties than do private sector investment decisions.' Discuss.

(L Jan. 1987)

- Use either the discounted cash flow or internal rate of return method to explain investment decisions.
- Private firms only calculate private costs and benefits. Public bodies include private and social costs and benefits in a cost–benefit analysis of investment decisions.
- The bulk of the essay should consider the difficulties involved in such a cost–benefit analysis.

*Solution 10.21*

Profit-maximising private firms only take into account the effect on their own costs and revenues of buying capital. The spill-over effects of investment are of no concern. Social-welfare-maximising public agencies, on the other hand, take full account of the social implications of buying capital. Public bodies have to include any indirect effects on third parties in their investment calculations.

The calculation of private costs is a relatively simple matter for the private firm. The cost of the machine can be found in a catalogue. There may be an element of uncertainty in estimating the probable net yield from the project in times of inflation or changing market conditions, but usually the firm can predict future private benefits. The business then buys new plant or machinery, provided that the return on the investment exceeds its cost.

Public bodies have to undertake a more detailed and involved cost–benefit analysis. For instance, a local authority considering building a by-pass around a town has first to *identify* and then *value* the likely social costs and benefits that arise in each year of the project. Private costs and benefits from building the by-pass are included at their market price. However, if market prices are distorted and do not accurately reflect true opportunity cost, alternative '*shadow*' prices will have to be calculated.

Money is also used as a unit of account for valuing external costs and benefits. For instance, the by-pass is likely to benefit motorists by reducing travel time. Multiplying the number of minutes saved by the average wage rate gives an estimated value of the resulting social benefit. If the scheme reduces the number of road accidents, reduced expenditure on medical treatment is included in the calculations. The benefit the by-pass brings to new travellers is another positive externality, which is included by estimating the increase in consumer surplus.

The wages of anyone unemployed before working on the bridge should not be included as a social cost, because they would not otherwise have produced anything. On the other hand, a monetary value is placed on the loss of landscape. If noise from the by-pass affects local residents, a sum is deducted in the cost–benefit analysis which represents that damage.

The authority must be particularly careful not to include irrelevant changes. For example, reduced travel time may increase the value of local houses but this is not a true benefit of the scheme.

All investment decisions have to calculate the present value of future net benefits. Benefits received in the future are worth less than the same benefit received now. Firms resolve this problem by discounting future benefits at a given rate of interest. For example, at an interest rate of 10% per annum, £550 in 1 year's time is worth only £500 now. Private firms use the current market rate of interest in their calculations. Public bodies have to calculate a social rate of discount which states the true opportunity cost of future benefits.

Finally, private investment decisions typically involve schemes with only a short life. Machines are expected to last only a few years before being replaced by an improved model. Public projects have a life-span measured in decades. Estimates of future supply and demand patterns, and demographic trends over a period of 20 years, make public sector investment decision peculiarly difficult and complex.

## 10.5 Solutions to Objective Questions

*Solution 10.2 Answer:* **D**

The conditions necessary for productive efficiency are explained in Section 10.1(a)(i).

**A** and **C** $\Rightarrow$ Are necessary but not sufficient conditions for productive efficiency. That is, by themselves **A** and **C** do not guarantee technical efficiency in an economy.

*Solution 10.3 Answer:* **E**

*Demerit goods*, such as cigarettes, harm consumers and impose costs on society in general. For example, the cost of treating lung cancer caused by smoking. Demerit goods are consumed in quantities above that which is socially desirable.

**D** $\Rightarrow$ Some demerit goods, such as alcohol, are not illegal and are readily available in the market.

*Solution 10.4 Answer:* **E**

Pareto criteria cannot be used to compare a change in resource use which makes some people better off but others worse off. Here equity criteria such as the Kaldor–Hicks test are used.

**D** ⇒ Is true but does not explain why Pareto criteria cannot be used in declining resource changes resulting in both gainers and losers.

*Solution 10.5   Answer:* **C**

*Market failure* occurs when a free market economy fails to reach a Pareto optimal allocation of resources. If the price of a good exceeds its marginal cost, underproduction occurs. In Figure 10.5, the area BAC illustrates market failure from setting output below the point where marginal cost equals price.

*Solution 10.6   Answer:* **E**

Adding together private and external benefits gives social benefits. Adding together private and external costs gives social costs. Subtracting social costs from social benefits gives net social benefits. If net social benefits are positive, general welfare can be increased by undertaking the project.

|  | Project J | Project K | Project L |
|---|---|---|---|
| Social benefit (£) | 200 | 190 | 250 |
| Social cost (£) | 215 | 160 | 240 |
| Net social benefit (£) | −15 | 30 | 10 |

*Solution 10.7   Answer:* **D**

Welfare is improved by fitting an extra filter, provided that the social benefit from the extra filter is greater than or equal to the social cost of installation.
   **A, B, E** ⇒ Ignore the social costs of installation.
   **C** ⇒ The decision to install extra filters requires a marginal and not total method of analysis.

*Solution 10.8   Answer:* **A**

If a firm has social costs which do not pass through the market (e.g. pollution), then the government should tax the enterprise so that the firm *internalises* the externality and incurs its true total costs.
   **C** ⇒ A study would only encourage the firm to produce more and, hence, increase negative externalities.
   **D** ⇒ Net social benefits are positive and therefore the firm should be allowed to carry on production.

*Solution 10.9   Answer:* **B**

Adding together private marginal cost (PMC) and external marginal cost (EMC) gives social marginal cost (SMC). The price consumers are willing to pay for an extra unit of a good is given by average revenue (AR) — remember that average revenue always equals price. The socially efficient level of output occurs when SMC = AR.
   At output level 3, SMC = PMC + EMC = 6 + 4 = 10 = AR.

*Solution 10.10    Answer:* **D**

The characteristics of a public good are explained in Section 10.1(d). It is difficult, if not impossible, to make consumption of flood control dependent on prior payment.

**A** and **C** are examples of merit goods which are rival and excludable products.

*Solution 10.11    Answer:* **A**

Cost–benefit analysis (CBA) is a method of evaluating investment projects to include *all* gains and benefits. The budget is a statement of how the government intends to raise money to finance its expenditure.

**D** ⇒ Although CBA is usually used in the evaluation of public-sector investment projects, there is no reason why it could not be applied to private-sector schemes.

*Solution 10.12    Answer:* **D**

*Marginal cost pricing* occurs when a firm makes price equal to marginal cost and fixes output where the MC curve intersects the demand curve.

*Solution 10.13    Answer:* **E**

*Break-even pricing* occurs when a firm makes price equal to average cost and fixes output where the average cost (AC) curve intersects the demand curve.

*Solution 10.14    Answer:* **B**

Maximising the (positive) difference between revenue and cost will result in maximum profit. The condition for profit maximisation is that the firm makes marginal cost equal to marginal revenue and fixes output where the MC and MR curves intersect.

*Solution 10.15    Answer:* **D**

A marginal cost pricing policy where output is increased up to the point where social marginal benefit equals social marginal cost maximises welfare.

*Solution 10.16    Answer:* **A**

A *positive externality* is a benefit from economic activity, accruing to a third party, for which no compensation is paid. Subsidising inter-city rail journeys is likely to reduce the volume of cars on motorways and city roads, thereby reducing the number of accidents.

*Solution 10.17    Answer:* **B**

**1** ⇒ A downward sloping demand curve indicates imperfect competition.
**2** ⇒ The firm has made price equal to marginal cost when fixing the level of output.
**3** ⇒ Is incorrect because no information is given as to whether or not the cost and revenue curves include externalities.

*Solution 10.18   Answer:* **A**

**1** ⇒ The non-excludability of public goods such as defence makes it impossible to link consumption with payment.
**2** ⇒ Since it is impossible to exclude free riders from consuming public goods, a private firm cannot produce such goods and make a profit.
**3** ⇒ Public goods are non-rival. For instance, once defence has been provided for one consumer, the cost of providing security for additional consumers is zero.

*Solution 10.19   Answer:* **B**

**1** ⇒ An optimal allocation of resources only takes place if firms take full account of the effect of externalities on third parties.
**2** ⇒ Monopolies may not produce where price equals marginal cost, or at minimum average cost.
**3** ⇒ In conditions of perfect competition where the government provides public goods and there are no externalities, the price mechanism ensures a Pareto optimal resource allocation.

# 11 National Income Accounting

## 11.1  Fact Sheet

### (a) Calculating National Income

*National income* is the money value of the goods and services produced by a country in one year. There are three methods of calculating national income.

### (i)  *The Income Method*

First calculate *total domestic income* by adding up all the money earned by people and firms in producing this year's output. Include:

(1) income from employment;
(2) income from self-employment;
(3) rent;
(4) gross trading profits of companies;
(5) gross trading surpluses of nationalised industries;
(6) an imputed charge for the consumption of non-traded capital.

Then proceed as in Figure 11.1

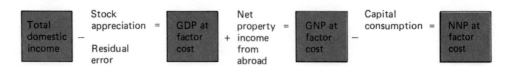

**Figure 11.1**   The income method

- GDP refers to *Gross Domestic Product* and is a measure of economic activity within the UK.
- GNP refers to *Gross National Product* and is a measure of UK citizens' activity all over the world.
- NNP refers to *Net National Product* and is the technical term for national income.
- *Stock appreciation* is the increase in the value of inventories brought about by inflation.

- *Residual error* occurs because income and expenditure data are collected from different sources. An amount is included to balance up the difference between these estimates.
- *Net property from abroad* is the difference between income received from UK ownership of overseas assets and income paid out to overseas owners of UK assets.

### (ii)  *The Expenditure Method*

First calculate *total domestic expenditure* by adding up all the money spent buying up this year's output. Include:

(1) consumers' expenditure (C);
(2) general government final consumption (G);
(3) investment expenditure (I) on:
    (a) gross domestic fixed capital formation (e.g. machinery, vehicles);
    (b) physical increases in stocks and work in progress.
Then proceed as in Figure 11.2.

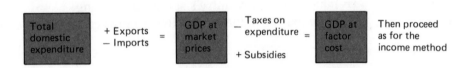

**Figure 11.2**  The expenditure method

### (iii)  *The Output Method*

The economy is divided into industrial sectors (e.g. construction). The value of *inputs* (purchases) is then deducted from the value of *outputs* (sales) to find each industrial sector's *value added*. For example:

sales − purchases = value added
£60b − £50b    = £10b

- Adding up each sector's value added, and including a imputed (estimated) value for the ownership of dwellings, gives *GDP at factor cost*.

It is important to understand the relationships shown in Table 11.1.

**Table 11.1**  National Income accounting equations

| | |
|---|---|
| National Income | ≡ National Expenditure ≡ National Output |
| GNP | = GDP + Net property income from abroad |
| NNP | = GNP − Capital consumption |
| Gross investment | = Net investment + Capital consumption |
| Factor cost | = Market prices − Expenditure taxes + Subsidies |

**(b) Problems in Calculating National Income Accounts**

Difficulties arise in the calculation of national income accounts (N.Y.A.) because of:
- (i) *double counting* if transfer payments (e.g. pensions), intermediate expenditures or outputs (e.g. components), and stock appreciation are included;
- (ii) unrecorded production in the *black economy*;
- (iii) *arbitrary definitions*:
    - (1) the imputed value of services from owner occupied houses is included in N.Y.A., while the imputed value of services of consumer durables (e.g. cars) is not;
    - (2) paid production (e.g. decorator) is included in N.Y.A., while unpaid production (e.g. DIY) is not.

**(c) Importance of National Income Accounts**

National Income Accounts provide data for:
- (i) showing the current allocation of resources;
- (ii) government economic planning;
- (iii) calculating trends within the economy;
- (iv) measuring a country's standard of living;
- (v) comparing standards of living between different countries.

**(d) Real and Money National Income**

- *Money* (or *nominal*) *national income* (M.N.Y.) is the value of this year's output at current prices.
- A *price deflator* is an index used to eliminate the effect of inflation. There are two main price indices in the UK:
    - (i) the *Retail Price Index* (RPI), covering only consumer goods and services;
    - (ii) the *GDP deflator*, covering both consumer and capital goods.
- *Real national income* (R.N.Y.) is the value of this year's output at constant prices and is calculated by using either of the following equations:

$$\text{R.N.Y.} = \frac{\text{M.N.Y.}}{\text{GDP deflator}} \times 100$$

$$\text{R.N.Y.} = \text{M.N.Y.} \times \frac{\text{price index of base year}}{\text{price index of current year}}$$

**(e) Measuring a Country's Standard of Living**

National income measures the value of goods and services produced by a country in a year. An increase in the value of national income implies an increase in economic welfare, unless:
- (i) the increase has been brought about by inflation;
- (ii) there is a corresponding increase in population;
- (iii) only a small fraction of the population receive the benefits because of an unequal distribution of income;

(iv) additional output results in negative externalities such as pollution;
(v) additional output is on non-consumer items such as defence;
(vi) increased output is the result of harder conditions of work or reduced leisure time.

The *standard of living* (SOL) refers to real national income per capita (person), and is calculated by using the equation:

$$\text{SOL} = \frac{\text{R.N.Y.}}{\text{population}}$$

Table 11.2 gives examples of calculating changes in a country's standard of living, over time.

**Table 11.2**  Calculating the standard of living

| Year | M.N.Y. (£m) | RPI (deflator) | R.N.Y. (£m) | Population (m) | SOL (£) |
|------|-------------|----------------|-------------|----------------|---------|
| 1989 | £20 000 | 100 | £20 000 | 5 | £4 000 |
| 1990 | £22 000 | 105 | £20 952 | 5 | £4 190 |
| 1991 | £24 000 | 110 | £21 818 | 5.5 | £4 970 |

- An increase in per capita R.N.Y. is one indicator of improved economic welfare.
- An increase in the percentage of the population owning consumer durables such as cars indicates a rise in overall living standards.
- A reduction in the amount of time taken by the average worker to earn sufficient money to buy given products indicates improved living standards.
- *Measurable Economic Welfare* (devised by Nordhaus and Tobin) adjusts national income figures for leisure, working conditions, unpaid housework and externalities, and excludes defence and police work.

### (f) Comparing Living Standards in Different Countries

Using per capita R.N.Y. to compare standards of living between countries is difficult, because:
(i) changes in the exchange rate affect the relative value of each country's national income;
(ii) different statistical procedures are used to calculate national income in different countries;
(iii) the extent of the black economy varies between nations;
(iv) the distribution of income varies between countries.

International comparisons can be made by contrasting the percentage of the population in each country owning particular consumer durables; by contrasting the amount of time taken in each country to earn sufficient money to buy given products; by contrasting mortality rates; or by contrasting measurable economic welfare.

## 11.2  Data Response

**Worked Example 11.1**

**Table 1**  Average weekly household income in the United Kingdom

|  | 1970 | 1975 | 1980 | 1983 |
|---|---|---|---|---|
| Gross weekly income | £35.40 | £72.87 | £147.18 | £187.86 |
| Weekly disposable income | £29.54 | £58.16 | £121.50 | £152.58 |

Source: Family Expenditure Survey

**Table 2**  The rental price index (1975 = 100)

| 1970 | 1975 | 1980 | 1983 |
|---|---|---|---|
| 54.2 | 100.0 | 195.6 | 248.6 |

Source: *Economic Trends*

**Table 3**  Selected commodities or services as a percentage of total household expenditures in the United Kingdom

|  | 1970 | 1975 | 1980 | 1983 |
|---|---|---|---|---|
| Housing | 12.6 | 13.1 | 15.0 | 16.8 |
| Fuel, light, and power | 6.3 | 5.5 | 5.6 | 6.4 |
| Food | 25.7 | 24.8 | 22.7 | 20.8 |
| Alcoholic drink | 4.5 | 5.1 | 4.8 | 4.8 |
| Tobacco | 4.8 | 3.6 | 3.0 | 2.9 |
| Clothing and footwear | 9.2 | 8.7 | 8.1 | 7.0 |
| Durable household goods | 6.5 | 7.4 | 7.0 | 7.2 |
| Transport and vehicles | 13.7 | 13.8 | 14.6 | 14.7 |
| Services | 9.0 | 9.9 | 10.8 | 11.3 |

Source: Family Expenditure Survey

(a) Explain the terms 'gross weekly income' and 'weekly disposable income'.
   **(2 marks)**
(b) Discuss whether the average household in the United Kingdom is better or worse off over the period shown in the data.  **(6 marks)**
(c)  (i) Summarise the significant features of the data in Table 3  **(4 marks)**
    (ii) Suggest the possible reasons which might explain the changes or the lack of change in the pattern of household expenditure shown in the data.
   **(8 marks)**
(AEB June 1986)

*Solution 11.1*

(a) Gross weekly income refers to the amount of money received by households before deductions for tax and national insurance. Weekly disposable income is the amount of 'take home' pay after deductions have been made and any benefits have been included from gross pay for income tax and national insurance.
(b) The data in Table 1 would seem to indicate a clear improvement in money income over the period specified. However, these raw data fail to take account of the effect of inflation on the purchasing power of weekly pay.

Real income is found by using the equation

$$\text{real income} = \frac{\text{money income} \times 100}{\text{retail price index}}$$

Using the data in Tables 1 and 2 gives the following information:

**Table 4**  Real weekly income

|  | *1970* | *1975* | *1980* | *1983* |
|---|---|---|---|---|
| Real gross weekly income (£) | 65.31 | 72.87 | 75.25 | 75.57 |
| Real weekly disposable income (£) | 54.50 | 58.16 | 62.12 | 61.38 |

Real gross weekly income has risen throughout the period. However, disposable income rises between 1970 and 1980 but falls between 1980 and 1983. In this period, households are able to buy fewer goods and services.

(c)  (i) The three items of household expenditure which absorb the largest proportion of household spending are: food, transport and vehicles, and housing. These three items have maintained their relative position throughout the period covered. However, while the percentage spent on housing (up $[16.8 - 12.6]/12.6 = 33\%$) and transport (up $[14.7 - 13.7]/13.7 = 7\%$) has risen consistently, the proportion spent on food has fallen continually and by 19%. Spending on tobacco (down 40%) and clothing (down 24%) has fallen, while spending on services has risen by 26%.

Spending on fuel, alcohol, durable household goods and transport is relatively stable, with a less than 1% change in the absolute proportion of each item.

(ii) A large increase in the proportion of the population owning their own homes has increased the demand for houses. Escalating house prices have forced would-be householders to take larger mortgages, with repayments accounting for a growing percentage of overall spending.

Food has a low income elasticity of demand coefficient. As incomes rise, a smaller proportion has been devoted to expenditure on food between 1970 and 1983. Services, on the other hand, have a high income elasticity of demand and now account for a higher percentage of spending. Items where the percentage spent has remained virtually static throughout the period are likely to have income elasticity of demand coefficients close to unity.

A movement in consumer taste away from tobacco smoking has caused a decline in relative spending.

## 11.3  Objective Questions

**Example 11.2**

Which one of the following is *not* a reason for a country collecting national income statistics:
A  to calculate changes in the standard of living
B  to calculate changes in the cost of living
C  to compare standards of living between countries
D  to provide data for private-sector firms
E  to estimate the rate of economic growth

## Example 11.3

Which one of the following is included in UK national income accounts:
A  the imputed value of direct production
B  the market value of the output of housewives
C  a charge for the depletion of non-renewable resources
D  an imputed rent from owner occupation of houses
E  the imputed value of undeclared economic activity


## Example 11.4

The national income accounts exclude all the following *except*:

A  intermediate expenditures       B  transfer payments
C  transfer earnings       D  residual error
E  balancing item


## Example 11.5

On reaching 65, a builder earning £10 000 per year sells his firm for £10 000 but stays on as consultant for a fee of £5000 per year. He receives an annual occupational pension of £5000. One of two assistants, each earning £5000, loses his job and is not eligible for state social security benefits. As a result, national income:

A  falls by more than £5000       B  falls by £5000
C  is unchanged       D  rises by £5000
E  rises by more than £5000


## Example 11.6

Gross national product exceeds gross domestic product by the amount of:

A  subsidies less expenditure taxes       B  transfer payments
C  income from abroad       D  imports
E  capital consumption


## Example 11.7

Which one of the following is the most accurate measure of a country's standard of living?

A  real national income       B  nominal national income
C  per capita real national income       D  per capita nominal national income
E  the domestic product deflator


*Examples 11.8–11.10 are based on the following table, which shows the value of inputs and outputs at different stages in the production of wooden tables.*

| Stage | Cost | Revenue |
|---|---|---|
| Plantation | 0 | 10 |
| Mill | 10 | 25 |
| Factory | 25 | 50 |
| Retailer | 50 | 70 |

| A | 20 | B | 25 | C | 50 | D | 70 | E | 85 |

On the basis of the above information, select from the options **A–E** above, the figure which corresponds to:

### Example 11.8

The value added by the retailer.

### Example 11.9

The value of final output.

### Example 11.10

The value of intermediate expenditures.

*Examples 11.11–11.14 make use of the following information concerning the national income accounts of an imaginary country.*

|  | *£(b)* |
|---|---|
| *Total final expenditure at market prices* | *22* |
| *Gross domestic product at market prices* | *20* |
| *Subsidies* | *1* |
| *Gross domestic product at factor cost* | *18* |
| *Gross national product at factor cost* | *18* |
| *Net national product at factor cost* | *17* |

| A | £0b | B | £1b | C | £2b | D | £3b | E | £4b |

On the basis of the above information, select from the options **A–E** the figure which corresponds to:

### Example 11.11

Taxes on expenditure.

### Example 11.12

Imports.

### Example 11.13

Depreciation.

### Example 11.14

Net property income from abroad.

*Examples 11.15–11.17 are based on the following national income statistics of a hypothetical country.*

|                     | £(b) |
|---------------------|------|
| Consumption         | 195  |
| Investment          | 55   |
| Government spending | 70   |
| Exports             | 68   |
| Imports             | 66   |
| Capital consumption | 38   |
| Indirect taxes      | 44   |
| Income from abroad  | 3    |

**A** £454b    **B** £388b    **C** £322b    **D** £278b    **E** £243b

Use the above data to select from options **A–E** the figure which measures:

**Example 11.15**

Total final expenditure at market prices.

**Example 11.16**

Gross domestic product at market prices.

**Example 11.17**

Net national product at factor cost.

**Example 11.18**

If, over the last twelve months, prices have gone up by 6%, population has increased by 2% and nominal national income has risen by 6%, then:
**A** real national income has increased  **B** real national income has decreased
**C** real income per head has increased  **D** real income per head has decreased
**E** real income per head is unchanged

**Example 11.19**

The table below gives information about a country in 1989, 1990 and 1991. In 1988 real GDP per head was £8200.

|      | GDP (£ millions) | GDP deflator index (1987 =100) | Population (millions) |
|------|------------------|-------------------------------|-----------------------|
| 1989 | 440 000          | 110                           | 50                    |
| 1990 | 450 000          | 120                           | 50                    |
| 1991 | 480 000          | 120                           | 51                    |

From the data, it can be deduced that real GDP per head:
    A  has increased in all three years
    B  has decreased in all three years
    C  has increased in 1989 and 1990 only
    D  has decreased in 1989 and 1990 only
    E  has remained constant


*Select your answers to Examples 11.20–11.23 by means of the following code*:
**A**  *if 1, 2 and 3 are all correct*
**B**  *if 1 and 2 only are correct*
**C**  *if 2 and 3 only are correct*
**D**  *if 1 only is correct*


## Example 11.20

Which of the following is (are) *not* necessarily equal to national income?
**1**  national wealth        **2**  national product        **3**  national output


## Example 11.21

Which of the following is (are) *not* included in national income calculated by the income method?
**1**  interest received by holders of government stocks
**2**  the prize received by a football pools winner
**3**  final consumption


## Example 11.22

All other things being equal, which of the following would increase the average standard of living of a country?
**1**  a rise in population and a proportionately greater increase in national product
**2**  no change in population and an increase in national product
**3**  a fall in population and no change in national product


## Example 11.23

When calculating final national income, it is necessary to exclude:
**1**  the purchase of a second-hand car
**2**  intermediate outputs
**3**  stock appreciation


# 11.4  Essays

## Example 11.24

Distinguish between wealth and welfare. Discuss whether increases in national income provide a suitable indication of improvements in welfare.

(AEB June 1987)

- Material welfare is the satisfaction derived from the consumption of wealth.
- National income is a narrow measure of a nation's wealth creation in a given time period.

169

- Include a discussion of the circumstances in which an increase in national income does and does not improve welfare.
- A detailed discussion of how national income accounts are calculated is *not* required.

*Solution 11.24*

Any asset which can be exchanged for money can be regarded as an item of wealth. There are two main types:
 (a) Material wealth consists of financial assets such as shares, and real assets such as property and consumer durables.
 (b) Human wealth consists of the skills, training and education of individuals. The consumption of material wealth satisfies the wants and needs of individuals. The higher an individual's rate of consumption the higher his *material* welfare. Hence, wealth and material welfare are interlinked.

A nation's stock of wealth allows it to produce an enormous variety of goods and services which can then be used to satisfy material wants and needs. National income is simply the money value of all final products provided during a year which flow through the markets. Hence, national income is a indicator of economic welfare.

However, an increase in national income does not automatically raise living standards. For instance, an increase in national income may be the result of an increase in the price level with output held constant, or an increase in output with prices held constant. Only the latter suggests an increase in material well-being. To measure changes in *real* as opposed to *money* national income, output is valued at constant prices by dividing current money national income by a general index of all prices, called the GDP deflator.

Yet an increase in real national income is still no guarantee that average living standards have improved. Any improvement in material standards could be negated by a proportionately larger increase in population. The actual standard of living of a nation is found by dividing real national income by the total population. Material well-being, then, increases only if per capita real national income increases.

It can be argued that per capita real national income is a restrictive, narrow welfare indicator. Official statistics only count final products sold in markets and ignore the value of non-market activities such as the output of unpaid house-keepers. The value of leisure time finds no place in national income accounts. Official statistics fail to take into account the impact of intangibles such as the quality of the environment on overall *social* welfare. The presence of negative externalities may cause the material and social welfare of a nation to diverge.

Nordhaus and Tobin have devised an alternative measure of social welfare: *measurable economic welfare*. Here real national income is adjusted to include an allowance for non-marketed output and leisure time, while expenditure on 'regrettable necessities' including defence, and the effects of negative external-ities such as pollution, are deducted. An improvement in measurable economic welfare indicates an improvement in social welfare.

There are a series of other non-economic measures which can also be used to indicate improvements in welfare over time. The United Nations publishes data on the infant mortality rates, suicides and road accidents of various countries. A fall in these figures implies an improvement in a nation's quality of life. Similarly, an increase in the proportion of the population owning various types of consumer durable such as video recorders, or a reduction in the time taken to earn sufficient money to buy given products, implies improved social welfare.

In conclusion, it has been shown that a country's stock of wealth helps determine the quantity of goods available for the satisfaction of material wants and needs. Increases in real per capita national income are a suitable indication of improvements in material welfare. A simultaneous and larger increase in negative externalities or reduced leisure would lower overall social welfare.

**Example 11.25**

Discuss the problems which might arise in attempting to compare the standard of living in the United Kingdom with that in (a) Brazil and (b) the Soviet Union.

(OLE 1986)

- Discuss various methods of measuring living standards.
- Detailed knowledge of the economic systems of Brazil and the Soviet Union is *not* expected.
- The UK is an example of a mixed economy; Brazil, a developing economy; and the Soviet Union, a planned economy.
- Place the emphasis of the essay on the problems of *comparing* living standards between countries.

*Solution 11.25*

The standard of living can be defined as real per capita income. Hence, international comparisons of living standards are usually made by referring to national income statistics. However, great care should be taken in using raw national income figures. Money national income states the value of this year's final marketed output at current prices. An increase in one country's nominal national income may be the result of inflation rather than an increase in total output. Therefore, national income divided by an index of all prices — for example, the GDP deflator — provides a better basis for comparison. Even then, real GNP alone is not an accurate guide to a country's standard of living. Real GNP is twice as high in the UK as in Brazil. Brazil has more than twice the population of the UK. Dividing real GNP by total population means that the average standard of living is four times higher in the UK than in Brazil.

A further adjustment is necessary to convert the figures of each country to the same currency. This can cause problems if the market rate of exchange of one country does not reflect different costs of living. For example, the amount of roubles exchanged for £1 at the official rate may buy fewer goods in the USSR that can be bought with £1 in the UK. Converting Soviet national income into sterling at the official rate of exchange would result in an overvaluation. Moreover, Brazil and the UK have floating exchange rates, and the resulting continual changes in the relative value of the two currencies make a direct comparison difficult.

Because Brazil has not yet reached the same stage of economic development as the UK, a range of activities included in the UK accounts go unrecorded in Brazil. Intense specialisation means that most UK citizens use markets to buy goods and services they have not had time to make themselves. Hence, UK national income figures include most of the economic activity which has taken place in the last year. Unmarketed and undeclared activity is only likely to account for a small percentage of total output. For example, the tax returns of a UK farmer are usually an accurate indicator for national income accountants of the value added by a farmer in any one year. By way of contrast, markets are less developed in Brazil because communities are more self-sufficient and practise less specialisation and exchange. The output of a Brazilian farmer will not be officially recorded if a crop is either consumed by the farmer or exchanged for other goods, or if income is not declared to the authorities.

Problems arise when different countries use different statistical procedures in calculating national income figures. For instance, the Soviet Union is a planned economy where resources are allocated by the state. Official prices are used to value output, but these may not reflect the relative value of goods and services consumed in the Soviet Union. Activities considered economic in the UK and included in national accounts are considered unproductive and excluded from USSR statistics. For instance, the output of entertainers is excluded for Soviet statistics but included in UK national accounts.

Different countries draw different boundaries between intermediate and final output. Most people travel to work. A large number of commuters in the UK use British Rail, and the value of their expenditure on travel, less the cost of inputs, is added to national income. In the USSR, public transport is considered an intermediate output — that is, a type of input — and is therefore not included in the accounts.

Physical conditions vary widely between Brazil, the UK and the USSR. The climate of the USSR is severe in winter; the climate of Brazil is not. Yet the national income of the USSR includes expenditure on heating, which Brazil does not have to undertake, and the value of the resources used to heat buildings is included in Soviet national income.

The extent of negative externalities and the proportion of national product spent on 'regrettable necessities' vary between countries. For example, defence spending in the USSR accounts for a larger percentage of GDP than in either Brazil or the UK.

International comparisons of standards of living may overcome the problems discussed by adopting alternative measures of welfare. The country where least time is taken by a worker to earn sufficient income to buy a given basket of goods is likely to enjoy the highest standard of living. Low suicide rates and low infant mortality rates also indicate a good quality of life.

## 11.5 Solutions to Objective Questions

*Solution 1.2   Answer:* **B**

Changes in the cost of living are calculated by using the retail price index. The uses of national income accounts are explained in Section 11.1 (c).

*Solution 11.3   Answer:* **D**

A decrease in the number of people renting accommodation reduces the income of landlords, and national income falls. An *imputed* (estimated) figure for the amount of income home owners could obtain by renting out their homes is included in the accounts.

*Solution 11.4   Answer:* **D**

By definition, the value of national income using the income or expenditure methods is the same. However, the sources of information used to collect income and expenditure figures are different. Income is adjusted to equal expenditure by the inclusion of a 'residual error'.

**E** $\Rightarrow$ Is an error term used in the balance of payments.

*Solution 11.5   Answer:* **A**

The pension of the builder (a transfer payment) and the money received from the sale of the firm (a transfer of ownership) are not included in national income. The fall in national income is: £5000 (the builder's reductions in earnings) + £5000 (the loss of the assistant's salary) = £10 000.

*Solution 11.6   Answer:* **C**

*Solution 11.7   Answer:* **C**

*Solution 11.8   Answer:* **A**

*Value added* is the difference between the value of inputs (costs) and outputs (revenue).

*Solution 11.9   Answer:* **D**

The value of final output can be calculated either by adding together the value added by each stage of production or by only counting the final output of the retailer.

*Solution 11.10   Answer:* **E**

The total amount of money spent on buying inputs gives the value of intermediate expenditures.

*Solution 11.11   Answer:* **D**

GDP at market prices − indirect taxes + subsidies = GDP at factor cost
(£20b)                       − (£3b)         + (£1b)     = (£18b)

*Solution 11.12   Answer:* **C**

Total final expenditure at market prices (£22b) less imports (£2b) gives GDP at market prices.

*Solution 11.13   Answer:* **B**

GNP at factor cost (£18b) minus depreciation (£1b) gives NNP at factor cost (£17b).

*Solution 11.14   Answer:* **A**

GNP at factor cost (£18b) less GDP at factor cost (£18b) gives net property income from abroad (£0b).

*Solution 11.15   Answer:* **B**

Consumption (£195b) + investment (£55b) + government spending (£70b) + exports (£68b) gives a total final expenditure at market prices of £388b.

*Solution 11.16   Answer:* **C**

Consumption (£195b) + investment (£55b) + government spending (£70b) + exports (£68b) − imports (£66b) gives a GDP at market prices of £322b.

*Solution 11.17   Answer:* **E**

GDP at market prices (£322b) − indirect taxes (£44b) + income from abroad (£3b) − capital consumption (£38b) gives a net national product of £243b.

*Solution 11.18   Answer:* **D**

**A** and **B** ⇒ Equal percentage increases in *nominal* (money) national income and prices means real national income is unchanged.
**C** and **E** ⇒ A 2% population increase with constant real national income means real income per head has decreased.

*Solution 11.19   Answer:* **D**

There are two stages in calculating real GDP per head:
  (i) divide GDP by the GDP deflator to find real GDP;
  (ii) divide real GDP by population.
*In 1989*: real GDP = (£440 000 ÷ 110) × 100 = £400 000
      real per head GDP = £400 000 ÷ 50 = £8000
*In 1990*: real GDP = (£450 000 ÷ 120) × 100 = £375 000
      real per head GDP = £375 000 ÷ 50 = £7500
*In 1991*: real GDP = (£480 000 ÷ 120) × 100 = £400 000
      real per head GDP = £400 000 ÷ 51 = £7843

*Solution 11.20   Answer:* **D**

Wealth is the current market value of all assets, including those created in previous years.

*Solution 11.21   Answer:* **B**

**1** ⇒ The interest received by the holders of government stocks is not included, as it is a payment on debt created in the past and is not related to current output.
**2** ⇒ Prizes from gambling are a type of transfer payment.
**3** ⇒ Final consumption is included in the expenditure method.

*Solution 11.22   Answer:* **A**

*Solution 11.23   Answer:* **A**

**1** ⇒ The car has already been included in previous accounts.
**2** ⇒ *Intermediate outputs* are the raw materials and components used in production. Only the value of final output is counted.
**3** ⇒ *Stock appreciation* is the increase in the value of stocks brought about by inflation and is therefore not included.

# 12 Income Determination

## 12.1 Fact Sheet

### (a) The Circular Flow of Income

The economy can be divided into a number of spending *sectors*:
  (i) households ($H$), whose expenditure is called *consumption* ($C$);
  (ii) firms ($F$), whose expenditure is called *investment* ($I$);
  (iii) government ($G$);
  (iv) international, referring to the difference between *exports* ($X$) and *imports* ($M$).

- A *closed* economy has no international trade (i.e. no $X - M$).
- An *open* economy takes account of international trade (i.e. includes $X - M$).
- The *circular flow of income* shows the flow of income and payments between domestic households and firms.

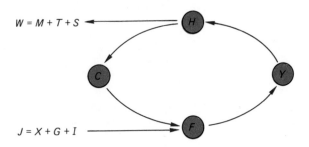

**Figure 12.1**   The circular flow of income in a four-sector economy

- *Injections* ($J$) are additions to the income of firms which do not normally arise from the expenditure of households. There are three types: investment, government and exports. Injections cause a rise in spending in the economy.
- *Leakages* or *withdrawals* ($W$) is any income not passed on in the circular flow. There are three types: savings, taxation and imports. Withdrawals reduce spending in the economy.

### (b) Consumption

*Consumption* is expenditure by households on goods and services which satisfy current wants.

- The *consumption function* in Figure 12.2 shows how much will be spent at different income levels, and is given by the equation:

$C = a + bY$

where $C$ = consumption, $a$ = *autonomous consumption* (what is spent when income is 0 and does not vary with income), $b$ = the marginal propensity to consume and $Y$ = National Income. $bY$ is *income-induced consumption*.

- As income rises, the amount spent rises depending on the value of the marginal propensity to consume. As national income rises, so the proportion spent begins to decline.
- The *average propensity to consume* (apc) is the proportion of total income spent: apc = $C/Y$.
- The *marginal propensity to consume* ($b$ or mpc) is the proportion of each extra pound spent by households, and is the change in consumption resulting from a change in income: $b = \Delta C/\Delta Y$.

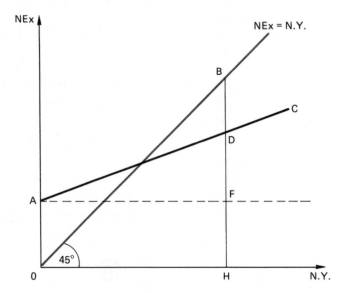

**Figure 12.2** Autonomous and induced consumption: 0A or HF = autonomous consumption = $a$; DH/BH = apc

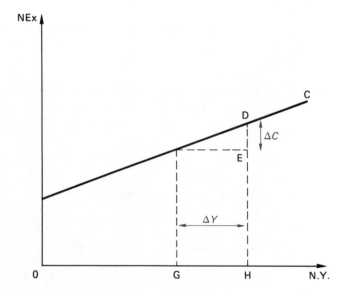

**Figure 12.3** The marginal propensity to consume: DE/GH = $b$

176

Influences on consumption include the level of income; credit facilities; distribution of income; the population's age structure; the quality and availability of consumer goods; the amount and distribution of wealth; expectations of inflation.

It is important to remember that there is more than one theory of consumption. Most economists agree that the main influence on consumption is income. However:

    (i) Keynesians believe that consumption is a function of *current income*. Therefore, the value of the marginal propensity to consume is high.

    (ii) Friedman's *Permanent Income Hypothesis* and Modigliani's *Life Cycle Hypothesis* argue that consumption is a function of estimated *lifetime income*. Therefore, the value of the marginal propensity to consume is low.

## (c) Savings

*Savings* is that part of *disposable income* (income less taxes) not spent on goods and services.

- The *savings function* shows how much will be saved at different income levels and is given by the equation

$$S = -a + sY$$

  where $S$ = savings; $-a$ = autonomous dissaving (the amount of $s$ when $Y = 0$); $s$ = the marginal propensity to save; $Y$ = National Income; $sY$ = induced saving. As income rises, both the amount saved and the proportion saved usually increase.

- The *average propensity to save* (aps) is the proportion of total income saved: aps = $S/Y$.

- The *marginal propensity to save* ($s$ or mps) is the proportion of each extra pound of disposable income not spent and is the change in saving resulting from a change in income: $s = \Delta S/\Delta Y$.

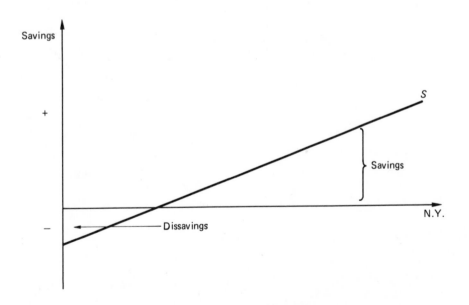

**Figure 12.4** The savings function

Influences on savings include the level of income; the rate of interest; the rate of inflation; the quality of financial institutions; general attitudes to the virtue of saving; government policies (e.g. tax concessions); expectations of inflation; advertising.

## (d) Investment

- *Investment* is expenditure on capital goods and changes in stocks.
- The *marginal efficiency of capital* is the expected rate of return on investment.
- The *accelerator theory* states that a given change in demand for consumer goods will cause a greater percentage change in demand for capital goods. So the level of planned investment is a function of changes in income: $I = (f)\ \Delta Y$.

The level of investment is also influenced by:
 (i) the rate of interest;
 (ii) the relative prices of capital and labour;
 (iii) corporation tax;
 (iv) technological change and innovation;
 (v) business expectations;
 (vi) profits/company liquidity.

## (e) Income Determination

Assuming a two-sector closed economy of households and firms, aggregate demand is made up of consumption and investment. There are two conditions necessary for equilibrium:
 (i) aggregate demand $(C+I)$ must equal national income (N.Y.);
 (ii) planned withdrawals (savings) must equal planned injections (investment).

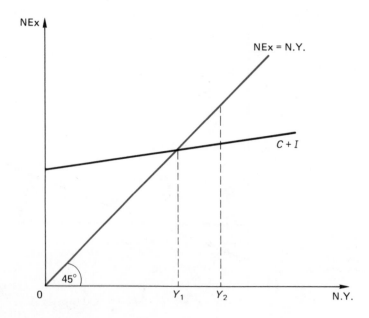

**Figure 12.5** Equilibrium in a two-sector closed economy

## (f) Disequilibrium Levels of National Income

*Disequilibrium* occurs when planned injections are not equal to planned withdrawals or when aggregate demand does not equal national income. For instance, at $Y_2$ in Figure 12.5, national output ($J$) is greater than aggregate demand ($K$). Firms are left with $J-K$ unsold goods which are added to stocks. In the next time period, these stocks are run down by laying off workers and income falls back towards $Y_1$.

## (g) The Multiplier

The *multiplier* ($k$) shows by how much income changes as a result of a change in an injection. The value of the multiplier is given by any of the following equations:

$$k = \frac{\Delta Y}{\Delta J} = \frac{1}{1-b} = \frac{1}{w}$$

where $b$ is the marginal propensity to consume, and $w$ is the marginal propensity to withdraw — that is, the proportion of each extra pound withdrawn from the circular flow.

To calculate the effect of changes in an injection on national income, use the equation:

$$\Delta Y = k \times \Delta J$$

For example, assume a three-sector closed economy where $b = 0.8$. An increase of £50m in government spending results in an increase in national income of $1/1 - 0.8 \times 50 = 5 \times 50 = 250$.

Note that:

  (i) $w = s$ in a two-sector closed economy;
  (ii) $w = s + t$ in a three-sector economy, where $t$ is the marginal propensity to tax;
  (iii) $w = s + t + m$ in a four-sector economy, where $m$ is the marginal propensity to import.

- The *multiplier effect* is the series of consumer incomes and expenditures generated by an initial change in an injection.

## (h) The Government Sector

*Government spending* ($G$) is an injection and *taxation* ($T$) is a leakage.

- The *marginal propensity to tax* ($t$ or mpt) is the proportion of each extra pound of income taken by the government, and is the change in tax resulting from a change in income: $\Delta T/\Delta Y$.
- A three-sector closed economy is in equilibrium when:
  (i) N.Y. $= C + I + G$;
  (ii) $S + T = I + G$.

## (i) The International Sector

*Exports* ($X$) add to income in the home economy and, hence, are an injection, whereas *imports* ($M$) result in income leaving the domestic circular flow of income and represent a leakage.

- The *marginal propensity to import* (*m* or mpm) is the proportion of each extra pound of disposable income spent on foreign-made goods, and is the change in expenditure on imports resulting from a change in income: $\Delta M/\Delta Y$.
- A three-sector open or four-sector economy is in equilibrium when:
  (i) N.Y. $= C + I + G + (X-M)$;
  (ii) $S + T + M = I + G + X$.


### (j) Aggregate Supply

Aggregate supply is the total of all planned production in a period at each level of prices. The aggregate supply (AS) curve in Figure 12.6 shows:
  (i) AS is horizontal if the economy is operating well below full employment and national income rises through an increase in output with constant prices;
 (ii) AS is upward-sloping if there are bottlenecks in some but not all markets and national income rises through an increase in both prices and output;
(iii) AS is vertical if the economy is at full employment and national income rises through an increase in prices with constant output.

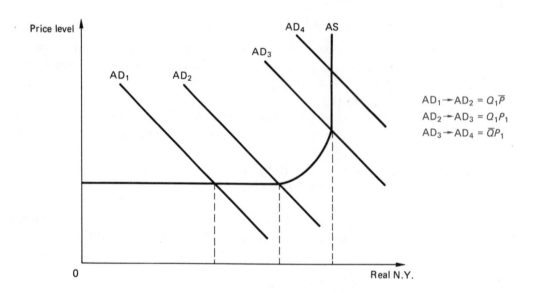

Figure 12.6  Aggregate supply and demand


### (k) Aggregate Demand

Aggregate demand is the total of all planned expenditure at each level of prices. The aggregate demand (AD) curves in Figure 12.6 are downward-sloping because:
  (i) The lower the rate of inflation the lower the rate of interest and, hence, the greater the demand for interest-sensitive investment and consumer goods.
 (ii) As prices fall, people's wealth buys more products.
(iii) As UK prices fall, consumers substitute domestically made goods for imports.

## (l) Changes in Aggregate Supply and Demand

- Supporters of supply-side economics argue that output is largely supply determined. The AS curve can be shifted to the right by:
  - (i) removing market distortions;
  - (ii) increasing incentives by reducing taxes on income.
- The AD curve shifts to the right if there is an increase in aggregate demand at each price level. This may be the result of more desired consumption, investment, government spending or international demand for UK products.

# 12.2  Data Response

**Worked Example 12.1**

Year 1: In a closed economy there is initially no government spending or taxation and the only injection is investment. National Income is £600m and mpc is 0.75 of disposable income.

Year 2: A government sector is introduced with a tax rate of 20% of N.Y. and government spending of £80m. Investment remains at the level prevailing in year 1 and mpc remains at 0.75 of disposable income.

Year 3: The country engages in international trade. Export earnings are £110m and $\frac{1}{6}$ of consumption is spent on imports. Government spending remains at £80m but investment rises by £20m. The tax rate stays at 20% of N.Y. and mpc at 0.75 of disposable income.

(a) Calculate the level of investment in Year 1.                                    **(2 marks)**
(b) Calculate the level of N.Y. and the budget deficit or surplus in Year 2.
                                                                                      **(6 marks)**
(c) Calculate the level of N.Y., the budget deficit or surplus and the balance of trade position in Year 3.                                                           **(8 marks)**
(d) Is the government's fiscal policy reflationary or deflationary?          **(2 marks)**
(e) Would you expect the mpc to remain constant as income changes?       **(2 marks)**

*Solution 12.1*

(a) In year 1, mpc is 0.75, so mps is $1 - 0.75 = 0.25$ and the multiplier is $1/0.25 = 4$. Investment is the only injection. N.Y. = injections × the multiplier. So investment = £600m/4 = £150m.

(b) In year 2, mpt is 0.2 and mps is $\frac{1}{4}$ of 0.8 (disposable income) — i.e. 0.2. So the multiplier is

$$\frac{1}{mpt + mps} = \frac{1}{0.2 + 0.2} = 2\tfrac{1}{2}$$

   Injections are £150m (investment) + £80m (government spending) = £230m. So N.Y. = £230m × $2\tfrac{1}{2}$ = £575m.

   The budget position is tax revenue − government spending. Tax revenue is $0.2 \times £575m$ = £115m. So the budget position is £115m − £80m = a budget surplus of £35m.

(c) In year 3, mpt is 0.2, mps is 0.2 and mpm is $\frac{1}{6}$ of consumption — i.e. $\frac{1}{6}$ of 0.6 = 0.1. So the multiplier is:

$$\frac{1}{mpt + mps + mpm} = \frac{1}{0.2 + 0.2 + 0.1} = 2$$

Injections are £110m (exports) + £80m (government spending) + £170m (investment) = £360m. N.Y. is £360m × 2 = £720m.

The budget position is 0.2 × £720m − £80m = £144m − £80m = a surplus of £64m.

The balance of trade is exports − imports = £110m − 0.1 × £720m = £110m − £72m = £38m surplus.

(d) The government's fiscal policy is deflationary. Tax revenue exceeds government expenditure, so the government will be reducing demand by taking more spending out of the economy than it is injecting.

(e) As income rises, mpc usually declines. People will spend a larger total amount but a smaller proportion of extra income, as the higher income enables them to save more.

## 12.3  Objective Questions

### Example 12.2

A man has a rise in income from £15 000 to £17 000. As a result, his saving rises from − £100 to £300. His mpc is:

**A**  0.2      **B**  0.3      **C**  0.4      **D**  0.6      **E**  0.8

### Example 12.3

The following table shows a country's consumption schedule:

| Income (£m) | Consumption (£m) |
| --- | --- |
| 0 | 60 |
| 100 | 130 |
| 200 | 200 |
| 300 | 270 |
| 400 | 340 |

$C$ is consumption and $Y$ is national income. Which of the following represents the consumption function?

**A**  $C = -60m + 0.3Y$      **B**  $C = 60m + 0.3Y$      **C**  $C = 60m + 0.7Y$
**D**  $C = -60m + 0.7Y$      **E**  $C = 60m - 0.7Y$

### Example 12.4

A closed economy has a National Income of £65m, a marginal propensity to save of 0.3 and a marginal propensity to tax of 0.1. If the government wishes to achieve the full employment level of N.Y. of £75m, it will have to increase government expenditure by:

**A**  £40m      **B**  £10m      **C**  £4m      **D**  £3.3m      **E**  £1m

## Example 12.5

An economy has a saving function $(S)$ which is given by the equation $S = -£500m + 0.2Y$ (where $Y$ is National Income). If the level of National Income is £5000m, what is the average propensity to save?

   **A**  0.1       **B**  0.2       **C**  0.6       **D**  0.8       **E**  0.9

## Example 12.6

If, in an economy, out of every additional £100 of National Income, £20 is taxed, £20 is saved and £10 is spent on imports, the value of the multiplier is:

   **A**  2       **B**  2.5       **C**  3.3       **D**  5       **E**  6

## Example 12.7

In the diagram below, as income increases from £15 000 to £17 000, what is the marginal propensity to consume?

   **A**  0.8       **B**  0.6       **C**  0.4       **D**  0.2       **E**  0.1

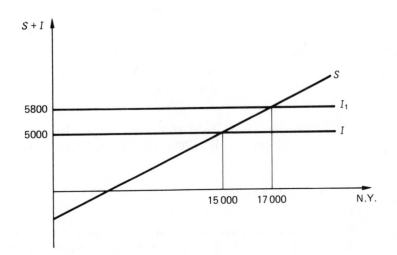

## Example 12.8

Which of the following represents a leakage from the circular flow?

   **A**  distributed profits              **B**  interest paid on bank loans
   **C**  national insurance contributions    **D**  investment
   **E**  exports

## Example 12.9

The diagram on page 184 shows the relationship between planned saving and planned investment.

If income is $0Y$, which distance represents actual investment?

   **A**  AB       **B**  BC       **C**  CY       **D**  AC       **E**  BY

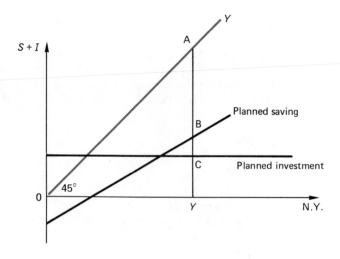

## Example 12.10

The table below refers to a closed economy:

| Income (£m) | Investment (£m) | Savings (£m) | Government spending (£m) | Taxation (£m) |
|---|---|---|---|---|
| 100 | 60 | 20 | 40 | 50 |
| 200 | 70 | 20 | 30 | 60 |
| 300 | 80 | 20 | 20 | 40 |
| 400 | 90 | 20 | 10 | 80 |
| 500 | 100 | 20 | 40 | 90 |

The equilibrium level of National Income is:
**A** £100m    **B** £200m    **C** £300m    **D** £400m    **E** £500m

## Example 12.11

$Y = C + I$ (National Income = Consumption + Investment). $I$ = £2500m and $C$ = £700m + 0.6$Y$. If the full employment level of National Income is £10 000m, by how much must investment be increased to achieve it?
**A** £200m    **B** £500m    **C** £800m    **D** £2000m    **E** £2500m

## Example 12.12

A firm makes 10 000 goods, using 20 machines. Each year 2 machines wear out. If demand for the good rises to 12 000, gross investment will increase by:
**A** 50%    **B** 100%    **C** 200%    **D** 300%    **E** 600%

## Example 12.13

In an economy, $Y$ (National Income) = $C$ (Consumption) + $I$ (Investment). If Consumption = 50m + 0.75$Y$, Planned Investment = £80m and National Income = £800m, Realised Investment will be:
**A** £50m    **B** £80m    **C** £100m    **D** £150m    **E** £200m

## Example 12.14

An economy with no taxation has a marginal propensity to consume of 0.8. Out of this, for every £10 spent £2.50 goes on imported goods. The current level of National Income is £350. The full employment level of National Income is £400m. To achieve full employment the government should inject spending of:

**A**  £10m      **B**  £20m      **C**  £25m      **D**  £40m      **E**  £50m

## Example 12.15

$C = 40 + bY$, $I = 30$, $X = 50$, $M = 60$ and $b = 0.8$ (where $C$ = consumption, $Y$ = income, $I$ = investment, $X$ = exports and $M$ = imports, and $b$ = the marginal propensity to consume). The equilibrium level of $Y$ will be:

**A**  550      **B**  400      **C**  300      **D**  275      **E**  250

## Example 12.16

If the marginal propensity to consume of all members of a closed economy are equal, then a rise in taxation of £5000m and of government expenditure of £5000m will cause National Income to:

**A**  remain constant                **B**  rise by more than £5000m
**C**  rise by £5000m                 **D**  rise by less than £5000m

## Example 12.17

The marginal propensity to tax is 0.2 and, out of disposable income, 0.25 is spent on imports and 0.25 is saved. The multiplier is:

**A**  $1\frac{1}{2}$      **B**  $1\frac{2}{3}$      **C**  $2\frac{1}{2}$      **D**  $3\frac{1}{3}$      **E**  $3\frac{1}{2}$

## Example 12.18

In a closed economy with no government sector, the consumption function is $C = £150m + 0.7Y$. At which level of N.Y. does the level of savings equal zero?

**A**  £2000m      **B**  £1800m      **C**  £1200m      **D**  £900m      **E**  £500m

## Example 12.19

An increase in government spending is likely to have a large impact on the level of employment when there is:

**A**  a high marginal propensity to import
**B**  a high marginal propensity to tax
**C**  a high marginal propensity to consume
**D**  a high level of stocks
**E**  full employment

## Example 12.20

Which of the following is concerned with how capital expenditure responds to a change in consumer expenditure?

**A**  the multiplier                **B**  the accelerator
**C**  the consumption function      **D**  the savings function

Example 12.21

The paradox of thrift suggests that:
A   a decision by people to save more can in the longer term result in a decrease in savings
B   a decision by people to save more will in the short term reduce investment
C   while total savings rise with income, the average propensity to save falls
D   while total savings rise with income, the marginal propensity to save tends to fall

Example 12.22

According to Keynesian analysis, consumption is a function of:
A   permanent income              B   current income
C   estimated lifetime income     D   previous income

Example 12.23

According to supply-side economics, which of the following could have caused the short-run aggregate supply curve to shift to the right?
A   an increase in demand for consumer goods
B   an increase in government spending
C   a reduction in the differential between earnings from employment and unemployment benefit
D   a reduction in marginal tax rates

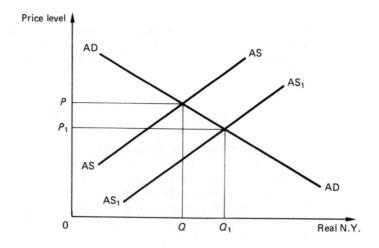

Select your answers to Examples 12.24–12.28 by means of the following code:
A   if 1, 2 and 3 are all correct
B   if 1 and 2 only are correct
C   if 2 and 3 only are correct
D   if 1 only is correct

186

Example 12.24

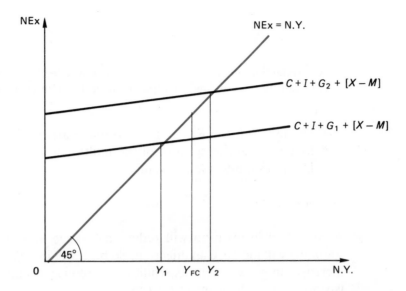

In the diagram above, the economy's initial economy level of National Income is $Y_1$ and $Y_{fe}$ is the full employment level of National Income. If the government raises its spending from $G_1$ to $G_2$, which of the following will occur?
1  output will rise        2  employment will rise    3  prices will rise

Example 12.25

A government wishing to reduce an inflationary gap may:
1  reduce government spending        2  reduce direct taxation
3  reduce the exchange rate

Example 12.26

In an economy, the marginal propensity to save is 0.2, the marginal propensity to tax is 0.16 and the marginal propensity to import is 0.04. National Income is currently £10 000m. The full employment level of N.Y. is £12 389m, and to achieve this level the government injects extra spending of £860m. Which of the following is/are true in this situation?
1  the multiplier is $2\frac{1}{2}$
2  at the new equilibrium level of N.Y. imports will be £650m
3  the injection is too expansionary

Example 12.27

According to Keynesian analysis, in a closed economy with no government sector, the equality of planned savings and planned investment is brought about by changes in:
1  National Income        2  interest rates        3  prices

Example 12.28

A downward multiplier effect could be caused by:
1  a decrease in government spending
2  a decrease in investment
3  a decrease in savings

## 12.4 Essays

**Example 12.29**

Are reductions in taxation likely to be less effective than increases in government expenditure in reducing unemployment in the United Kingdom?

(OLE 1986)

- Discuss both the Keynesian and monetarists' viewpoints.
- Make use of the concept of the multiplier.
- Discuss supply-side economics.

*Solution 12.29*

A reduction in taxation will reduce a leakage and an increase in government spending will increase an injection. So both will increase N.Y. Keynesians favour increases in government expenditure to reduce unemployment, while monetarists advocate reductions in taxation.

Keynesians believe that an increase in government expenditure will have a larger impact on aggregate demand and, hence, employment. This is because the recipients of government spending are likely to have a higher marginal propensity to consume than are taxpayers. The recipients of government spending may include the unemployed, the low-paid and pensioners, all of whom will spend a high proportion of extra income. In contrast, the main beneficiaries of tax reductions are likely to be the rich, and they will tend to save rather than spend a high proportion of extra income. So one leakage, taxation, will in part be offset by another leakage, savings.

Government spending will enter the circular flow, causing National Income (N.Y.) to rise by a multiple amount. If, for example, mpc is 0.75, a rise in government spending of £400m will cause N.Y. to rise by £400m × 4 (the multiplier) = £1600m. The resulting increase in demand is likely to stimulate output and employment. The diagram shows that an increase in government spending causes a rise in N.Y. from $Y$ to $Y_1$.

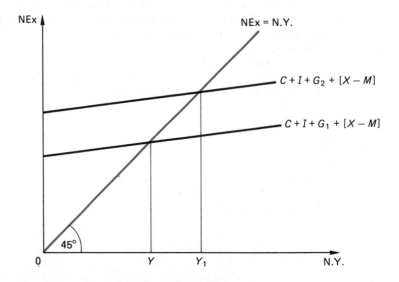

However, unemployment will not fall if there was initially full employment, if there were already underemployed workers, if existing workers work overtime, if there is an increase in productivity or if the rising demand is met from abroad.

Monetarists believe that an increase in government spending can reduce the rate of unemployment below the natural rate for a short period. However, they think that, in the longer term, increases in government spending will succeed only in raising inflation. Indeed, they consider that past attempts to reduce unemployment through increased government spending financed by borrowing has resulted in inflation, which, in turn, has caused unemployment due to the resulting reduction in domestic competitiveness.

Monetarists believe that increasing supply will be more effective in increasing output and employment than increasing demand. They favour microeconomic policies to improve the efficiency of product, capital and labour markets. One measure they advocate to create incentives to raise productivity is a reduction in taxation. They argue that this will cause existing workers to work harder and, by increasing the gap between paid employment and unemployment benefit, will also reduce voluntary, frictional and search unemployment.

**Example 12.30**

Describe the interrelationships between consumption, investment and income, and discuss how a change in each one will affect the other two.

- Stress the interrelationships between the three variables in Keynesian analysis.
- Make use of the multiplier and accelerator concepts.
- Discuss how an increase in one variable will cause the other two to increase.

*Solution 12.30*

Income, consumption and investment are all interrelated and are important variables in Keynesian analysis.

Income equals consumption plus investment. If investment and/or consumption rise, income will increase. Keynes used Kahn's concept of the multiplier to show that not only will income increase, but also it will rise by a multiple amount.

A rise in investment and a rise in autonomous consumption are injections into the circular flow of income which will result in a multiple rise in N.Y. For instance, if investment increases by £50m and mpc is 0.8, the final rise in N.Y. will be £50m × 5 = £250m. The diagram shows that a rise in investment from $I$ to $I_1$ causes N.Y. to increase from $Y$ to $Y_1$.

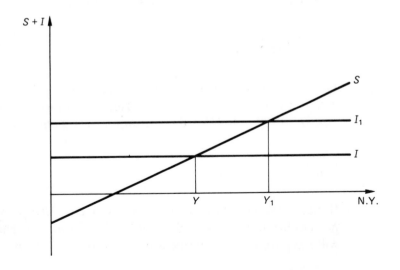

Just as a rise in investment will result in a rise in income, so an increase in income will cause a rise in private-sector investment. The accelerator theory, incorporated by Keynes into his analysis, states that a given percentage rise in demand for consumer goods will induce a greater percentage rise in demand for investment goods. For instance, if 100 goods are usually produced by 10 machines and 1 machine wears out each year, then demand for capital goods will be 1 per annum. Should consumption rise by 50% to 150 goods, demand for capital goods would rise by 500% to 6 machines, 1 of which will be to replace a worn-out machine and 5 will represent net investment. However, if income is increasing, government investment may be reduced. Part of government investment may be undertaken to influence the level of aggregate demand in the economy. When private-sector demand is low, the government may inject investment into the economy to raise aggregate demand. Conversely, if private-sector demand is high, a government may reduce investment in order to offset inflationary pressures.

A rise in income will induce a rise in consumption. Income is the main influence on consumption. While investment is likely to increase by a greater percentage than the rise in income which has brought it about, consumption is likely to rise by a smaller percentage than income. Keynes pointed out that, when income rises, a person's or a society's spending is also likely to rise. However, the proportion of total income spent (the average propensity to consume) and the proportion spent out of extra income (the marginal propensity to consume) are likely to decline. When a person or a society is poor, the whole of his or its income is likely to be spent. Indeed, there may be dissaving — that is, spending more than income by borrowing or drawing on past savings. However, as income rises, there will be increased opportunities for saving, so, while both saving and spending will rise, the proportion devoted to consumption is likely to decline.

Consumption and investment are not only components of national income, they are also influences on the level of that income and are, in turn, influenced by income.

## 12.5 Solutions to Objective Questions

*Solution 12.2   Answer:* **E**

The man's savings rise by £400 when his income rises by £2000. So his mps is $400/2000 = 0.2$. $1 - \text{mps} = \text{mpc}$. So $\text{mpc} = 1 - 0.2 = 0.8$.

*Solution 12.3   Answer:* **C**

The consumption function shows the relationship between income and consumption — i.e. $C = a + bY$. In this case, autonomous consumption ($a$) is £60m and mpc is $70/100 = 0.7$. So the consumption function is $C = £60m + 0.7Y$.

*Solution 12.4   Answer:* **C**

If mps is 0.3 and mpt is 0.1 the multiplier is: $1/(\text{mps} + \text{mpt}) = 1/0.4 = 2\frac{1}{2}$. The gap between present and desired N.Y. is £10m. To achieve this, the government will have to increase its spending by $£10m/2\frac{1}{2} = £4m$.

*Solution 12.5   Answer:* **A**

If the savings function is $S = -£500m + 0.2Y$, then, when N.Y. is £5000m, total savings will be $-£500m + 0.2 \times £5000m = £500m$. So aps = £500m/£5000m = 0.1.

*Solution 12.6   Answer:* **A**

In this case, the multiplier is:

$$\frac{1}{\text{mpt} + \text{mps} + \text{mpm}} = \frac{1}{0.2 + 0.2 + 0.1} = \frac{1}{0.5} = 2$$

*Solution 12.7   Answer:* **B**

When income rises by £2000, savings rise by £800, so mps = 800/2000 = 0.4. So mpc is $1 - 0.4 = 0.6$.

*Solution 12.8   Answer:* **C**

National Insurance contributions are a tax and so reduce the amount of income passed round the economy.
   **A** and **B** $\Rightarrow$ Distributed profits and interest are incomes earned within the economy and form part of the circular flow.
   **D** and **E** $\Rightarrow$ Investment and exports are injections into the circular flow.

*Solution 12.9   Answer:* **E**

Actual investment consists of planned investment plus changes in stocks. As planned savings exceed planned investment, there are unsold stocks represented by the distance BC. So actual investment is C$Y$ (planned investment) + BC (rise in stocks) = B$Y$.
   The answer could also be derived from the knowledge that actual investment = actual savings and that actual savings = planned savings. So B$Y$ = B$Y$.
   **A** $\Rightarrow$ AB = consumption.

*Solution 12.10   Answer:* **D**

The equilibrium level N.Y. is where planned injections equal planned withdrawals. In a closed economy this will be where:
investment + government spending = savings + taxation — i.e.

$$90 + 10 \qquad\qquad = \qquad 20 + 80$$

which occurs where N.Y. is £400m.

*Solution 12.11   Answer:* **C**

There are two ways of working out this answer:
   (1) When N.Y. is £10 000m, $C = £700m + 0.6 \times £10\,000m = £6700m$. So investment needs to be £10 000 − £6700m = £3300m. It is currently £2500m, so there needs to be an increase of £800m.
   (2) Initially injections = investment + autonomous consumption — i.e. £2500m + £700m = £3200m. mps is $1 - 0.6 = 0.4$, so the multiplier is

$1/0.4 = 2\frac{1}{2}$. N.Y. is initially £3200m $\times$ $2\frac{1}{2}$ = £8000m. To raise N.Y. by £2000m, it will be necessary to raise investment by £2000m/$2\frac{1}{2}$ = £800m.

*Solution 12.12   Answer:* **C**

Each machine makes 10 000 ÷ 20 = 500 goods, and the firm originally buys two machines. To produce an extra output of 2000, it will need additional machines of 2000 ÷ 500 = 4. So the firm will purchase a total of 6 machines — 2 replacement and 4 to expand output (net investment). Thus, gross investment (depreciation + net investment) rises from 2 to 6 — i.e. an increase of 4/2 × 100/1 = 200%.

*Solution 12.13   Answer:* **D**

Realised investment is actual investment and includes both planned investment and changes in stock. $C = 0.75 \times$ £800m = £650. So savings = $Y -$ £650m = £150m. Since actual investment = actual savings, actual investment will be £150m. This consists of £80m (planned investment) + £70m unsold stock (£720m consumer goods made but only £650m sold).

*Solution 12.14   Answer:* **B**

mps is 0.2, mpm is 0.25 of 0.8 — i.e. 0.2. So the multiplier is: $1/0.4 = 2\frac{1}{2}$. To raise N.Y. by £50m, the government should inject £50m/$2\frac{1}{2}$ = £20m.

*Solution 12.15   Answer:* **C**

The equilibrium level of $Y$ will be where:
$Y = C + I + (X - M)$
$Y = 40 + 0.8Y + 30 + (50 - 60)$
$0.2Y = 40 + 30 - 10$
$Y = 300$

*Solution 12.16   Answer:* **C**

According to the balanced budget multiplier theorem, if the mpcs of taxpayers and recipients of government spending are equal then a rise in government spending and taxation of equal amounts will cause N.Y. to rise by the amount of the change. For instance, if mpc is 0.8, a rise in taxation of £5000m will cause private spending to fall by £5000m $\times$ 0.8 = £4000m. Public spending increases by £5000, so the net injection of spending is £5000m $-$ £4000m = £1000m. mps is 0.2, so the multiplier is $1/0.2 = 5$. Thus, N.Y. will rise by £1000m $\times$ 5 = £5000m.

*Solution 12.17   Answer:* **B**

mpt is 0.2, disposable income is 0.8. mpm is 0.25 $\times$ 0.8 = 0.2 and mps is 0.25 $\times$ 0.8 = 0.2. Thus, the multiplier is:

$$\frac{1}{\text{mpt} + \text{mpm} + \text{mps}} = \frac{1}{0.6} = 1\tfrac{2}{3}$$

*Solution 12.18   Answer:* **E**

When N.Y. is £500m, consumption will be: £150m + 0.7 × £500m = £150m + £350m = £500m. $Y - C = S$. So £500m − £500m = 0.

*Solution 12.19   Answer:* **C**

A high mpc will mean a high multiplier — i.e. if mpc is 0.9, the multiplier will be 10. Thus, a rise in government spending of £50m will cause N.Y. to rise by £50m × 10 = £500m. The larger the rise in N.Y. the greater the likely increase in employment.

   **A** and **B** ⇒ A high mpm and a high mpt will both reduce the size of the multiplier.

   **D** and **E** ⇒ If there is full employment and a high level of stocks, then a rise in demand resulting from government spending will not cause a significant increase in output or employment.

*Solution 12.20   Answer:* **B**

The accelerator theory states that a given change in demand for consumer goods will cause demand for capital goods to change by a greater percentage.

   **A** ⇒ The multiplier is concerned with how N.Y. changes as a result of a change in an injection — e.g. investment.

*Solution 12.21   Answer:* **A**

The paradox of thrift suggests that if people save more, planned saving will exceed planned investment. National Income will decrease as entrepreneurs experiencing unsold stocks reduce output. As N.Y. falls, savings will fall until planned savings are again in equilibrium with planned investment.

   **B** ⇒ In the short term, a decision by people to save more will increase both actual savings and actual investment.

   **C** and **D** ⇒ As income rises, total savings, aps and mps all rise.

*Solution 12.22   Answer:* **B**

According to Keynesian analysis, the main determinant of consumption is current income.

   **A** ⇒ Milton Friedman and other supporters of the permanent income hypothesis suggest that consumption depends on permanent income. So, if people experience what they expect to be a short-term change in income, they may not alter their consumption.

   **C** ⇒ Franco Modigliani and Albert Ando developed the Life Cycle Hypothesis, which states that people estimate the income they are likely to earn over their lifetime and on this base a lifetime consumption plan.

*Solution 12.23   Answer:* **D**

The aggregate supply curve will shift to the right if the productivity of the factors of production increases. Supporters of supply-side economics urge tax cuts to increase the attractiveness of paid employment and the productivity of workers.

   **A** and **B** ⇒ Would influence demand initially rather than supply.

$C \Rightarrow$ Supply-side supporters argue that, if the differential between earnings from employment and unemployment benefit is narrowed, this will reduce the incentive for workers to increase productivity.

*Solution 12.24    Answer:* **A**

Initially equilibrium income $Y_1$ is below the full employment level of $Y_{fe}$. When the government increases its spending to $G_2$, N.Y. rises beyond the FE level to $Y_2$. As income rises to the FE level, output and employment will rise. When it passes beyond the FE level, output and employment cannot increase any further and the rise in demand is likely to result in a rise in prices.

*Solution 12.25    Answer:* **D**

An inflationary gap occurs when aggregate demand exceeds the FE level of N.Y. To remove the gap, it will be necessary to reduce demand and a reduction in government spending will lower demand.

$2 \Rightarrow$ Lower direct taxation will increase disposable income and demand.

$3 \Rightarrow$ A lower exchange rate is likely to increase exports, which will result in higher domestic incomes and demand.

*Solution 12.26    Answer:* **D**

The multiplier is:

$$\frac{1}{\text{mps} + \text{mpt} + \text{mpm}} = \frac{1}{0.2 + 0.16 + 0.04} = 2\tfrac{1}{2}$$

An injection of £860m will cause N.Y. to rise by £860m $\times$ $2\tfrac{1}{2}$ = £2150m. The gap between present and desired N.Y. is £2389m. So the injection is not sufficiently expansionary. There is a shortfall of £2389m $-$ £2150m = £239m. At the new level of N.Y. of £12150m imports will be £12150m $\times$ 0.4 = £486m.

*Solution 12.27    Answer:* **D**

It is changes in N.Y. which restore equilibrium. If, for instance, planned investment is greater than planned savings, N.Y. will rise until planned savings increase to the same amount.

*Solution 12.28    Answer:* **B**

A downward multiplier can be caused by either an increase in a leakage or a reduction in an injection. Government spending and investment are both injections into the circular flow, and if they decrease, N.Y. will fall.

$3 \Rightarrow$ A reduction in savings will cause a rise in N.Y.

# 13 Money and Banking

## 13.1 Fact Sheet

### (a) Barter

- *Barter* is the direct exchange of goods. Trade was originally carried out by barter but this posed three main problems:
  - (i) the need for a *double coincidence of wants*;
  - (ii) the difficulty of agreeing on a rate of exchange;
  - (iii) the difficulty of storing wealth in the form of goods.

  However, there has recently been an increase in international barter (*counter-trade* or *counter-purchase*) because of uncertainty about exchange rate movements and concern about Third World debt.

### (b) Functions and Characteristics of Money

- *Money* is any item which is widely accepted as payment for products. Money has the following functions:
  - (i) *Medium of exchange*  Money is used to buy goods.
  - (ii) *Measure of value* (unit of account)  Money is used to compare the value of goods, services and factor rewards.
  - (iii) *Store of value*  Money is used to hold wealth (savings).
  - (iv) *Standard for deferred payments*  Money is used to enable people to borrow and lend agreed amounts.
- The most important characteristic of money is general acceptability. If a commodity ceases to be acceptable, it will cease to act as money.
- The most widely used types of money in the UK are notes and coins and bank deposits. The transfer of bank deposits via cheques, etc., accounts for approximately 90% by value of all transactions.
- *Near money* or *quasi-money* consists of assets which perform some but not all the functions of money and which can be quickly turned into money.

### (c) Measures of the Money Supply

There is some debate as to which items to include in the money supply. The UK *monetary aggregates* include:
- (i) *Narrow* measures, which concentrate on money which is used mainly as a medium of exchange:
  - (1) $M_0$, which consists of notes, coins and commercial banks' balances at the Bank of England;
  - (2) $M_1$, which includes $M_0$ items + sight (current) bank accounts;
  - (3) $M_2$, which consists of notes, coins, sight bank accounts, retail deposit accounts, building society accounts and national savings bank accounts.

(ii) *Broad* measures concentrate on money kept as a store of value and on which interest is paid:

   (1) $M_3$, which consists of $M_1$ items + time (deposit) accounts and sterling certificates of deposit;

   (2) $M_{3c}$, which includes $M_3$ measures + foreign currency bank deposits;

   (3) $M_4$, which is essentially $M_3$ + building society shares and deposits and sterling certificates of deposit;

   (4) $M_5$, which includes $M_4$ items + private sector holdings of money market instruments (e.g. treasury bills), certificates of tax deposits and national savings instruments.

### (d) Financial Intermediaries

- *Financial intermediaries* are institutions which channel funds from people and institutions wishing to lend to those wishing to borrow.
- The *monetary sector* includes authorised institutions, the National Giro-bank, the Banking department of the Bank of England and some of the banks of the Channel Islands and the Isle of Man.
- *Authorised institutions* are banks which meet the Bank of England's (BOE) statutory prudential requirements, including having adequate capital and liquidity and conducting their business with integrity and appropriate professional skills.
- The *money market* includes institutions concerned with short-term borrowing and lending:
  - (i) The *primary banking system* consists of institutions which have the main function of providing a money transmission service — e.g. commercial banks and discount houses.
  - (ii) The *secondary banking system* includes institutions which accept large deposits from a relatively small number of depositors and which do not have a high street branch network — e.g. merchant banks and consortium banks.
- The *capital market* includes institutions concerned with long-term borrowing and lending.
- The *Stock Exchange* provides a market for second-hand shares and securities. *Bears* sell shares expecting their price to fall, while *bulls* buy shares expecting their price to rise. *Stags* buy newly issued shares expecting their price to rise.

**Table 13.1** Examples of financial intermediaries

| Institution | Functions |
| --- | --- |
| Commercial banks | Provide customers with the three traditional services of accepting deposits, acting as agents for payment, lending, plus a wide range of other services |
| Discount houses | Borrow from the commercial banks and other institutions at short notice and use this money to buy treasury bills, commercial bills and other financial assets |
| Merchant banks | Accept bills of exchange, arrange and underwrite the issue of new shares, provide credit and advice to companies |
| Building societies | Accept deposits, lend to house buyers, and since the 1986 Building Societies Act have offered a wide range of banking services |

## (e) Investment Finance

Firms wishing to buy capital goods may use:
  (i) *Internal finance*  Retained profits account for between 60% and 70% of all investment finance.
  (ii) *External finance* in the form of:
     (1) issuing new shares (e.g. a *rights issue*);
     (2) borrowing from financial institutions or the general public in the form of debentures.

## (f) Commercial Banks' Balance Sheets

*Liabilities* are the money owed by commercial banks and consist mainly of deposits (accounts). *Assets* are the various resources owned by the bank. The profitability of assets tends to increase as their liquidity is reduced. Banks seek to maximise the amount of profitable but illiquid assets held, while maintaining sufficient liquid assets to meet their customers' demand for cash.

**Table 13.2**  Balance sheet of a commercial bank

| Liabilities (D) | Assets (A) |
|---|---|
| (1) Sight deposits<br>(2) Time deposits | (4) Cash in till<br>(5) Balances at the BOE<br>(6) Money at call and short notice<br>(7) Treasury and other bills<br>(8) Short-term investments |
|  | (9) Investments<br>(10) Advances<br>(11) Property |
| (3) Total liabilities | (12) Total assets |

(1) Customers' current accounts.
(2) Customers' deposit accounts.
(3) Total amount of money owed by the bank to customers.
(4) Cash in till held on the premises.
(5) Operational accounts used to settle interbank debts at clearing and to draw out cash when necessary.
(6) Money lent at call or short notice (7 days) to the discount houses.
(7) Short-term (91 days) loans to the government or companies.
(8) Government and local authority stocks (securities or bonds) with less than a year to run.
(9) Government securities, etc., with more than 1 year to run.
(10) Loans to customers.
(11) The value of bank premises, etc.
(12) Total amount of bank claims on other people.

  • Items (4)–(8) of the balance sheet are the *liquid* or *reserve assets* of the bank.
  • The liquid asset ratio ($\phi$) is the proportion of overall deposits held in liquid form.

## (g) Credit Creation

  • *Credit creation* refers to the commercial banks' ability to create money in the form of bank accounts. Assume a single-bank system where the only liability is money held as sight deposits; cash is the only liquid asset. The bank keeps 10% of its liabilities in cash ($\phi = 10\%$) and lends out the rest. Any loan is spent only to be redeposited by shopkeepers, etc. Figure 13.1 shows in simplified form the effect on the bank's balance sheet of an initial deposit of £200.

Step 1: £200 cash is deposited

Balance sheet 1

| Liabilities | Assets |
|---|---|
| £200 sight deposit | £200 cash |
| £200 | £200 |

Step 2: £180 cash is lent out

Balance sheet 2

| Liabilities | Assets |
|---|---|
| £200 sight deposit | £20 cash |
| | £180 loan |
| £200 | £200 |

Step 3: £180 cash is redeposited

Balance sheet 3

| Liabilities | Assets |
|---|---|
| £380 sight deposit | £200 cash |
| | £180 loan |
| £380 | £380 |

Eventually:

Final balance sheet

| Liabilities | Assets |
|---|---|
| £2000 sight deposit | £200 cash |
| | £1800 loan |
| £2000 | £2000 |

**Figure 13.1** Simple credit creation

- In the final balance sheet, the bank now holds 10% of its overall liabilities ($D$) in cash ($C$): $D = 1/\phi \times C$.
- Through a process of deposits, loans, redeposits, loans, etc., the bank has created £1800 of credit.
- The bank or credit multiplier ($1/\phi$) shows by how much total liabilities (accounts or *low-powered money*) can increase as a result of a rise in liquid assets (*high-powered money*) deposited in the banking system.
- Using the equation $\Delta D = 1/\phi \times \Delta R$, it is possible to calculate the change in liabilities ($\Delta D$) following a change in reserve assets ($\Delta R$). Assume $\phi = 12\frac{1}{2}\%$ and that a monopoly bank's liquid assets increase by £2m:

$$\Delta D = 1/\phi \times \Delta R = 1/12.5/100 \times £2m = 1/0.125 \times £2m = 8 \times 2m = £16m$$

As loans are redeposited and then lent out, liabilities eventually increase by £16m — that is, £14m of credit has been created.

### (h) Functions of the Bank of England

(i) Issues bank notes. The BOE has sole responsibility in England and Wales for the printing, issue and distribution of notes.

(ii) Issues and manages the national debt.

(iii) Acts as the government's bank. Tax revenues and current government expenditure are recorded in the Exchequer Account.

(iv) Acts as banker to the monetary sector. Authorised institutions keep 0.45% of their eligible liabilities at the BOE and the clearing banks also maintain operational balances.

(v) Acts as lender of last resort. The BOE will always lend to the discount houses and thereby ensures sufficient liquidity in the monetary sector to maintain confidence.

(vi) Supervises the monetary sector, checking that authorised institutions follow prudent policies and maintain adequate liquidity ratios.

(vii) Carries out government monetary policy — e.g. conducting open market operations (see Chapter 14, Section (e)).

(viii) Manages the Exchange Equalisation Account, which is a Treasury account operated by the BOE to buy and sell sterling to influence the exchange rate.

(ix) Acts as banker to other countries that want to keep their reserves in sterling on deposit in London.

(x) Meets with other central banks to discuss, e.g., international liquidity.

## 13.2 Data Response

**Worked Example 13.1**

The balance sheet of the Bank of England for 11 August 1983 was as follows:

| Liabilities | £m | Assets | £m |
|---|---|---|---|
| Issue Department: | | | |
| Notes in circulation | 11 436 | Government securities | 5 394 |
| Notes in Banking Dept. | 4 | Other securities | 6 046 |
| | 11 440 | | 11 440 |
| Banking Department: | | | |
| Capital | 15 | Government securities | 466 |
| Public deposits | 42 | Advances and other accounts | 1 137 |
| Special deposits | 0 | Premises, equipment and other securities | 983 |
| Bankers' deposits | 615 | Notes and coin | 4 |
| Reserves and other accounts | 1 918 | | |
| | 2 590 | | 2 590 |

(Source: *Bank of England Quarterly Bulletin*, December 1983)

With reference to the balance sheet, show how these items reflect the various functions of a central bank.

(L Jan. 1986)

*Solution 13.1*

The division of the Bank of England's balance sheet indicates the functions of the two departments.

The Issue Department has responsibility for the note issue, and the Bank of England is the only bank in England and Wales with the right to issue notes. Notes in circulation are ones which have been issued on instructions from the

Treasury, while notes in the Banking Department are those held to meet the demand for notes from commercial banks.

In the UK, the note issue is entirely fiduciary. It is no longer backed by gold but by government securities. Government securities consist of gilt-edged securities and Treasury bills. Other securities include commercial bills. If the government wishes to increase the notes in circulation, it may instruct the Bank of England to engage in open market operations, buying securities in exchange for money.

The Banking Department carries out all the other functions of the Bank of England. The public deposits reflect the Bank of England's role as the government's bank. Government revenue is paid into these accounts and expenditure is paid from these accounts. The inflows and outflows are very large but the balance is kept small. The Bank of England manages the National Debt, and the public deposits include the dividend accounts.

The Bank of England is also banker to the banking sector. The banks keep deposits at the Bank of England. Operational balances are used to settle interbank debts at clearing and as a source of notes and coins. Non-operational balances equal to 0.45% of each bank's eligible liabilities are kept to meet Bank of England requirements.

When the Bank of England engages in open market operations, it influences the banks' operational balances, and, as these are regarded as liquid assets, their ability to lend.

The Bank of England may also seek to change the quantity of banks' liquid assets and their ability to lend by calling for or releasing special deposits. These are expressed as a percentage of the banks' eligible liabilities and are kept at the Bank of England. The banks cannot count these as liquid assets. The balance sheet shows a nil figure for special deposits, so on the day it was drawn up the Bank was holding no special deposits.

Other accounts include accounts of foreign central banks, international institutions, staff and a few private customers. The private accounts are a reminder of the Bank's former role as a commercial bank. The Bank now has regular contact with other central banks and international organisations. Reserves are the retained profits of the Bank.

Capital is another item which is a reminder of the Bank's past. It is the share capital taken over when the Bank was nationalised.

On the assets side of the Banking Department section of the balance sheet, the government securities are short- and long-term securities, and represent loans to the government. Advances and other accounts include loans to the discount houses and other customers of the Bank. As 'lender of last resort' the Bank of England will always lend to the discount houses. It may do this to influence interest rates.

Premises, equipment and other securities refer mainly to the Bank's fixed assets — i.e. those items the Bank owns and will keep for a long period of time.

Notes and coins represent an opposite entry to that in the liability section of the Issue Department section of the balance sheet. They are issued to the commercial banks when requested.

## 13.3   Objective Questions

### Example 13.2

The essential condition for an item to act as money is that:
A   it is portable
B   it is legal tender
C   it is generally acceptable
D   it is backed by gold
E   it is homogeneous

### Example 13.3

Debenture holders are:
A   part-owners of a public limited company
B   creditors of a company
C   holders of government long-term stock
D   holders of government short-term stock
E   shareholders entitled to receive arrears of dividends

### Example 13.4

Which financial institution underwrites the weekly treasury bill tender?
A   discount houses
B   merchant banks
C   finance houses
D   commercial banks
E   the Bank of England

*Examples 13.5–13.7 refer to four assets and one liability of a commercial bank:*
A   *money at call*
B   *operational balances at the Bank of England*
C   *treasury bills*
D   *advances to customers*
E   *customers' current accounts*

### Example 13.5

Which of the items constitutes the largest figure on the assets side of a commercial bank's balance sheet?
A       B       C       D       E

### Example 13.6

Which is a liability of a commercial bank?
A       B       C       D       E

### Example 13.7

Which of the assets is the most liquid?
A       B       C       D       E

**Example 13.8**

A Special Deposit is
A money kept at the Bank of England by a clearing bank to settle debts with other banks
B money called in from commercial banks which is frozen at the Bank of England and which cannot count as liquid assets
C money kept at the Bank of England by commercial banks to meet the 0.45% cash ratio deposit requirement
D money lent by commercial banks to discount houses
E negotiable bearer securities issued by the commercial banks, usually for large denominations

**Example 13.9**

In which of the following ways can a commercial bank add to the money supply?
A cashing cheques for bank customers
B making advances to customers
C responding to a Bank of England call for special deposits
D printing bank notes
E increasing its liquidity ratio

**Example 13.10**

The bank multiplier would be increased by:
A a reduction in the bank's liquidity ratios
B an increase in the use of cash by the public
C an increase in the demand for loans
D an increase in liquid assets
E an increase in cash deposited in the bank

**Example 13.11**

A commercial bank which has liquid assets of £400m and which keeps a 20% liquidity ratio can support maximum deposits of:
A £50m      B £80m      C £800m      D £2000m      E £8000m

**Example 13.12**

A bank keeping a liquidity ratio of 10% receives a cash deposit of £240m. On the basis of this additional cash, the maximum additional deposits it could create would be:
A £960      B £1200      C £2160      D £2400      E £2640

**Example 13.13**

A bank which keeps a $12\frac{1}{2}$% liquidity ratio experiences a reduction in liquid assets of £90. If the bank's holdings of liquid assets was previously just meeting its liquidity ratio, the withdrawal of cash will cause a total decrease of liabilities of:
A £7.2      B £11.25      C £90      D £720      E £1125

**Example 13.14**

The opportunity cost of holding wealth in the form of cash may include the loss of all the following *except*:
A   interest     B   dividends     C   liquidity     D   capital gains


**Example 13.15**

Which type of security's yield is likely to fluctuate the most?
A   a cumulative preference share         B   a non-cumulative preference share
C   a debenture                          D   a gilt-edged security
E   an equity

*Select your answers to Examples 13.16–13.19 by means of the following code*:
A   *if 1, 2 and 3 are all correct*
B   *if 1 and 2 only are correct*
C   *if 2 and 3 only are correct*
D   *if 1 only is correct*


**Example 13.16**

When a commercial bank makes a loan to a customer:
1   its liabilities rise                  2   its assets rise
3   the money supply increases


**Example 13.17**

Which of the following is/are part of the money market?
1   an investment trust     2   a commercial bank     3   a discount house


**Example 13.18**

Which of the following assets are held by commercial banks at the Bank of England?
1   special deposits                     2   balances at Central Bank
3   money at call


**Example 13.19**

Which of the following are included in the $M_4$ measure of the money supply?
1   notes and coins                      2   current accounts
3   building society deposits

# 13.4   Essays


**Example 13.20**

Comment on the structure of the balance sheet of a commercial bank and explain what factors govern its composition.

(NISEC 1985)

- Define assets and liabilities and give examples.
- Devote most attention to assets.
- Discuss the influence on the composition of the balance sheet of liquidity, profitability and government action.

*Solution 13.20*

A bank's balance sheet will show the assets and liabilities. Banks, unlike other firms, list their assets in order of the most liquid first. Liabilities are divided into current and long-term items. A bank's assets will be matched by its liabilities.

A bank's liabilities consist of obligations to pay out money in the future. Customers' deposits account for the largest percentage of liabilities. Current (sight) accounts are used mainly to make payments, while deposit accounts are used mainly for saving. The customers have effectively lent money to the banks and are entitled to have this money returned to them on demand in the case of most current accounts and within 7 days in the case of deposit (time) accounts. The quantity and value of accounts will be influenced by competition from other financial institutions, government policy and customers' desire to hold cash.

Other liabilities include capital, which is the money which has been subscribed by the bank's shareholders, and reserves, which is profit earned in previous years which has been retained to reinvest in the bank. A bank may also have issued certificates of deposit to raise money and may, at any one time, have tax payments and dividend payments due.

A bank's assets are what the bank owns. Banks have to balance liquidity and profitability, and the structure of their assets is also influenced by the action and requirements of the Bank of England, carrying out government policy.

The banks' most liquid asset is cash, whereas its most illiquid asset, excluding premises, is advances. However, the more liquid an asset is the less profitable it is. For instance, there is no financial return from holding cash in till. Banks keep liquid assets in order to meet their customers' demand for cash. Most banks keep 15–18% of their assets in a liquid form. Liquid assets include cash, operational balances at the Bank of England, money at call, treasury bills, commercial bills, and local authority and government bonds with less than a year to run.

A bank will wish to lend as much as possible, since it earns most profits from advances. Indeed, advances account for the greatest percentage of a bank's assets. How much a bank can lend will be influenced by demand for loans, suitability of customers, government policy and the liquidity ratio which the bank decides it should keep. Banks appreciate that, every time they give a loan, they create a deposit, and, since some of this may be taken out in the form of cash, they have to ensure that the loans are backed by a sufficient amount of liquid assets. Banks discuss their liquidity ratios with the Bank of England, which will approve prudential ratios.

The second most profitable bank asset is investments, which consist mainly of gilt-edged securities, government bonds and company bonds.

The nature and size of the liabilities and assets may, at any one time, be influenced by the Bank of England in furtherance of government policy. The government may wish to encourage bank lending in order to increase demand, investment and employment. On the other hand, the government may attempt to reduce bank lending at a time of inflation.

One method which the BOE may adopt to reduce the money supply by means of reducing bank lending will actually result in an additional asset, or possibly an increase in that asset. The asset involved is special deposits, but this is a very illiquid asset. The BOE can tell the banks to deposit a given percentage — e.g.

2% — of their total liabilities in special deposits at the BOE. These are frozen, in the sense that commercial banks cannot use these deposits or count them in their liquid assets until they are released by the BOE. If the banks were only just holding what they regarded as a safe quantity of liquid assets, the call for special deposits may force them to reduce their loans.

However, the main method which the BOE now employs to influence the money supply is open market operations. This method will affect initially the banks' balances at the BOE, and later probably another asset.

Another method which the BOE may employ is funding. This involves selling fewer short-term government assets and more long-term assets in an attempt to reduce the banks' liquid assets and, hence, their ability to lend. This method is likely to result in the quantity of treasury bills held by the banks being reduced, and may result in a reduction in banks' advances unless they are able to increase other liquid assets such as commercial bills.

The BOE requires authorised institutions to keep 0.45% of their eligible liabilities in non-operational balances at the Bank.

Thus, a bank's balance sheet will contain a range of assets influenced by the need for liquidity, the desire for profitability and government action. The quantity and type of liabilities will be influenced by the competitive strength of banks in relation to other financial institutions and government policy.

**Example 13.21**

Explain briefly what is meant by the money supply. Why might a government seek to control the rate of growth of the money supply?

(AEB June 1987)

- Very briefly define money.
- Briefly discuss the main but not all measures of the money supply.
- Consider why the government measures the money supply.
- Concentrate on the relationship between changes in the money supply and inflation, but also consider how the changes in the money supply will affect other objectives.

*Solution 13.21*

The money supply is a measure of the items which fulfil the functions of money. These functions are to act as a medium of exchange, unit of account, store of value and standard for deferred payments. An item which carries out these functions will have a number of characteristics, the most important of which is to be generally acceptable.

The main components of the UK money supply are notes, coins, bank and building society accounts. There are a number of official measures of the money supply, which include different items. At any one time, the government is likely to concentrate on one or two measures. In recent years, $M_0$ (essentially notes, coins and banks' operational balances at the Bank of England), $M_3$ (notes, coins, banks' sight and time accounts) and $M_4$ (notes, coins, banks' sight and time accounts and building society accounts) have received the greatest attention.

One reason why governments measure the money supply is as an indicator of economic trends and the state of financial markets. For instance, a rapid growth of base money ($M_0$) will indicate a future rise in bank accounts.

Another reason is that the government may wish to use changes in the money supply as a policy instrument or objective, to influence one of its four main macroeconomic objectives. These are low inflation, a balance of payments equilibrium, full employment and growth. To achieve the last two objectives, a government may wish to increase the money supply, perhaps by means of encouraging bank lending. However, to achieve the first two objectives, it may seek to reduce the growth of the money supply and the level of demand.

A government whose main objective is to reduce inflation, and which believes that inflation is caused by the money supply growing too rapidly and at a rate exceeding the growth of output, will place considerable emphasis on controlling the growth of the money supply.

Monetarists argue that a rise in the money supply will increase people's money balances. They will use some of this addition to purchase goods and services. The rise in demand will, after a period of time, cause producers to raise their prices. To illustrate this analysis, the monetarists make use of the quantity theory. They suggest that if $V$ (velocity of circulation) and $T$ (transactions) are presumed to be constant, then a rise in $M$ (money supply) will cause an percentage rise in $P$ (prices).

Monetarists wishing to see a reduction in the growth of the money supply may urge a decrease in the PSBR (public-sector borrowing requirement) and possibly control of bank lending.

Some monetarists favour announcing targets for the growth of monetary aggregates. They argue that this may help to convince people that the government is taking steps to control prices and thereby reduce expectations of inflation, which can affect wage claims and price rises. They also suggest that this will also impose discipline on a government which will not want to be seen failing to meet its targets.

If the banks are increasing their lending, this may not only contribute towards inflation, but also worsen a current account deficit. People borrowing from the banks may purchase imports, and the rising home demand may cause some producers to divert goods from the export to the home market.

In contrast, some economists argue that a failure of bank lending to keep pace with demand for loans can cause problems. During inflation, entrepreneurs will face rising costs and are likely to try to borrow more from the financial sector. If they are unable to raise sufficient funds, they may go out of business, thereby causing unemployment.

The money supply may be regarded as an indicator, target and policy instrument, and it plays a particularly important role in monetarist analysis and policy. However, it is difficult to know which measure/measures of the money supply to use, and economists have found that, once one measure is under control, others start to move in undesired directions.

## 13.5   Solutions to Objective Questions

*Solution 13.2   Answer:* **C**

An item may possess many of the desirable characteristics of money, but, if it ceases to be generally acceptable, it will cease to act as money and people will use another item.

**A** and **E** $\Rightarrow$ Are regarded as important qualities for money to possess but they are not as significant as acceptability.

**B** $\Rightarrow$ The main form of money in the UK is bank accounts, which are not legal tender.

**D** $\Rightarrow$ The vast majority of money — i.e. all bank accounts, building society accounts and most cash — is not backed by gold and so is fiduciary issue.

*Solution 13.3   Answer:* **B**

Debenture holders lend money to a company and so are owed money by the company. They are creditors who receive interest.

    **A** ⇒ Shareholders.

    **C** and **D** ⇒ Holders of government securities.

    **E** ⇒ Cumulative preference shareholders.

*Solution 13.4   Answer:* **A**

A number of financial institutions and individuals buy treasury bills. However, it is only the discount houses which are committed to purchase any treasury bills not taken up through the competitive bidding process. In return for carrying out this function, the discount houses are able to use the Bank of England's 'lender of last resort' facility.

*Solution 13.5   Answer:* **D**

Commercial banks hold a range of current and fixed assets. However, their most profitable activity is lending, and advances account for the largest single item in their assets, usually in excess of 60%.

*Solution 13.6   Answer:* **E**

Customers' current accounts are liabilities, as a commercial bank has an obligation to pay these out to the customer on demand.

    **A, B, C, D** ⇒ Are all assets, items that the bank possesses.

*Solution 13.7   Answer:* **B**

A commercial bank can draw out money from its operational balances at very short notice. Operational balances are regarded as very liquid assets, usually the next most liquid after cash in till.

*Solution 13.8   Answer:* **B**

Special deposits represent a proportion of a bank's eligible liabilities which may be required to be placed with the Bank of England. They earn the going rate of interest but cannot be counted as liquid assets.

    **A** ⇒ Balances at the Bank of England.

    **C** ⇒ Non-operational balances at the Bank of England.

    **D** ⇒ Money at call.

    **E** ⇒ Certificates of deposit.

*Solution 13.9   Answer:* **B**

When a bank makes a loan to a customer, it opens up an account for the customer and this account will be included in most money supply measures.

    **A** ⇒ Cashing cheques will increase one form of money, cash, and reduce another, bank accounts. However, if more cash is withdrawn than is deposited in a period, a bank may have to reduce its loans, which will lower the money supply.

    **C** ⇒ Responding to a call for special deposits will reduce a commercial bank's liquid assets and so probably its ability to lend.

$D \Rightarrow$ Commercial banks do not print notes.

$E \Rightarrow$ Increasing its liquidity ratio will reduce a bank's ability to lend.

*Solution 13.10    Answer:* **A**

The bank multiplier shows by how much a change in liquid assets will affect a commercial bank's total liabilities and loans. It is found by using the ratio: 100%/ liquid assets ratio. A reduction in the liquidity ratio would increase the bank multiplier. For example, if the liquidity ratio was originally 25%, the bank multiplier would be 100%/25% = 4. If the liquidity ratio was then reduced to 10%, the bank multiplier would increase to 100%/10% = 10.

$B \Rightarrow$ An increase in the use of cash by the public may cause banks to increase their liquidity ratios to ensure that they can meet their customers' demand for cash. This would reduce the bank multiplier.

$C, D, E \Rightarrow$ Are unlikely to change the bank multiplier — merely bring it into effect.

*Solution 13.11    Answer:* **D**

If a bank has a liquidity ratio of 20%, it has a bank multiplier of 100%/20% = 5. Thus, liquid assets of £400m will enable the bank to have total deposits of £400m × 5 = £2000m.

*Solution 13.12    Answer:* **C**

A bank with a liquidity ratio of 10% has a bank multiplier of 100%/10% = 10. A cash deposit of £240m will enable total liabilities to increase by £240m × 10 = £2400m. This includes the account given to the customer who deposited the £240m. As a result, additional loans of £2400m minus the initial deposit could be created — i.e. £2400m − £240m = £2160m.

*Solution 13.13    Answer:* **D**

The bank multiplier works in reverse. A liquidity ratio of $12\frac{1}{2}$% will mean a bank multiplier of 100%/$12\frac{1}{2}$% = 8. Thus, a reduction in liquid assets of £90 will cause a fall in total liabilities of £90 × 8 = £720.

*Solution 13.14    Answer:* **C**

In choosing to hold wealth in the form of cash, a person forgoes the opportunity to hold other financial assets which may earn interest or dividends or the opportunity to hold, e.g., antiques or land, which may appreciate in value. However, the return which a person does receive from cash is the highest form of liquidity possible.

*Solution 13.15    Answer:* **E**

'Equities' is another term for shares. The dividend paid on ordinary shares may fluctuate considerably, depending on the profits firms earn and their decisions on the proportion of profits to distribute to shareholders and the proportion to plough back into the business. Indeed, a shareholder may receive no dividends.

A and $B \Rightarrow$ Preference shareholders are paid before ordinary shareholders and usually receive a fixed dividend out of profits — e.g. 10%.

**C** and **D** $\Rightarrow$ Debenture holders and gilt-edged security holders receive a fixed rate of interest.

*Solution 13.16   Answer:* **A**

When a commercial bank gives a customer a loan, which is an asset of the bank, it opens an account for the person, which is a liability. As bank accounts are regarded as money, the money supply will increase.

*Solution 13.17   Answer:* **C**

The money market consists of institutions which engage in short-term borrowing and lending. Most of the activities of the discount houses are concentrated in the money market, and the commercial banks are part of the money and capital markets.

**1** $\Rightarrow$ An investment trust is concerned primarily with long-term lending and borrowing, and is part of the capital market.

*Solution 13.18   Answer:* **B**

Special deposits and balances at Central Bank (another term for balances at the Bank of England) are both held by commercial banks at the Bank of England.

**3** $\Rightarrow$ Money at call represents money that the commercial banks have lent to the discount houses and, hence, will be held in the latter institution.

*Solution 13.19   Answer:* **A**

All the items are included in the new measure of the money supply, which seeks to take into account the importance of building societies as financial intermediaries. It includes all the items covered in $M_3$ plus building society deposits.

# 14 Monetary Economics

## 14.1  Fact Sheet

### (a)  Changes in the Money Supply

The UK money supply may increase as a result of:
  (i)   credit creation by the banking sector;
  (ii)  note issue by the Central Bank;
  (iii) a net inflow of sterling from abroad;
  (iv)  an increase in the public-sector borrowing requirement.

### (b)  The Importance of the Money Supply

Monetarists believe that changes in the money supply have a direct and significant impact on the economy. Keynesians believe that the effects are more complex and difficult to predict.

- The *transmission mechanism* shows the stages and ways in which a change in the money supply affects national income, prices and/or employment. There is still much controversy between Keynesians and monetarists over the exact working of the transmission mechanism.

#### (i)  *Keynesian Transmission Mechanism*

Increase in money supply $\Rightarrow$ increase in people's money balances $\Rightarrow$ increase in demand for bonds $\Rightarrow$ increase in the price of bonds $\Rightarrow$ fall in the rate of interest $\Rightarrow$ increase in investment $\Rightarrow$ multiplier effect $\Rightarrow$ increase in N.Y. $\Rightarrow$ increase in output $\Rightarrow$ increase in employment.

#### (ii)  *Monetarist Transmission Mechanism*

Increase in money supply $\Rightarrow$ increase in people's money balances $\Rightarrow$ people using 'surplus' money to demand more goods and services $\Rightarrow$ increase in prices.

### (c)  Monetary Policy

*Monetary policy* is a set of measures which seek to control aggregate demand, mainly by influencing the supply of money or the price of money (the rate of interest). To achieve a given macro-objective (e.g. stable prices), a government will use *policy instruments*, which operate initially on targets.

**Table 14.1** Examples of monetary policy

| Instrument | Intermediate target | Ultimate target | Objective |
| --- | --- | --- | --- |
| Funding | Banks' liquid assets | Volume of bank credit | Inflation |
| Base rate | Structure of interest rates | Exchange rate | Current account |
| Special deposits | Banks' liquid assets | Interest rates | Inflation |
| Open market operations | Structure of interest rates | Volume of bank credit | Employment |

### (d) Monetary Policy Targets

(i) Growth of the money supply. The *Medium-term Financial Strategy* was introduced in 1980, setting out plans for monetary growth for several years ahead, in addition to including targets for public spending, taxation and the PSBR.

(ii) The level and structure of interest rates.

(iii) The exchange rate. A government may seek to influence exchange rates by altering interest rates, and buying and selling currencies.

(iv) The total volume of spending which can be influenced by, e.g., changes in interest rates.

(v) The volume of bank credit. The commercial banks' ability to create credit can have a significant impact on the money supply.

### (e) Control of Credit Creation

The Bank of England (BOE) is responsible for carrying out the government's monetary policy. The following measures restrict the ability of banks to create credit, although some have not been used by recent governments.

(i) *Open market operations*, where the BOE sells short-term government securities and bills, thereby reducing commercial banks' liquid assets and raising interest rates.

(ii) *Funding*, where the BOE issues more long-term securities and fewer short-term securities, thereby reducing commercial banks' liquid assets.

(iii) The *Minimum Lending Rate* (MLR) is the rate, announced in advance, at which the BOE will lend to the discount houses. MLR influences other market interest rates. An increase in MLR discourages borrowing and so reduces the ability of banks to create credit.

(iv) *Interest rate policy* The BOE may operate a number of undisclosed interest rate bands at which it will discount bills, raising or lowering these bands to influence the structure of interest rates in the money market.

(v) *Special deposits* are when the BOE calls for compulsory loans from the commercial banks, thereby reducing commercial banks' liquid assets.

(vi) An increase in the *liquid asset ratio requirement* reduces the amount of liabilities a commercial bank can have from a given volume of liquid assets.

(vii) *Quantitative controls* on lending involve the BOE setting an upper limit on the volume of bank lending.

(viii) *Qualitative lending guidelines* involve requesting banks to direct lending to particular groups and/or restrict lending to other groups.

(ix) *Moral suasion* The BOE can informally try to persuade commercial banks to change their lending policy.
(x) *Monetary base control* involves the BOE regulating base money.

- *Overfunding* occurs when the BOE sells to the non-bank sector more government securities than is necessary to finance the current PSBR.


### (f) Fiscal and Monetary Policy

Fiscal policies have an impact on the money supply and interest rates, and so have implications for monetary policy. For example, a rise in government spending may increase the budget deficit, and subsequently may cause a rise in the money supply and/or interest rates.


### (g) The Public-sector Borrowing Requirement

The *public-sector borrowing requirement* is the difference between the total income and expenditure of the public sector. This borrowing can be financed by:
  (i) Borrowing from the BOE, which is likely to increase the money supply via a rise in the high-powered monetary base.
  (ii) Borrowing from the commercial banks by selling treasury bills, which is likely to increase the money supply via a rise in commercial banks' liquid assets.
  (iii) Borrowing from the non-bank private sector by selling government securities, which some argue may crowd out private investment.
  (iv) Borrowing from overseas residents will result in a rise in interest payments on national debt going abroad.

- Other government policies have implications for the PSBR. For instance, *privatisation* and setting spending limits for local authority (*rate-capping*) both have the effect of reducing the PSBR, thus reducing the rate of growth of the money supply.


## 14.2 Data Response


**Worked Example 14.1**

Study the extract below and then answer questions (a) to (g).

M3, the most widely used measure of broad money which includes notes, coin and bank accounts, grew by a seasonally adjusted 0.4 per cent in February but this still left the rise over the year at 20.4 per cent.

Any encouragement from the drop compared with January's 22.4 per cent will be shortlived, since it was due more to a sharp rise between January and February last year than the slowdown this year.

Although bank lending grew by £2.6 billion compared with £4 billion on average in the past six months, this seemed to be due more to the building societies' growing share of the mortgage market than any real slowdown in lending.

The broader money measure M4, which adds in building society accounts, grew by 16 per cent over the year to February. Total lending was up £4.2 billion compared with an average of £5.1 billion in the last six months.

The best-behaved money measure is the narrow M0 — notes, coin and bankers' cash at the Bank of England — which fell by a seasonally adjusted 0.1 per cent, although the rise over the year to February still came in at 5.3 per cent compared with last month's 4.8 per cent.

The reason is the fall in M0 at this time last year, which the Treasury expects to lead to above target growth at the beginning of 1988–9. The present target of 2–6 per cent will come down to 1–5 per cent from April.

(Source: *The Guardian*, 19 March 1988)

(a) What is the difference between narrow and broad measures of the money supply?
**(2 marks)**

(b) Why did bank lending grow more slowly than in the previous six months?
**(2 marks)**

(c) Explain what is meant by the statement: 'The best-behaved money measure is the narrow M0'?
**(3 marks)**

(d) What does the M4 measure of the money supply include?
**(1 mark)**

(e) Why may a government announce targets for the growth of monetary aggregates?
**(4 marks)**

(f) Why may an increase in bank lending cause inflation and why may inflation cause an increase in bank lending.
**(4 marks)**

(g) Discuss two measures which the Bank of England could employ to reduce bank lending.
**(4 marks)**


*Solution 14.1*

(a) Narrow money measures include assets which represent immediate purchasing power — i.e. assets used mainly as a medium of exchange. Broad money measures include not only assets used as a medium of exchange, but also those used as a temporary store of value — i.e. immediate and potential purchasing power.

(b) The article suggests that the growth in bank lending fell because of the increase in the building societies' share of the mortgage market. So people were still borrowing more but the proportion borrowed from different institutions changed.

(c) M0 was the best-behaved money measure in the sense that its growth stayed within the government-set target. From February 1987 to February 1988 it grew at 5.3%, which was within the 2–6% target.

(d) The M4 measure includes notes, coins, bank accounts and building society accounts.

(e) Some economists suggest that a government should announce targets for the growth of monetary aggregates in order to impose discipline on the government's monetary policy and to reduce expectations of inflation. If a government announces that it wants M3 to grow at, e.g., 8%, then it will be possible to assess whether the government has achieved its objective. If people believe that a government is determined to control the money supply, it may convince them that the rate of inflation will fall. The expectation of lower inflation may result in a fall in wage claims and price increases.

(f) An increase in bank lending will add to the money supply and spending. If output does not rise in line with spending, then demand will exceed supply and prices will rise. During periods of inflation, bank lending may increase. Producers may seek to borrow more to cover increased costs of production, and consumers may wish to borrow more to buy more expensive goods. If the rate of inflation exceeds the rate of interest charged, then debtors will gain by borrowing and buying assets which will appreciate in value. In real terms, they will pay back less than they borrowed, while certain assets may rise in price by more than the rate of inflation.

(g) The Bank of England could engage in open market operations to reduce the money supply. Selling government securities to the non-bank private sector will reduce bank customers' accounts, which, in turn, will reduce commercial banks' operational balances at the Bank of England. The reduction in the banks' liquid assets may result in a fall in bank lending. The Bank of England could also lower the banking sector's liquid assets by funding. This involves selling fewer short-term government securities, which are liquid assets, and more long-term government securities, which are not liquid assets.

## 14.3 Objective Questions

**Example 14.2**

The money supply can be increased by all the following *except*:
A  commercial banks lending to their customers
B  the government borrowing from the Bank of England
C  the issue of treasury bills to the banking sector
D  the sale of long-term bonds to the general public
E  the issue of new notes by the Bank of England

**Example 14.3**

The Bank of England sells government securities to the public. This will tend to:
A  reduce the money supply and have no effect on interest rates
B  reduce the money supply and raise interest rates
C  reduce the money supply and lower interest rates
D  increase the money supply and raise interest rates
E  increase the money supply and lower interest rates

**Example 14.4**

Funding involves:
A  buying and selling government securities to influence the money supply
B  reducing the size of the national debt
C  borrowing from the eurocurrency market
D  issuing more long-term and fewer short-term government securities
E  financing government expenditure by means of taxation

**Example 14.5**

If the Bank of England wishes to decrease the commercial banks' ability to lend, it would not:
A  sell government securities
B  engage in funding
C  release special deposits
D  request the banks to reduce their loans
E  force up the rate of interest

## Example 14.6

If the Bank of England calls in special deposits, which one of the following measures is a commercial bank likely to adopt to maintain its desired liquidity ratio?
A   borrow from the Bank of England
B   reduce the rate of interest charged to borrowers
C   reduce the investments held
D   reduce their liabilities
E   reduce their capital

## Example 14.7

Which of the following measures would be defined as an expansionary monetary policy?
A   the purchase by the Central Bank of government securities from members of the public
B   a reduction in indirect taxation
C   the conversion of short-term government debt into long-term government debt
D   an increase in special deposits
E   an increase in government spending

## Example 14.8

A sale of government securities to the non-bank private sector by the Bank of England is likely to be followed by all the following *except*:
A   a fall in the price of government securities
B   a fall in the money supply
C   a fall in the rate of interest
D   a fall in bank lending
E   a rise in short-term foreign capital inflows

## Example 14.9

Which of the following means of financing government spending is likely to lead to the greatest increase in the money supply?
A   the sale of national savings certificates to the general public
B   the sale of government securities to the general public
C   the sale of treasury bills to the banking sector
D   an increase in direct taxation
E   an increase in indirect taxation

## Example 14.10

If a government's prime objective is to reduce unemployment by increasing demand, the monetary policy it is most likely to adopt is to:
A   sell government securities to the non-bank private sector
B   call in special deposits
C   sell fewer treasury bills and more long-term government securities
D   lower the rate of interest

*Select your answers to Examples 14.11, 14.12 by means of the following code*:
A   *if 1, 2 and 3 are all correct*
B   *if 1 and 2 only are correct*
C   *if 2 and 3 only are correct*
D   *if 1 only is correct*

### Example 14.11

Which of the following is/are monetary policy measures?
1 changes in the deposit on hire purchase payments
2 interest rate changes
3 special deposits

### Example 14.12

The public-sector borrowing requirement may be regarded as:
1 a policy instrument
2 an intermediate policy objective
3 an economic indicator

## 14.4 Essays

### Example 14.13

Why does the public-sector borrowing requirement have implications for the Bank of England's ability to control the money supply?

(OLE June 1985)

- Define the PSBR.
- Discuss how the PSBR may be financed.
- Discuss how the financing of the PSBR can affect the money supply and interest rates.

*Solution 14.13*

The public-sector borrowing requirement (PSBR) is the difference between the public sector's total income and its total expenditure. It consists of borrowing by the central government and borrowing by local authorities and public corporations from non-government sources. As the main component is central government borrowing, the PSBR is closely related to the budget deficit.

The size of the PSBR and how it is financed will have implications for monetary policy. There are four main methods of financing the PSBR: borrowing from the BOE; borrowing from the banking sector; borrowing from the non-bank private sector; and borrowing from abroad.

The government can always borrow from the BOE. When a government does this, it actually sells government securities to the BOE in return for an increase in the note issue. This is sometimes referred to as 'printing money' or resorting to the printing press. The new currency issue will immediately add to the money supply, and, when it is deposited into the commercial banks, it will enable a multiple expansion of the money supply to occur.

Similarly, if the government borrows from the commercial banks by selling them treasury bills, this will add to the money supply by increasing the banks' liquid assets and, hence, their ability to lend.

The government may also choose to borrow from overseas. The effect on the money supply will depend on whether foreign currency is borrowed or sterling is held in the UK or sterling is held abroad. Borrowing sterling initially held abroad would have the greatest impact on the money supply, increasing the supply of high-powered money. However, all three possibilities represent a 'drain' on national resources in interest rate payments.

Borrowing from the non-bank private sector by selling government securities and National Savings Certificates will have a neutral effect on the money supply. Bank deposits will fall as people write out cheques drawn on the commercial banks to buy the government securities. However, this may be offset by the increase in bank deposits arising from the injection of government spending. Some economists claim that this source of finance can have the disadvantage of public investment crowding out private-sector investment as a result of interest rates rising.

In practice, the largest part of the PSBR, usually at least 70%, is financed by the sale of gilt-edged securities to the non-bank sector — e.g. to pension funds and insurance companies. Most of the rest is accounted for by borrowing from the banking sector. The least important source is borrowing from the overseas sector.

Financing the PSBR may affect the money supply, either directly or indirectly through the price of money (interest rate). The money supply or the rate of interest may change in a direction the government does not want. For instance, when selling securities to finance the PSBR, the BOE will lose, to a certain extent, the quantitative control over the money supply and its price. When the BOE sells government securities, it does not know how much people will be willing to pay for the securities. So it does not know how many it will have to sell and, hence, what the price of bonds will be and what the rate of interest will be. A fall in the price of securities will raise interest rates and increase the cost of servicing the National Debt. Similarly, increasing the banking sector's liquid assets may have an uncertain expansionary effect on the money supply, depending on the banks' initial holdings of liquid assets and the demand for loans.

Governments recognise that fiscal policy has implications for the money supply. A government which believes that inflation is caused by the money supply increasing more rapidly than output may seek to reduce the PSBR in order to slow down the rate of growth of the money supply.

**Example 14.14**

Describe the various methods by which the Government might try to control the money supply, and comment on their possible success.

(SUJB June 1987)

- Discuss open market operations, special deposits, funding and interest rate changes.
- Discuss how commercial banks may get round monetary control measures.
- Discuss conflicts of government policies.

*Solution 14.14*

In attempting to control the money supply, the government may encounter a number of difficulties, including deciding what to control, conflicts of objectives and, particularly if trying to reduce the money supply or its growth, a conflict of interest with commercial banks.

A government can itself add to the money supply by borrowing from the BOE or the banking sector to finance the PSBR. In seeking to control the money supply, a government may try to reduce the PSBR or at least reduce its growth.

However, the size of the PSBR may move in a direction not desired by the government. A recession, for instance, will cause tax revenue to fall and expenditure on benefits to rise and the PSBR to increase.

Commercial banks can also create money and, indeed, have an incentive to do this, since lending is their most profitable activity. Thus, if a government attempts to reduce their lending, they are likely to seek ways round the policy.

One of the most common methods a government can employ to reduce bank lending is open market operations. This will involve the BOE selling government securities to the non-banking sector. People will pay for these with cheques drawn on the commercial banks. When these are settled at clearing, the commercial banks' balances at the BOE will be reduced. As these balances count as liquid assets, the commercial banks may be obliged to reduce their loans. Banks decide what they regard to be a safe liquidity ratio after consulting with and gaining the approval of the BOE. If open market operations do not result in the ratio being reduced below their desired rate, the banks may not be obliged to reduce their loans.

Open market operations may also have some undesirable consequences for a government. The sale of government securities will reduce their price and raise the rate of interest. A higher interest rate will increase the cost of servicing the National Debt, may raise the exchange rate and may have an adverse effect on investment, employment and growth.

When the BOE calls for special deposits, banks have to place a percentage of their total liabilities with the Central Bank. These deposits cannot be counted in the banks' liquid assets and may oblige them to reduce their loans. However, again the banks may not have to take any action if their liquid assets are reduced to a level which they still regard to be adequate.

Funding, which is the issue by the government of more long-term and fewer short-term government securities, will also not be effective if the commercial banks can replace treasury bills by other liquid assets — e.g. commercial bills.

The BOE may influence interest rates by using an undisclosed interest rate band. It may announce that it is prepared to buy bills from the discount houses but without stating a price. If the money market is short of funds, discount houses will offer bills to the BOE. These will only be purchased when the BOE is satisfied with the price (and, hence, the rate of interest). If the BOE wishes to lower interest rates, it will increase the price it is willing to pay, and when it wishes to raise interest rates, it will lower the price. In exceptional circumstances, it may also reintroduce MLR at a rate lower than the market rate, to encourage lending, or at a higher rate, to discourage lending. However, a reduction in interest rates will not succeed in increasing bank lending if people and firms do not want to borrow. Similarly, a rise in interest rates may not deter borrowers if there is a consumer boom or if the expected yield from investment is rising.

In addition to the problems of controlling bank lending, there are problems of defining what to control. Whenever one form of money is brought under control, another grows more rapidly than is desired.

A government's success in controlling the money supply will also be affected by other government policies. For instance, interest rates may be altered to influence the exchange rate, and the purchase or sale of currencies for this purpose may also influence the money supply.

# 14.5  Solutions to Objective Questions

*Solution 14.2   Answer:* **D**

The public will be likely to pay for government securities by writing cheques drawn on accounts at the commercial banks. At clearing, this will cause a transfer of money from the commercial banks' balances to the government's account at the BOE. The resulting reduction in the commercial banks' balances at the BOE will reduce their liquid assets, and the money supply.

*Solution 14.3   Answer:* **B**

The sale of government securities will reduce the money supply. The increase in the supply of government securities will also reduce their price. The price of government securities and interest rates vary inversely. Thus, a fall in the price of government securities will be accompanied by a rise in interest rates.

*Solution 14.4   Answer:* **D**

Funding involves converting short-term into long-term government debt, usually with the intention of reducing the availability of liquid assets for commercial banks.

*Solution 14.5   Answer:* **C**

If the BOE had been holding special deposits and then released them, this would cause an increase in the commercial banks' liquid assets. With more liquid assets, the banks would be able to increase lending.

*Solution 14.6   Answer:* **D**

The BOE has the right to tell banks to deposit a percentage of their eligible liabilities with the Bank. To meet such a call, the commercial banks will have to transfer money to the BOE. This will be taken out of their liquid assets. To maintain the proportional relationship between liquid assets and liabilities, the banks are likely to reduce their liabilities in line with the reduction in liquid assets. For instance, a call for special deposits reduces liquid assets from £12m to £10m, while liabilities are £80m. If a liquidity ratio of 15% is considered to be desirable, liabilities are likely to be reduced to £67m.

*Solution 14.7   Answer:* **A**

An expansionary monetary policy is one which increases the supply of money and/or reduces the rate of interest and thereby increases demand. The purchase of government securities by the BOE from members of the public will cause money to transfer from the government to the commercial banks' balances at the BOE. This will enable the commercial banks to lend more, which, in turn, will cause an increase in the money supply.
  **B** and **E** $\Rightarrow$ Are examples of expansionary fiscal policies.
  **C** and **D** $\Rightarrow$ Are examples of restrictionist monetary policies.

*Solution 14.8   Answer:* **C**

The sale of government securities will increase the supply of bonds, which will result in a fall in their price and a rise in the rate of interest. It will also cause a fall in the money supply and bank lending. Foreign capital may be attracted by the higher domestic interest rates.

*Solution 14.9   Answer:* **C**

The sale of treasury bills to the banking sector will increase their supply of liquid assets, which will enable an increase in bank lending to occur.

   **A, B, D, E** ⇒ Are likely to have a neutral effect on the money supply. This is because the increase in bank deposits resulting from the injection in government spending is likely to be offset by a fall in bank deposits arising from increased taxation or the purchase of government securities.

*Solution 14.10   Answer:* **D**

Lowering the rate of interest will be likely to stimulate borrowing and spending.

   **A, B, C** ⇒ Are all likely to reduce bank lending and demand.

*Solution 14.11   Answer:* **A**

HP regulations, interest rates and special deposits all influence the amount of credit in the economy and are all monetary policy measures.

*Solution 14.12   Answer:* **A**

The PSBR has been used as a policy instrument, an intermediate policy objective and an economic indicator. For instance, Keynesian governments have increased the PSBR to increase demand in the economy, while monetarist governments have aimed to reduce the PSBR and have interpreted the PSBR as an indicator of likely monetary expansion and inflation.

# 15 Unemployment

## 15.1 Fact Sheet

### (a) Definition of Unemployment

*Unemployment* occurs when people who are willing and able to work are unable to find suitable paid employment. It is a stock, the size of which is influenced by inflows and outflows and the duration of unemployment experienced.

- *Full employment* does not mean that everyone is employed. In a dynamic economy there will always be some workers changing jobs (frictional unemployment), and some people choosing not to take up paid employment (voluntary unemployment).
- *Over-full employment* occurs when the number of vacancies exceeds the number of unemployed.

### (b) Measurement of Unemployment

In the UK, official unemployment figures include those claiming unemployment benefits.

- *Seasonally adjusted* unemployment figures take out the effects of seasonal factors such as weather, which result in unemployment being unusually high or low in certain months.

Table 15.1 gives examples of adjustments that some suggest should be made to the official figures.

**Table 15.1**  Measuring unemployment

| Some economists/politicians believe the following should be included | Some economists/politicians believe the following should be omitted |
| --- | --- |
| Unemployed over-60s | Severely disabled people |
| Discouraged workers | School-leavers |
| Those in government special employment measures | Claimants working in the 'black' economy |
| Unemployed not entitled to benefits | Claimants who are not looking for work |
| Those on short-time working | Mentally and physically handicapped people |
| Those who choose not to register | Those in between jobs |
| Students on vacation | |

The *unemployment rate* is:

$$\frac{\text{registered unemployed}}{\text{working population}} \times \frac{100}{1}$$

## (c) Types and Causes of Unemployment

**Table 15.2** Types and causes of unemployment

| Type of unemployment | Description |
| --- | --- |
| Frictional | Or *transitional*, occurs when workers are temporarily unemployed while moving from one job to another |
| Search | A form of frictional unemployment when workers do not accept the first job offered but remain unemployed while searching for a better job |
| Causal | Another form of frictional unemployment when workers are unemployed in between short periods of employment |
| Seasonal | Those who are unemployed as a result of seasonal fluctuations in demand and/or changes in weather conditions |
| Structural | Those out of work because of a permanent decline in the demand for an industry's products |
| Regional | Those out of work are disproportionately concentrated in particular regions, largely as a result of these areas being dependent on declining industries |
| Technological | A form of structural unemployment due to the introduction of new automated methods of production |
| International | Those out of work due to a fall in demand for domestically produced goods |
| Cyclical | Or *mass* or *demand-deficient*: those out of work because of a lack of aggregate demand |
| Involuntary | Workers without a job who are willing and able to work at current wage rates |
| Voluntary | Workers without a job who prefer to live on benefits |

Figure 15.1 illustrates Keynes's explanation of unemployment caused by insufficient aggregate demand. At the full employment level of National Income ($Y_{fe}$), output is $J$, while aggregate monetary demand is only $K$. The *deflationary gap* of $J - K$ causes cyclical unemployment.

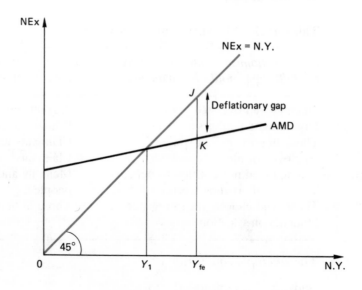

**Figure 15.1** A deflationary gap

### (d) The Natural Rate of Unemployment

A monetarist concept, the *natural rate of unemployment* (NRU) is the level of unemployment that is associated with a constant rate of inflation. At the NRU, the demand for labour is equal to the number of people prepared to supply their labour for the prevailing wage rate. Any unemployment is 'voluntary' and arises from labour market imperfections.

### (e) The Costs of Unemployment

These are influenced by the numbers unemployed and the length of time they are unemployed. They include:
  (i) Cost to the economy from lost production which can never be regained.
  (ii) Cost to the government in the form of:
      (1) lost revenue from, e.g., income tax, National Insurance contributions, VAT;
      (2) increased expenditure on unemployment and other benefits, special employment schemes, extra retirement redundancy payments in the public sector.
  (iii) Cost to the individual, usually in the form of:
      (1) decreased income;
      (2) loss of status, alienation and frustration;
      (3) reduced chance of regaining employment the longer unemployed.

### (f) Remedies for Unemployment

**Table 15.3**  Remedies for unemployment

| Type | Remedy |
| --- | --- |
| Frictional and search | May be reduced by improved vacancy information services and retraining |
| Causal and seasonal | Finding other activities during slack periods; employ students, retired people or work overtime during peak employment periods |
| Structural | Improve occupational mobility through retraining; import protection for declining industries |
| Regional and technological | Regional policies; retraining and import protection for particular industries |
| International | Lowering the exchange rate; imposing import controls |
| Cyclical | Increasing aggregate demand by expansionary fiscal and/or monetary policy. In addition, the Cambridge Economic Policy Group believe in imposing general import controls to ensure that rising demand goes on domestic goods and providing protection while UK industry is restructured |
| The natural rate of unemployment | Monetarists suggest supply-side policies widening the gap between unemployment and employment income by reducing direct taxes and unemployment benefits; reducing trade union power; and improving the mobility of labour |

## 15.2 Data Response

**Worked Example 15.1**

Seasonally adjusted annual averages

| Year | % change in RPI | % UK unemployment | UK unemployment (thousands) | Unfilled vacancies (thousands) |
|------|-----------------|-------------------|------------------------------|--------------------------------|
| 1983 | 4.9 | 10.8 | 2969.7 | 137.3 |
| 1984 | 5.1 | 11.1 | 3046.8 | 150.2 |
| 1985 | 5.0 | 11.3 | 3163.3 | 162.1 |
| 1986 | 5.5 | 11.5 | 3185.1 | 188.8 |

Sources: Adapted from the *Annual Abstract 1988* and the *Employment Gazettef1, January 1988.*

It is estimated that only about one-third of all vacancies are notified to job centres and that approximately one-quarter of all appointments are made through job centres.

In any period, some of the vacancies may be in different areas of the country from the areas in which the unemployed are, may require different skills and qualifications from those possessed by the unemployed, or may be for jobs which the unemployed are unwilling to do.

(a) Do the figures support the relationship between inflation and unemployment indicated by the Phillips curve? **(5 marks)**
(b) Explain how a fall in the inflation rate can reduce unemployment. **(5 marks)**
(c) Discuss the relationship between vacancies and unemployment in the period 1983–6. **(4 marks)**
(d) Why might the proportion of vacancies notified to job centres (i) increase or (ii) decrease during times of high unemployment? **(4 marks)**
(e) '. . . some of the vacancies . . . may be for jobs which the unemployed are unwilling to do'. What types of unemployment may this describe? **(2 marks)**

*Solution 15.1*

(a) The Phillips curve suggested that high inflation would be associated with low unemployment, and vice versa. It implied a trade-off relationship between inflation and unemployment. Between 1983 and 1984 both unemployment and inflation increased; between 1984 and 1985 inflation fell, while unemployment rose; and between 1985 and 1986 both again showed an increase. So, for most of the period, unemployment and inflation moved in the same direction, in contradiction of the Phillips curve.

(b) A fall in the inflation rate could make UK goods more competitive at home and abroad. If the UK inflation rate falls below that of the UK's main competitors, then demand for exports should rise, while demand for imports should fall. The extent to which unemployment will fall will depend on the original level of unemployment, how much output rises, the relative costs of labour and capital, and changes in technology.

(c) Between 1983 and 1986 both unemployment and vacancies rose, and the number of unemployed considerably exceeded the number of vacancies. The number of unemployed per vacancy fell throughout the period:

| Year | No. of unemployed per unfilled vacancy |
|------|----------------------------------------|
| 1983 | 21.6 |
| 1984 | 20.3 |
| 1985 | 19.5 |
| 1986 | 16.9 |

(d) During times of high unemployment, employers may be keener to notify vacancies to job centres, as they believe that people possessing higher skills and qualifications will be registered there. However, it is possible that a smaller proportion of vacancies may be notified, since employers may be able to fill vacancies relatively easily and quickly through, e.g., word of mouth, 'in-house' publications and newspaper advertisements.

(e) A situation where there are jobs available which the unemployed do not take up may describe voluntary or search unemployment. The former occurs when people are unwilling to work, and the latter occurs when people do not accept the first job offered but remain unemployed while seeking a better job.

# 15.3 Objective Questions

**Example 15.2**

Which group of workers is most likely to experience causal unemployment?
A   accountants      B   actors      C   chiropodists
D   teachers      E   undertakers

**Example 15.3**

As a result of a decrease in demand for blankets, several blanket mills are closed down and the workers are made redundant. This is a result of:
A   demand deficiency unemployment    B   seasonal unemployment
C   causal unemployment      D   residual unemployment
E   structural unemployment

**Example 15.4**

The natural rate of unemployment is the rate:
A   at which unemployment is zero
B   at which inflation is zero
C   at which inflation is constant
D   at which all unemployment is involuntary
E   below which it is impossible to lower unemployment, both in the short term and the long term, by increasing aggregate demand

**Example 15.5**

The government attempts to reduce cyclical unemployment by means of expansionary fiscal policy. The impact of the policy in lowering unemployment would be reduced by:
A   a high marginal propensity to consume
B   a high marginal propensity to import

**C**  a low marginal propensity to save
**D**  a low exchange rate
**E**  a low rate of real interest

## Example 15.6

Which of the following would increase a deflationary gap?
**A**  an increase in government spending
**B**  an increase in export revenue
**C**  an increase in savings
**D**  an increase in investment
**E**  a reduction in taxation

## Example 15.7

Which of the following conditions will ensure full employment in an economy?
**A**  a balanced budget
**B**  a balance of payments equilibrium
**C**  planned savings equalling planned investment
**D**  total leakages from the circular flow of income equalling total injections
**E**  none of the above

*Select your answers to Examples 15.8–15.10 by means of the following code:*
**A**  *if 1, 2 and 3 are all correct*
**B**  *if 1 and 2 only are correct*
**C**  *if 2 and 3 only are correct*
**D**  *if 1 only is correct*

## Example 15.8

An increase in which of the following would reduce the natural rate of unemployment?
**1**  labour mobility       **2**  unemployment benefit       **3**  government expenditure

## Example 15.9

Which of the following groups is/are included in the government's official unemployment figures?
**1**  unemployed men aged 60-plus
**2**  people who register for unemployment benefit but who are not actively seeking employment
**3**  people who are claiming benefit while working in the 'black economy'

## Example 15.10

Immobility of labour will tend to increase the duration of which of the following types of unemployment?
**1**  frictional                   **2**  structural                   **3**  regional

## 15.4  Essays

**Example 15.11**

'Increases in public expenditure lead to lower unemployment and eventually to a reduction in public expenditure; public expenditure cuts lead to higher unemployment and to increased public expenditure.' Critically discuss this statement.

(AEB June 1985)

- Discuss why a rise in public expenditure may be thought to be likely to increase employment and why some economists would argue that it may have the opposite effect.
- Discuss the initial and subsequent effects of changes in public expenditure.
- Consider how a rise in public expenditure may be financed.

*Solution 15.11*

Keynesians argue that a rise in public expenditure will cause N.Y. to rise by a multiple amount. Draw figure solution 12.29 diagram 1. As demand rises, output will increase. The initial rise in public expenditure on, e.g., roads should result in more people being employed, and the multiple rise in aggregate monetary demand and output should raise employment by a further and larger amount. However, unemployment will not fall if there was initially full employment, underemployed workers or changes in technology.

Even if an increase in public expenditure is financed by an equal rise in taxation, this will still cause a rise in N.Y. which should lead to higher employment. For instance, if the mpc is 0.75, then a rise in government spending of £100m and a rise in taxation of £100m will cause an initial net rise in spending of £25m (£100m government spending − £75m fall in spending resulting from the rise in taxation). This will cause a multiple rise in N.Y. of £25m × 4 = £100m.

As N.Y. increases and employment rises, public expenditure on unemployment and other benefits should fall. The initial rise in public expenditure will cause a rise in tax revenue in the longer term and a fall in public expenditure.

Cuts in public expenditure may be expected to have the opposite effects to those of an increase. The multiplier works in reverse. A fall in public expenditure, which is a reduction in an injection, will cause N.Y. to fall by a multiple amount. As demand decreases, output will be reduced. This is likely to result in a rise in unemployment, unless entrepreneurs believe that the decrease in demand is temporary and so hoard labour or employers were initially short of labour.

The rise in unemployment will reduce tax revenue and, unless the level of benefits is changed, will increase expenditure on unemployment and other benefits. Expenditure on special employment schemes may also increase and, if falling demand encourages students to stay on in education, there will be extra expenditure on education.

Monetarists would not entirely agree with this analysis. They argue that an increase in government spending may reduce unemployment in the short term. However, as entrepreneurs compete for factors of production and less efficient factors are employed, costs will rise and output will return to, or near, its previous level but at higher prices. Monetarists believe that a government is unable to reduce unemployment below the natural rate in the long term by increasing demand.

Indeed, some argue that increases in government spending may increase rather than decrease employment. If financed by increased taxation, then there will be a reduction in incentives for firms and workers. If financed by borrowing from the Bank of England or the banking sector, the money supply is likely to increase. Monetarists argue that this will cause a rise in prices, and, if it results in fewer home-produced goods being sold, unemployment may rise. They also believe that government borrowing can crowd out private-sector investment by taking a proportion of what they believe is a limited supply of funds available and by raising interest rates through the increased sale of government securities. If private-sector investment falls by more than the amount by which public expenditure rises, unemployment may rise.

Monetarists urge the reduction in the growth of public expenditure so that government borrowing and the growth of the money supply can be decreased. They believe that this will lower inflation, which, in turn, will increase international competitiveness and result in a rise in output and employment.

**Example 15.12**

Discuss the view that the official unemployment statistics in the United Kingdom are not an accurate reflection of the number of people unable to find work.

(L Jan. 1986)

- Discuss the official measures of unemployment.
- Discuss other possible measures.
- Consider why official figures may overstate and why they may understate the level of unemployment.

*Solution 15.12*

Unemployment arises when people willing and able to work in paid employment cannot find employment. In the UK, people are officially classified as unemployed if they are claiming benefits at unemployment benefit offices. One total commonly used is the seasonally adjusted total, excluding school-leavers. This includes registered unemployed, excluding those under 18 who have not entered employment since leaving school, and is adjusted to take out the effects of seasonal factors which result in unemployment being unusually high or low in certain months. Other totals are the unadjusted unemployment figure and the seasonally adjusted unemployment figure.

There is a debate as to how true a reflection official figures are of the number of people looking for a job. Until October 1982, the UK unemployment figures were based on the number of people who registered at job centres. There are a number of groups of people seeking employment who would have been included in the former measure but not the current one. These include married women who are seeking employment but, because they did not pay the full National Insurance contribution, are not entitled to unemployment benefit; unemployed men over 60 who are still seeking employment; those who choose not to register; students on vacation; and school-leavers seeking their first job.

Some countries measure unemployment by conducting surveys asking a sample of households how many of their members are seeking employment. This method would pick up groups not included in the UK official figures: for instance, discouraged workers — i.e. those who would like a job but have dropped out of the labour market. Some people may stay on in education, and married women may give up looking for work. Also, people in special employment schemes would be likely to state that they are seeking employment. There are a number of people in part-time employment who are seeking full-time employment, people who have taken early retirement and people past retirement age who would still like to work.

However, some economists argue that the official figures, far from understating the true level of unemployment, overstate the true level. They argue that some people who claim benefit are not really looking for work and are content to live on the benefits they receive. They also suggest that some of the official unemployed are actually working in the 'black economy' and not declaring their jobs or earnings. Some also urge that workers who are frictionally unemployed — that is, between jobs — should also be omitted from the figures.

Most economists believe that the official figures need to be analysed carefully. In addition to the total figure, consideration should be given to the inflow (those joining the figures), the outflow (those leaving the figures), the duration of time people are unemployed and the groups most affected by unemployment.

## 15.5 Solutions to Objective Questions

*Solution 15.2    Answer:* **B**

Causal unemployment occurs when workers who are usually employed on a short-term basis are laid off. Actors are frequently 'resting' — i.e. unemployed between roles. Accountants, chiropodists, teachers and undertakers are usually employed on a more regular and long-term basis than are actors.

*Solution 15.3    Answer:* **E**

This is an example of unemployment arising from an industry experiencing a decline in demand for its products, which is structural unemployment. Demand-deficiency unemployment arises as a result of a lack of aggregate demand, seasonal owing to changes in demand occurring at particular times of the year and when weather conditions prevent production. Causal unemployment occurs when there are irregular layoffs, and residual unemployment refers to those people who would be likely to be unemployed even when demand is high.

*Solution 15.4    Answer:* **C**

According to monetarists, the natural rate of unemployment is when inflation is stable but not necessarily zero.

    **A** $\Rightarrow$ At the natural rate, there is likely to be some unemployment in the form of those who are not prepared to work at that wage rate and people in between jobs.

    **D** $\Rightarrow$ Monetarists argue that the unemployment above the natural rate is voluntary and not involuntary.

    **E** $\Rightarrow$ Monetarists believe that, while it is not possible to reduce unemployment below the natural rate in the long term by increasing demand, it is possible to do so in the short term but only at the expense of accelerating inflation.

*Solution 15.5    Answer:* **B**

Cyclical unemployment arises from a lack of aggregate demand. Expansionary fiscal policy will increase demand. However, a high mpm will mean that a significant proportion of the extra demand will create increased employment abroad rather than at home.

229

**A, C, D, E** ⇒ Are all likely to mean that a high proportion of the extra demand generated will be spent on domestic output. A high mpc means that a high proportion of extra income will be spent. A low mps means, and a low rate of interest suggests, that a small proportion of extra income will be saved and, hence, a high proportion spent. A low exchange rate will mean that the price of imports is high while the price of exports is low, so not much of the extra demand will be spent on foreign goods and services.

*Solution 15.6   Answer:* **C**

A deflationary gap exists when aggregate monetary demand is below the level required to ensure full employment — people demand fewer goods and services than the labour force could produce.

**A, B, D, E** ⇒ Would all tend to increase demand for domestic goods and services and, hence, reduce the gap.

**C** ⇒ An increase in savings would reduce demand and increase a deflationary gap.

*Solution 15.7   Answer:* **E**

None of the conditions will ensure full employment.

**A, B, C** ⇒ Are each only part of the composition of aggregate demand.

**D** ⇒ Will mean that the economy is in equilibrium, but Keynes argued that an economy can be in equilibrium at any level of employment and not necessarily at the full-employment level. Indeed, without planning, it would be very unlikely to be at this level.

*Solution 15.8   Answer:* **D**

Monetarists believe that the level of employment and, hence, unemployment is determined by the demand for and supply of labour. They think that the natural rate of unemployment would be reduced by anything which increases the supply of and/or the demand for labour at the equilibrium wage rate. An increase in labour mobility will result in people moving more quickly from job to job, increasing the supply of labour and so reducing frictional unemployment.

**2** ⇒ They think that an increase in unemployment benefit would reduce the supply of labour by increasing voluntary unemployment.

**3** ⇒ Monetarists believe that, although increased government spending may raise demand for labour in the short term, in the long term it will succeed only in causing an acceleration in the inflation rate, while unemployment will return to the natural rate.

*Solution 15.9   Answer:* **C**

While many would agree that those who are not actively seeking employment and those working in the black economy are not really unemployed, if they register, they will be counted. Indeed, it is difficult to assess which claimants are looking for work and who may be illegally claiming benefit.

*Solution 15.10   Answer:* **A**

Immobility will increase the duration of all the types of unemployment mentioned, since, in every case, limits on a person's ability to move to another area or to another occupation would reduce his/her chances of finding another job quickly.

# 16 Inflation

## 16.1 Fact Sheet

### (a) Definition of Inflation

*Inflation* is a persistent rise in the general price level and, hence, a sustained fall in the value of money.

- *Creeping inflation* is a low rate of inflation.
- *Hyperinflation* is a very high rate of inflation which can cause major economic problems and political instability.
- *Stagflation* is a situation of high inflation and high unemployment.
- *Slumpflation* occurs when there is high inflation, high unemployment and negative growth.

### (b) Measuring Inflation

(i) The *Retail Price Index* (RPI) is the most widely used index of general consumer prices.

(ii) The *Tax and Price Index* (TPI) measures average household purchasing power, including the effects of changes in indirect taxes as well as prices.

(iii) *Producer Price Indices* (PPI) measure changes in material and product prices, and give an indication of the future trend of retail prices.

(iv) *Pensioners' Retail Price Index* (PRPI) indicates price changes in goods and services purchased by the retired.

(v) The *GDP deflator* is the most widely used index of general prices for both consumers and producers.

- These measures are *weighted* indices, which means that particular importance is attached to items which form a large proportion of expenditure or output.

### (c) Cost Push Inflation

*Cost push* inflation occurs when a cost of production (e.g. wages) increases and firms put up prices to maintain profits. Causes of cost push inflation include:

(i) Wage increases which may result from:

    (1) a *wage–price spiral*, when wage increases raise prices, thereby encouraging further wage demands, etc.;

    (2) a *wage–wage spiral*, when a wage increase in one industry sets off a series of wage claims in other industries so as to maintain differentials.

(ii) *Imported inflation* from overseas increases in the prices of goods imported into the UK.

(iii) An increase in the price of imports as a result of a depreciation of sterling. See Section 19.1(a).

### (d) Demand Pull Inflation

*Demand pull* inflation occurs when aggregate demand exceeds aggregate supply. In Figure 16.1, an increase in a component of aggregate monetary demand (AMD) means that total demand ($J$) exceeds the full employment value of output ($K$). An *inflationary gap* of $J-K$ results.

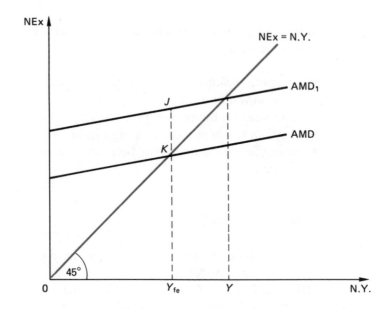

**Figure 16.1** An inflationary gap

Monetarists argue that, if the growth of the money supply exceeds the growth of output, prices will eventually rise. Fisher's *Quantity Theory of Money* states:

$$MV = PT$$

where $M$ is the money supply; $V$ is the velocity of circulation (i.e. the number of times one unit of currency changes hands); $P$ is average prices; and $T$ is the number of transactions (goods bought).

- Monetarists assert that $V$ and $T$ are constant in the short term. Any increase in $M$ must necessarily increase $P$.
- However, Keynesians argue that at less than full employment an increase in $M$ causes an increase in $T$, as more output is made, leaving prices unchanged. $V$ rises in times of boom and falls during depressions.

### (e) The Effects of Inflation

- Low inflation may stimulate investment if prices are increased before wages rise.

The costs of inflation include:
- (i) *Shoe leather costs* The high opportunity cost of holding money means people hold lower money balances and make frequent journeys to banks, building societies, etc.
- (ii) *Menu costs*, as a result of changing price tags, slot machines, etc.
- (iii) *Fiscal drag* occurs when people's money income rises, dragging them into higher tax brackets. A higher percentage of real income is paid in tax.
- (iv) Uncertainty may reduce investment and increase the resources devoted to planning.
- (v) The Balance of Payments will be adversely affected if the country's inflation rate is higher than that of competitors and there are no offsetting exchange rate changes.
- (vi) Labour unrest may occur as workers seek wage rises to maintain real income.
- (vii) Expectations of inflation may arise, further fuelling inflation.
- (viii) *Money illusion* may occur where people confuse changes in nominal balances with changes in real balances.
- (ix) Arbitrary redistribution of income and wealth may occur, as shown in Table 16.1.

**Table 16.1** Redistribution of income through inflation

| From | To |
| --- | --- |
| Taxpayers | The government |
| Holders of the National Debt | The government |
| Savers | Borrowers |
| Creditors | Debtors |
| Workers in weak trade unions, non-unionised labour and those on fixed incomes | Those who can raise their incomes by more than the rate of inflation |
| Domestic producers | Foreign producers with lower inflation rates |

### (f) Methods of Adapting to Inflation

- (i) Firms and households may include *indexation* in contracts, automatically adjusting prices and wages to the inflation rate.
- (ii) Firms may use *inflation accounting* and adjust costs, revenue, value of stock, etc., in line with inflation.

### (g) Remedies for Inflation

The measures taken to cure inflation depend on whether price increases are caused by demand pull or cost push factors.
- (i) Demand pull inflation remedies:
    - (1) deflationary fiscal policy, where increased taxes and/or reduced government spending lowers aggregate demand;
    - (2) deflationary monetary policy, where reducing the growth of the money supply and/or raising the rate of interest lowers demand;
    - (3) stimulating output by improved productivity, labour relations, etc.

(ii) Cost push inflation remedies:
  (1) imposing *prices and incomes policies* to freeze price and income increases — the wage–price and wage–wage spirals are broken;
  (2) subsidising production, to reduce costs;
  (3) reducing indirect taxes, to reduce prices;
  (4) raising the exchange rate, to reduce the cost of imported materials and components and to force domestic producers and exporters to remain competitive with foreign producers.

## (h) Inflation and Unemployment

(i) The *Phillips curve* implies a trade-off relationship between inflation and unemployment. For instance, in Figure 16.2 the percentage change in money wages is high when unemployment is low.

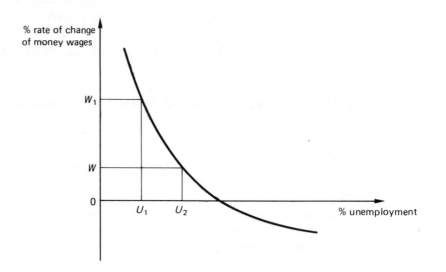

**Figure 16.2** The Phillips curve

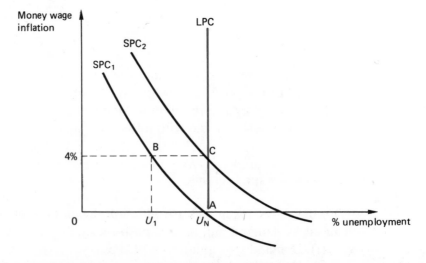

**Figure 16.3** An expectations-augmented Phillips curve. $SPC_1$ and $SPC_2$ are short-term Phillips curves. LPC is the long-term Phillips curve at the NRU. Economy initially on $SPC_1$ curve at $U_N$ at point A. Government reduces unemployment to $U_1$ by increasing demand. This causes prices and wages to rise. Move to point B. Higher wages and costs result in a rise in unemployment to $U_N$ but at a higher expected rate of inflation on $SPC_2$. Move to point C

(ii) The *expectations-augmented Phillips curve* reflects the monetarist view that there is no long-term inflation–unemployment trade-off. Any attempt to reduce unemployment below the natural rate will only succeed in accelerating the rate of inflation (see Figure 16.3).

(iii) The *Rational Expectations Hypothesis* suggests that there is no long-term or short-term trade-off. Supporters argue that people base their actions on past experiences of inflation and their expectations of current and future government policies. On average, they correctly forecast the results of current economic events and policies, and do not suffer from money illusion.

# 16.2 Data Response

**Worked Example 16.1**

'Unemployment seems to be an unavoidable side effect of curing inflation, just as going to bed is of an operation, and there are many policies that simultaneously add to unemployment and inflation, just as staying in bed may produce illness (though not appendicitis). I know of no example of a country that has cured substantial inflation without going through a transitional period of slow growth and unemployment. I know of no example of a country that has experienced accelerating inflation without running into serious economic difficulties. Japan, Great Britain, Chile and Brazil illustrate both propositions. All got into serious economic difficulties as a side effect of accelerating inflation. All went through a transitional period of slow growth and unemployment in curing — or at least reducing — inflation.

Why is unemployment a side effect of curing inflation? Because a cure changes the economic environment in ways that were not widely anticipated by the economic actors and that they misinterpret. The only cure for inflation is to reduce the rate at which total spending is growing.'

Source: M. Friedman, condensed from *Newsweek*, 12 November 1979

(a) How might 'accelerating inflation' result in 'serious economic difficulties'?
**(6 marks)**

(b) Why does the author consider that 'slow growth and unemployment' are necessary in alleviating inflation? **(7 marks)**

(c) The author states that 'the only cure for inflation is to reduce the rate at which total spending is growing'. Discuss other policies that might be adopted to cure inflation. **(7 marks)**

(L June 1986)

*Solution 16.1*

(a) Accelerating inflation can result in a number of problems. Rising inflation will reduce a country's international competitiveness and is likely to result in a deterioration in its current account position. Output and employment may fall if more goods are bought from foreign rather than domestic producers. There may be a reduction in capital inflows if inflation reduces the real rate of interest below that prevailing in other countries. There will be an arbitrary redistribution of income, and labour unrest may arise due to the need to press for wage rises to maintain living standards. Inflation will impose a number of costs on individuals and firms. People will have to spend time estimating future inflation, and firms will have to change their prices and the value of their assets and stocks on a regular basis. If hyperinflation occurs, confidence in the currency will decrease and there may be political and economic instability.

(b) Milton Friedman and other monetarists believe that inflation is caused by an excessive growth of the money supply and expectations of inflation. To reduce inflation, they urge a reduction in the rate of monetary growth. There is some dispute among monetarists as to whether the reduction in the rate of monetary expansion should be gradual or sharp. However, all accept that the initial effect of reducing the growth of the money supply is likely to be a sharp rise in the level of unemployment above the natural rate, as the fall in output precedes the fall in inflation.

When the government reduces the growth of the money supply, prices will initially rise faster than the nominal money supply. This will cause a fall in aggregate demand, a reduction in output and a rise in involuntary unemployment. When workers are convinced that the government will maintain a tight monetary policy and that inflation will fall, they will ask for lower increases in money wages. The rise in unemployment will also exert downward pressure on wages. How long and how high unemployment rises will depend mainly on how fast wages adjust. If workers are prepared to accept a drop in living standards for a while, then they will price themselves back into work relatively quickly. However, if workers are resistant or misinterpret the 'changes in the economic environment', unemployment may continue at a level above the natural rate for some time.

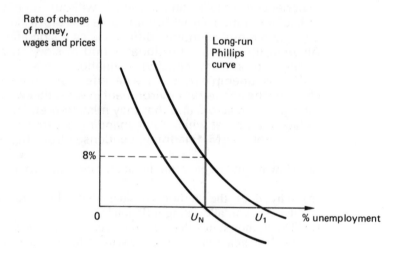

The diagram shows that initially the economy is experiencing 8% inflation and unemployment is at the natural rate of $U_N$. To eliminate inflation and inflationary expectations, unemployment would have to rise to $U_1$.

(c) The policies which will be adopted to cure inflation will depend on what is believed to be the cause of inflation and views on the effectiveness of the policies. Economists who consider that inflation results from increases in costs of production may urge the implementation of a prices and incomes policy. They argue that this will reduce price rises while avoiding the adverse effects of deflationary policies — in particular, rises in unemployment. Economists who consider that inflation has resulted from demand exceeding supply may urge a reduction in demand. This could be achieved by deflationary fiscal and/or monetary policy. The article refers to reducing the growth of spending. This could be achieved by reducing government spending, increasing taxation, reducing the growth of the money supply or raising interest rates. An alternative to reducing demand is increasing output. This will only be a viable policy if the economy is below the full-employment level. A rise in the exchange rate may also be employed to reduce inflationary pressures. The fall in import prices will lower the cost of finished imported goods, some UK producers' costs of production and possibly wage claims. The lower import prices may also increase pressure on domestic producers to keep their prices low in order to remain competitive at home and abroad.

# 16.3  Objective Questions

**Example 16.2**

The weights in the retail price index indicate:
A   which goods have risen by more than the average rise in prices
B   by how much the prices of goods have changed
C   the relative amount spent on each category of good
D   that each item has been given an index number of 100 in the base year
E   seasonal fluctuations in price

**Example 16.3**

The following information shows a country's consumer expenditure pattern on four goods and the price indices of these commodities for two years.

| Commodity | Index of prices in year 1 | Index of prices in year 2 | Consumers' expenditure (£ million) in year 1 |
|-----------|-----------|-----------|-----------|
| W | 100 | 80 | 300 |
| X | 100 | 110 | 200 |
| Y | 100 | 120 | 100 |
| Z | 100 | 150 | 400 |

Between years 1 and 2 the general level of prices has:
A   remained the same       B   risen by 4.5%       C   risen by 12%
D   risen by 18%            E   risen by 60%

**Example 16.4**

Which of the following groups is most likely to benefit from a period of higher than anticipated inflation?
A   standard-rate taxpayers
B   people claiming unemployment benefit
C   creditors
D   non-unionised labour
E   the government

**Example 16.5**

Demand pull inflation may initially be caused by:
A   an increase in bank credit
B   an increase in profit margins

**C**　an increase in wages
**D**　an increase in the price of imported raw materials
**E**　an increase in rent


## Example 16.6

An inflationary gap is said to exist when:
**A**　aggregate demand is greater than the full-employment level of National Income
**B**　visible exports exceed visible imports
**C**　leakages exceed injections at the full-employment level of National Income
**D**　government spending exceeds government revenue
**E**　the full-employment level of National Income exceeds the equilibrium level of National Income


## Example 16.7

In conditions of full employment, which of the following would be most likely to lead to inflation?
**A**　a rise in the expenditure on imports
**B**　an increase in income tax
**C**　a reduction in government expenditure
**D**　an increase in labour productivity
**E**　a rise in demand for exports


## Example 16.8

If a government believes that inflation is the result of cost push factors and it wishes to reduce inflation, which of the following measures is it most likely to adopt?
**A**　an increase in income tax
**B**　a reduction in government expenditure
**C**　a rise in interest rates
**D**　a reduction in the growth of the money supply
**E**　the imposition of a prices and incomes policy


## Example 16.9

In year 1, an economy has a money supply of £400 and a velocity of circulation of 6, and it produces 800 goods. In year 2 the velocity of circulation and the level of output remain constant, but the money supply increases to £600. According to the quantity theory, this will cause the price level to rise by:
**A**　$£1\frac{1}{2}$　　　**B**　£3　　　**C**　$£4\frac{1}{2}$　　　**D**　£6　　　**E**　£10


## Example 16.10

In the diagram opposite, $U_N$ is the natural rate of unemployment, $SPC_1$, $SPC_2$, $SPC_3$ and $SPC_4$ are short-run Phillips curves associated with successively higher levels of inflationary expectations, and LPC is the long-run, vertical Phillips curve. If inflationary expectations are at 6% and a government wishes to eliminate wage inflation, it would have to permit unemployment in the short run to change to:
**A**　$U_1$　　　**B**　$U_2$　　　**C**　$U_3$　　　**D**　$U_4$　　　**E**　$U_5$

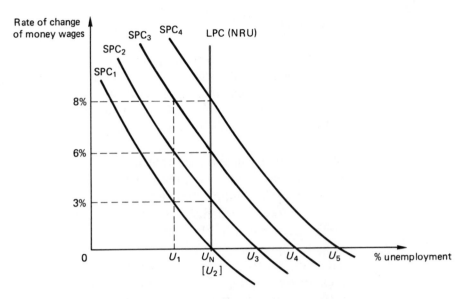

*Select your answers to Examples 16.11, 16.12 by means of the following code*:

**A** *if 1, 2 and 3 are all correct*
**B** *if 1 and 2 only are correct*
**C** *if 2 and 3 only are correct*
**D** *if 1 only is correct*

### Example 16.11

Which of the following must occur as a result of inflation?
1 debtors will gain and creditors will lose
2 the volume of exports will decline
3 the domestic purchasing power of the currency will decline

### Example 16.12

Which of the following may result in inflationary pressure in an economy with full employment?
1 an increase in the budget deficit
2 an increase in government spending matched by an equal increase in taxation
3 an increase in the current account deficit

## 16.4 Essays

### Example 16.13

Analyse the proposition that the United Kingdom government cannot avoid eventually introducing a formal prices and incomes policy for the whole economy
(OLE 1985)

- Define a prices and incomes policy and consider its main purpose.
- Consider the causes of inflation.
- Discuss different views on the need for a prices and incomes policy.

*Solution 16.13*

A formal prices and incomes policy is a deliberate government measure to influence prices and incomes. An incomes policy may be introduced for a number of purposes, including reducing poverty and establishing equal pay. However, the most common form of incomes policy, particularly when combined with a prices policy, is to reduce rises in incomes in an attempt to lower inflation.

Monetarists reject the idea that inflation is caused by cost push factors, and most dislike prices and incomes policies, not only because they believe they are an inappropriate solution, but also because they consider that they interfere with the free market mechanism. Government intervention in pricing and factor income decisions will, they argue, reduce efficiency and result in a fall in aggregate supply.

The monetarists believe that rises in money incomes are the result rather than the cause of inflation. They believe that inflation is of a demand pull nature resulting from an excessive growth of the money supply. They argue that large public-sector borrowing requirements have been financed partly by increasing the money supply, and that this has led to a rise in demand and a rise in prices. Their solution to inflation is to control the money supply.

However, some monetarists would favour, during times of high inflation, indexation of wages, and possibly some other incomes and prices, in order to reduce expectations of inflation. Some would also acknowledge that the government may wish to restrict public-sector pay settlements, to avoid a growth of the PSBR and to encourage low rises in incomes to avoid inflation accelerating.

Most Keynesians believe that inflation is the result of cost push factors, including wage rises and increases in the cost of raw materials and fuel. Workers are now concerned with real wages, so that, for instance, a rise in import prices may provoke wage claims to restore workers' living standards. Workers are also very concerned about their differentials and there is often a wage–wage spiral.

However, not all economists who believe that inflation is caused by cost push would advocate a prices and incomes policy. Rises in incomes and prices may be reduced by other measures, including deflation and raising the value of the exchange rate. For instance, reducing government expenditure, which causes unemployment to rise, is likely to result in a reduction in wage claims.

Although one advantage claimed for a prices and incomes policy is that it enables inflation to be reduced without raising unemployment, there are a number of problems associated with a prices and incomes policy. As there are millions of prices, they are difficult to monitor, and new products, seasonal food and imports may pose problems. Entrepreneurs will probably try to find ways round controls by, e.g., quality deterioration or by reducing quantity or weight. They will also probably be asked to be made exceptions because of, e.g., rises in raw material costs.

Similar problems arise with incomes policies. Exceptions will be claimed on the grounds of low pay, productivity, labour shortages and comparability. There will be a conflict of interest between high-paid workers, who will favour percentage increases, and low-paid workers, who will favour flat-rate pay increases. Unions and employers will find ways round the policy — e.g. fringe benefits, upgrading and overtime — and, once an incomes policy is removed, incomes may rise significantly.

The main motive behind introducing a prices and incomes policy would be to reduce inflation. A government will not be obliged to introduce such a policy if inflation is not a problem. A government faced with the problem of inflation will also not implement a formal prices and incomes policy if it can lower price and income rises by persuasion or other means or if it believes that inflation is caused by other factors and/or that prices and incomes policies will be ineffective and will result in market distortions.

**Example 16.14**

Is inflation only harmful if it is at a rate above that prevailing in other countries?

- Consider the effects of inflation on a country's external position.
- Also consider the effects on a country's internal position.

*Solution 16.14*

Inflation, which is a persistent rise in the general price level, may have detrimental effects, not only externally, but also internally. The internal effects can occur even if the country has a lower inflation rate than that of other countries.

If the UK's inflation rate is higher than that of other countries, then the UK's products will become less competitive both at home and abroad. This is likely to result in a fall in export revenue and a rise in import expenditure. Investment in the UK may be discouraged. So there is likely to be an adverse effect on the UK's balance of payments position and employment. It may also result in a fall in the exchange rate, which will accelerate inflation.

Inflation, especially if it is above a creeping level, will also probably be undesirable, because of the internal effects. Inflation will affect the distribution of income, and this can create social tension. For instance, unions will have to press for wage rises merely to keep pace with inflation — i.e. to maintain real wages. Members of weak unions — e.g. USDAW — are more likely to suffer a decline in real wages than are members of strong unions.

The effects of inflation can be alleviated by index linking wages and or benefits. However, if, e.g., unemployment benefit is not raised in line with inflation, then the unemployed will experience a fall in their real living standards. In contrast, house owners may benefit, since the value of their property is likely to rise by more than the rate of inflation, while the real cost of their mortgage payments is likely to fall.

Creditors may suffer and debtors may gain if the rate of interest does not rise in line with inflation. Fiscal drag may occur, although the government could eliminate this effect by adjusting tax brackets in line with inflation.

There will be costs involved in living with inflation. Firms will incur menu costs, having to adjust prices regularly, and time and effort may have to be taken in estimating future inflation. Firms and individuals may also experience shoe leather costs.

Government measures to reduce inflation may have an adverse effect on other economic objectives, particularly growth and full employment. Deflationary monetary policy and fiscal policy will reduce demand and, hence, tend to result in lower output and employment, at least in the short term.

One possible advantage of inflation may arise if it is at a low level and is of a demand pull nature. This is because a situation where demand exceeds supply may make entrepreneurs optimistic about the potential returns which can be earned from expanding output.

However, inflation, particularly of a high level, will have effects within a country as well as on its competitive position abroad. While it is possible to alleviate some of the internal effects, some may cause inconvenience, disruption and possibly hardships. For a number of countries, including the UK, a reduction in international competitiveness will be significant, but it is not the only adverse effect which the country may suffer as a result of inflation.

## 16.5 Solutions to Objective Questions

*Solution 16.2 Answer:* **C**

The index of retail prices is a weighted price index. This means that the price changes of different categories of goods are multiplied by weights. These weights indicate what proportion of consumer expenditure is devoted to the different categories. For instance if, out of a total expenditure of £100m, £30m is spent on food, then food will receive a weighting of 3/10.

*Solution 16.3 Answer:* **D**

To determine the change in the general price level, it is necessary to multiply the price change of each commodity by its weighting. The total of the weighted price changes gives the answer.

| Commodity | Weight | | Price change | Weighted price change |
|---|---|---|---|---|
| W | $\dfrac{3}{10}$ | $\times$ | $\dfrac{20}{1}$ | $= -6\%$ |
| X | $\dfrac{2}{10}$ | $\times$ | $\dfrac{10}{1}$ | $= 2\%$ |
| Y | $\dfrac{1}{10}$ | $\times$ | $\dfrac{20}{1}$ | $= 2\%$ |
| Z | $\dfrac{4}{10}$ | $\times$ | $\dfrac{50}{1}$ | $= 20\%$ |
| | | | | $\overline{18\%}$ |

*Solution 16.4 Answer:* **E**

The government is a net debtor and so is likely to have to pay lower real interest. The government may also raise more revenue if fiscal drag occurs. Other options are incorrect.

A and B $\Rightarrow$ Standard-rate taxpayers and the unemployed will experience a fall in living standards if tax rates and benefits are not adjusted in line with inflation or if there is a lagged response. Even if fiscal drag is avoided and unemployment benefits are raised in line with inflation, the two groups will not be better off, merely no worse off.

C $\Rightarrow$ Creditors are likely to lose during a period of higher than anticipated inflation, since the real rate of interest is likely to fall.

D $\Rightarrow$ Similarly, non-unionised labour is likely to suffer, since it will be in a weak position to maintain real wages.

*Solution 16.5   Answer:* **A**

An increase in bank credit will mean that firms and consumers will have more to spend and the resulting increase in demand may result in demand pull inflation.

**B, C, D, E** ⇒ Are likely to increase costs of production and so might result in cost push inflation.

*Solution 16.6   Answer:* **A**

An inflationary gap occurs when aggregate demand is greater than the output which can be produced when there is full employment.

**B** ⇒ Describes a balance of trade gap.

**C** and **E** ⇒ Describe a deflationary gap.

**D** ⇒ Describes a budget deficit.

*Solution 16.7   Answer:* **E**

An increase in demand for exports will mean more money coming into the country while goods are going out. Thus, there will be more money and fewer goods to spend it on. With full employment, it will be difficult to produce more goods and an inflationary gap is likely to develop, with demand exceeding supply.

**A, B, C** ⇒ Would all reduce demand and, hence, inflationary pressure.

**D** ⇒ Would result in more goods being available and, assuming no increase in wages, a fall in the inflation rate.

*Solution 16.8   Answer:* **E**

Cost push inflation arises when prices are pushed up by increases in the costs of production, such as wages. One possible solution is a prices and incomes policy which aims to limit rises in prices and incomes while avoiding deflation. All the other measures mentioned are designed to reduce demand — **A** and **B** by fiscal measures and **C** and **D** by monetary measures — and so would be more likely to be implemented if it was believed that the inflation was caused by demand pull.

*Solution 16.9   Answer:* **A**

The Quantity Theory is represented by the formula $MV = PT$ or $P = MV/T$. In year 1, the price level is:

$$P = MV/T = 400 \times 6/800 = 2400/800 = £3$$

In year 2, the price level is:
$$P = MV/T = 600 \times 6/800 = 3600/800 = £4\tfrac{1}{2}$$

So the price level has risen from £3 to £4½ — i.e. by £1½. The money supply increases by 50%, causing a 50% rise in the price level.

*Solution 16.10   Answer:* **D**

If inflationary expectations are at 6%, the economy is on Phillips curve $PC_3$. On this curve, $U_4$ is the rate of unemployment that will reduce the rate of change of money wages to zero, since $U_4$ is where $PC_3$ cuts the zero percentage rate of change of money wages line. In the long term, when the expected rate of inflation equals the actual rate of inflation, unemployment will return to the natural rate of $U_N$.

*Solution 16.11   Answer:* **D**

If prices rise, each unit of currency (e.g. each £1) will be able to buy fewer goods and services.

**2** and **3** $\Rightarrow$ May occur but will not necessarily occur. Debtors will gain and creditors will lose if the inflation rate exceeds the rate of interest — i.e. if there is negative rate of interest. However, the rate of interest may rise in line with inflation and even possibly above it. Whether the volume of exports decreases or not will depend on a number of factors, including the inflation rate experienced in other countries. Indeed, if the home country's inflation rate is below that of rival countries, her exports will become more and not less competitive.

*Solution 16.12   Answer:* **B**

**1** $\Rightarrow$ An increase in the budget deficit will represent an injection of spending into the economy, which, if it cannot be matched by a rise in output, may result in a rise in prices.

**2** $\Rightarrow$ An increase in government spending matched by an equal increase in taxation will cause N.Y. to rise, since the recipients of government spending will be likely to have a higher mpc than taxpayers.

**3** $\Rightarrow$ An increase in a current account deficit may reduce inflationary pressure, since it will mean an inflow of goods and services and an outflow of money.

# 17 International Trade

## 17.1 Fact Sheet

### (a) Problems of International Trade

*International trade* is the exchange of goods and services between countries.
Problems arise over:
- (i) currencies;
- (ii) language;
- (iii) distance;
- (iv) customs/tastes;
- (v) foreign competition;
- (vi) import restrictions;
- (vii) legal and technical regulations;
- (viii) possible delays in payment.

### (b) Benefits of International Trade

- (i) A greater variety of goods for consumers.
- (ii) A larger market allows domestic producers greater scope for economies of scale.
- (iii) An opportunity to obtain goods which the country cannot produce itself. This accounts for a very small percentage of the goods the UK imports.
- (iv) Consumers' welfare may increase as a result of lower prices resulting from international competition.
- (v) Trade with other countries may lead to the spread of technology.
- (vi) International specialisation raises output.

### (c) Absolute and Comparative Advantage

The main advantage claimed for international trade is higher world output. The theories of absolute advantage and comparative advantage explain how output may be increased by specialisation and trade.

- *Absolute advantage* exists when a country can produce more of a product per resource unit than another country.
- *Comparative advantage* exists when a country can produce a product at a lower opportunity cost than its trading partners.

**Table 17.1** An example of comparative advantage

| Country | Monthly output per resource unit | |
| --- | --- | --- |
| | cars | boats |
| A | 2 | 4 |
| B | 4 | 10 |

While country B has an absolute advantage in the production of both goods, A has a comparative advantage in the production of cars. A sacrifices only 2 boats for 1 extra car (4 boats/2 cars), while B has to forgo $2\frac{1}{2}$ cars (10 boats/4 cars).

### (d) Costs of International Trade

  (i) *Infant industries* may not be able to become established if faced with competition from foreign companies with lower costs due to greater economies of scale.

 (ii) *Declining industries* may decline rapidly, causing a significant rise in unemployment.

(iii) Foreign producers may engage in *dumping* (i.e. selling surplus output at a low price, even sometimes below average cost) in the home market.

(iv) A country may become dependent on other nations for products — e.g. weapons, food — which may be cut off during periods of dispute or war.

 (v) A country may experience the disadvantages of overspecialisation, including diseconomies of scale, vulnerability to sudden changes in demand and unemployment.

### (e) Pattern of UK International Trade

The UK is a major trading country, importing and exporting mainly manufactured goods from and to mainly developed countries.

**Table 17.2** The UK's main trading partners in 1986

| | Most important sources of UK imports | Most important recipients of UK exports |
| --- | --- | --- |
| 1 | West Germany | USA |
| 2 | USA | West Germany |
| 3 | France | France |
| 4 | Netherlands | Netherlands |
| 5 | Japan | Belgium and Luxembourg |
| 6 | Italy | Irish Republic |
| 7 | Belgium and Luxembourg | Italy |
| 8 | Norway | Sweden |
| 9 | Irish Republic | Spain |
| 10 | Switzerland | Canada |

Source: *Monthly Digest of Statistics*, January 1988

## (f) Protectionism

*Protectionism* protects domestic industries from foreign competition by means of tariffs and non-tariff barriers. The main forms of restrictions are:
- (i) *Tariffs* (also called customs duties), which are a tax on imported goods. This is the most common form of restriction. In addition to protecting domestic industries, tariffs may be imposed to raise revenue.
- (ii) *Quotas* are limits on the quantity of a commodity which is allowed to enter the country.
- (iii) *Exchange control* occurs when a government controls the availability of foreign currency. This often involves a limit on the foreign exchange available to importers.
- (iv) *Physical control* occurs when a ban is placed on the export or import of a certain good or on trade with a particular country or countries.
- (v) *Subsidies* act as a form of import restriction by lowering the price of home-produced goods and, hence, making imports less competitive.

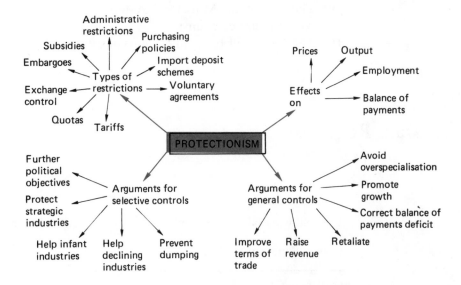

**Figure 17.1** Types of, effects of and reasons for import restrictions

## (g) Regional Economic Groupings

There are two main types of groupings:
- (i) A *free trade area* is a group of countries which removes tariff barriers between member countries but allows each member to decide on its own tariff policy towards non-members. For instance, the European Free Trade Area (EFTA).
- (ii) A *customs union*, which, in addition to removing tariffs between members, also imposes common external tariffs on non-members. For instance, the European Economic Community (EEC).

## (h) The European Economic Community

The EEC was established in 1957 by France, West Germany, Belgium and The Netherlands. It currently has 12 members. Its main policies include:

247

(i) The *Common Agricultural Policy* (CAP), which has the following main aims:
   (1) to increase agricultural productivity;
   (2) to ensure a fair standard of living for the agricultural community;
   (3) to stabilise markets through price intervention (see Figure 3.3);
   (4) to ensure the availability of supplies to consumers at reasonable prices.

   While most would agree that the EEC has been successful with the first two aims it has not achieved (3) and (4). The high support prices have resulted in large surpluses and considerable expenditure. CAP usually takes up 60% of the EEC budget.

(ii) Energy policy, which has the following main aims:
   (1) to control the consumption of energy resources;
   (2) to increase the Community's coal production;
   (3) to increase the use of solid fuels and nuclear power.

(iii) Regional policy: the EEC Regional Development Fund assists regional development areas in member countries.

(iv) The European Monetary System seeks to stabilise exchange rates between member countries.

(v) The EEC will be a single market after 1992, with no trade barriers.

# 17.2 Data Response

## Example 17.1

The following table shows imports as a percentage of home demand.

Import Penetration

| Imports/home demand | 1982 (%) | 1983 (%) | 1984 (%) | 1985 (%) | 1986 (%) |
|---|---|---|---|---|---|
| Manufacturing industries | 29.0 | 31.1 | 33.4 | 34.3 | 34.3 |
| Class: | | | | | |
| Metals | 33 | 36 | 43 | 45 | 48 |
| Chemicals and man-made fibres | 34 | 36 | 39 | 41 | 41 |
| Motor vehicles and their parts | 47 | 52 | 51 | 50 | 51 |
| Food, drink and tobacco | 16 | 17 | 18 | 18 | 18 |
| Textile industry | 39 | 41 | 44 | 44 | 45 |
| Paper, printing and publishing | 19 | 20 | 21 | 21 | 21 |

Source: Adapted from *Annual Abstract of Statistics* (HMSO), 1988

(a) Which industries experienced higher than average import penetration and which ones experienced lower than average import penetration throughout the time period shown? **(3 marks)**

(b) In which industry was the growth in import penetration greatest in percentage terms between 1982 and 1986? **(2 marks)**

(c) What may have caused the increase in import penetration between 1982 and 1986? **(5 marks)**

(d) Briefly describe four types of import restrictions which a government could impose or increase to reduce import penetration. **(5 marks)**

(e) What other measures, apart from import restrictions, could a government take to reduce import penetration? **(5 marks)**

*Solution 17.1*

(a) Metals, chemicals and man-made fibres, motor vehicles and their parts and the textile industry all experienced higher import penetration than the average for manufacturing industries. Food, drink and tobacco, and paper, printing and publishing experienced lower than the average import penetration.

(b) The growth of import penetration can be measured by using the equation:

$$\frac{(1986 \text{ import penetration} - 1982 \text{ import penetration})}{1982 \text{ import penetration}} \times \frac{100}{1}$$

For metals, this converts to:

$$\frac{(48\% - 33\%)}{33\%} \times \frac{100}{1} = \frac{15}{33} \times \frac{100}{1} = 45.5\%$$

(c) Reasons include:
   (i) lower prices of imports due to high value of the £ during the 1980s;
   (ii) the superior quality and better after-sales service of some foreign producers;
   (iii) foreign subsidies;
   (iv) rises in UK prices.

(d) (i) Tariffs (custom duties) may be used to protect home producers and/or to raise revenue. They may be specific or *ad valorem*. Whether the main effect is on the price or the quantity of imports will depend in part on the elasticity of demand.

   (ii) Quotas are physical limits on the quantity of a good that can be imported. They are usually enforced by licences, and may result in shortages or higher prices if placed on raw materials.

   (iii) Exchange control involves the government controlling the availability of foreign currency. Importers wanting to pay overseas suppliers have to apply to obtain foreign currency. The government can thereby determine the nature and quantity of imports.

   (iv) An embargo involves a ban on the import of certain goods (e.g. drugs) or a boycott of trade with certain countries (e.g. South Africa).

(e) A government could introduce deflationary fiscal and/or monetary policy. A reduction in government spending, an increase in taxation, a rise in interest rates or a fall in the growth of the money supply will be likely to result in a reduction in demand for all goods, including imports.

A government could also devalue the currency. This would lower export prices and raise import prices. The rise in import prices could result in UK goods becoming more price-competitive.

A government could also encourage consumers and government departments to buy UK goods by, e.g., an advertising campaign or giving preference to UK firms when placing orders.

# 17.3 Objective Questions

### Example 17.2

A country is said to have a comparative advantage in the production of a good when:

A  it can produce more of it than any other country
B  it accounts for a greater percentage of total world sales in the product than in any other product it produces
C  it has captured a larger percentage share of the world market than any other country
D  it can produce it at a lower opportunity cost than its trading partners
E  it employs more workers in its production than in any other activity

### Example 17.3

With respect to the table below, which of the following statements is correct?

| Units of resources required to: | Country A | Country B |
|---|---|---|
| produce one TV | 30 | 60 |
| produce one radio | 10 | 40 |

A  country B has an absolute advantage in the production of both products
B  country B has an absolute advantage in the production of TVs
C  country A has a comparative advantage in the production of TVs
D  country B has a comparative advantage in the production of radios
E  none of the above statements is correct

*Examples 17.4 and 17.5 are based on the following information:*

|  | Cuba | USA |
|---|---|---|
| Output of cigar units per factor input | 30 | 10 |
| Output of sugar units per factor input | 90 | 50 |

### Example 17.4

Which of the following is true of the situation above?

A  the USA has an absolute advantage in the production of both sugar and cigars
B  Cuba has an absolute advantage in the production of both sugar and cigars
C  the USA has an absolute advantage in the production of sugar and Cuba has an absolute advantage in the production of cigars
D  the USA has a comparative advantage in the production of cigars
E  Cuba has a comparative advantage in the production of sugar

### Example 17.5

Which of the following exchange rates will benefit both Cuba and the USA?

A  1 cigar for 6 sugar     B  1 cigar for 5 sugar     C  1 cigar for 4 sugar
D  1 sugar for 8 cigar     E  1 sugar for 6 cigar

## Example 17.6

The following table shows the output per factor input in two products:

|                | UK  | Nigeria |
|----------------|-----|---------|
| Units of iron  | 240 | 48      |
| Units of steel | 80  | 16      |

If the assumptions are made that there are no trade barriers and no transport costs, which of the following is most likely to occur?
A   the UK will import iron and steel from Nigeria
B   Nigeria will import iron and steel from the UK
C   the UK will export iron to Nigeria and import steel from Nigeria
D   Nigeria will export iron to the UK and import steel from the UK
E   there will be no trade between the two countries in the products concerned

## Example 17.7

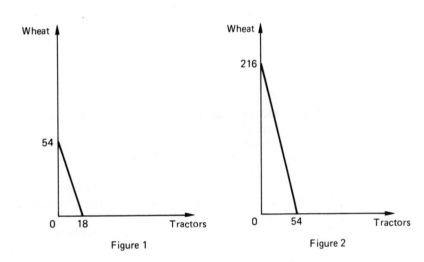

Figure 1                    Figure 2

Figure 1 shows the production possibility curve of country A and Figure 2 shows the production possibility curve of country B.
   In this case, which of the following is most likely to occur?
A   no trade, since country B is better at making both products
B   no trade, since the opportunity cost ratios are identical
C   no trade, since country A is better at making both products
D   country A will tend to export wheat to country B
E   country B will tend to export wheat to country A

## Example 17.8

Which of the following would reduce the level of protection faced by domestic producers in the home market?
A   the introduction of exchange control
B   an increase in VAT
C   a reduction in the level of import quotas
D   a rise in tariffs
E   an agreement to implement reciprocal tariff concessions proposed by GATT

## Example 17.9

Before the imposition of a tariff, the domestic price of good T is $P_X$ and domestic producers supply SA. Domestic demand is represented by DA. When the country engages in free international trade, the total world supply is represented by SB and the price is $P_Y$. The imposition of a tariff on the product causes price to rise to $P_Z$. The tariff will result in domestic producers increasing their output by:

**A** OC       **B** CD       **C** DE       **D** EF       **E** FG

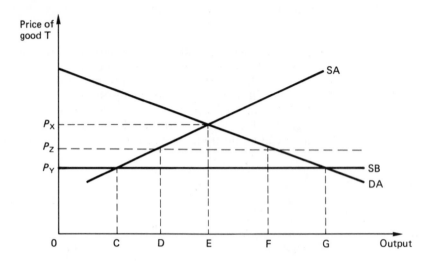

## Example 17.10

Which of the following is the main feature which distinguishes a customs union from a free-trade area?

**A** only the free-trade area has no tariff barriers between members
**B** only the free-trade area requires members to adopt a common external tariff with non-members
**C** only the customs union has no tariff barriers between members
**D** only the customs union requires members to adopt a common external tariff with non-members
**E** only the customs union maintains tariffs between member countries

*Select your answers to Examples 17.11 and 17.12 by means of the following code:*
**A** *if 1, 2 and 3 are all correct*
**B** *if 1 and 2 only are correct*
**C** *if 2 and 3 only are correct*
**D** *if 1 only is correct*

## Example 17.11

The following table shows the costs of producing a unit of coal and a unit of wheat in two countries in $s:

|  | Country A | Country B |
|---|---|---|
| Cost per unit of coal | 10 | 50 |
| Cost per unit of wheat | 4 | 12 |

Which of the following is/are true?
1   country B has the absolute advantage in producing both coal and wheat
2   country A will specialise in coal
3   country B will export wheat

## Example 17.12

The table below shows the output per factor unit in two countries:

|       | Country Y | Country Z |
|-------|-----------|-----------|
| Cloth | 9         | 30        |
| Beef  | 3         | 6         |

Which of the following exchange rates would be acceptable to both countries:
**1**   1 beef for 4 cloth    **2**   2 beef for 3.3 cloth    **3**   3 beef for 2 cloth

# 17.4   Essays

## Example 17.13

Discuss the case for and against increased protection for manufacturing industry in the UK.

(WJEC June 1986)

- Distinguish between arguments for selective and general import controls.
- Concentrate on the arguments rather than detailed descriptions of the different types of import controls.
- Include a discussion of the CEPG case.

*Solution 17.13*

Protection limits the entry of goods into a country. It is usually imposed to protect domestic industries. The main argument against protection is that it prevents full advantage being taken of the principle of comparative advantage, which states that world output will be higher when countries specialise and engage in free trade. Moreover, protection may reduce choice, reduce competition, create shortages, increase inefficiency and provoke retaliation.

However, some economists argue that selective import controls should be placed on particular goods or goods from particular countries. These calls for selective controls are backed by a number of arguments. One reason given is that protection will be necessary to enable infant industries to grow and take advantage of economies of scale.

At the other end of the industry age span, protection may be used to help industries decline gradually. The idea is that this will permit natural wastage to occur and avoid a sudden increase in unemployment.

Selective import controls may also be used to prevent dumping, when foreign companies sell products at or below cost price. *Predatory pricing* benefits domestic customers in the short term. In the longer term, artificially low prices may eliminate domestic firms. Foreign producers can then use their monopoly position to raise prices.

General import controls may improve the terms of trade so that each export can be exchanged for more imports. This will occur if the imposition of tariffs forces foreign producers to reduce their prices in order to remain competitive.

Import restrictions may also enable a country to diversify and avoid over-specialisation. If a country is highly specialised, there is a danger that it will suffer if there is a fall in world demand or if there are supply problems. Protection of strategic industries guarantees a domestic supply of essential goods.

In some developing countries, import controls are used to raise revenue, and both developing and developed countries may use import controls to gain a strong bargaining position or to retaliate against other countries' trade restrictions. However, the danger is that a trade war may develop.

Countries may also use import controls to correct or prevent a balance of payments deficit. However, import controls are usually only used as a last resort, and are likely to be combined with other measures to reduce the underlying tendency to purchase a high level of imports.

The Cambridge Economic Policy Group urge the adoption of a system of general import controls in order to restructure the UK economy. They do not wish to reduce imports, merely to control their growth and to prevent an injection of government spending, designed to stimulate the UK economy, being largely spent on foreign imports. Their main idea is that a protective wall will enable UK industry to regain its efficiency and growth, creating a situation of full employment.

**Example 17.14**

Explain the theory of comparative advantage. To what extent is it a satisfactory explanation of the basis of international trade?

- Distinguish between absolute and comparative advantage.
- Explain comparative advantage and then consider the assumptions underlying the theory.
- Keep the numerical example simple. It should be designed to illustrate economic theory and not to prove elaborate mathematical skill.

*Solution 17.14*

The theory of comparative advantage states that, provided that opportunity cost ratios differ, even a more and a less efficient country will benefit from specialisation and trade with each other. However, the simplicity and unreality of some of the assumptions on which the theory is based have led to a number of reservations being made about its applicability to the real world.

It is relatively straightforward to ascertain that countries with absolute advantages in different products will benefit from specialisation and trade.

However, David Ricardo, in developing the theory of comparative advantage, went further. He stated that both countries will benefit from specialisation and trade, even if one country is more efficient at making both products concerned, provided that it is even better at making one of the two. It is relative and not absolute efficiency which is crucial.

|  |  | UK | USA |
|---|---|---|---|
| Units of output per factor: | cars | 10 | 50 |
| Units of output per factor: | wheat | 20 | 200 |

In the example given above, the USA has the absolute advantage in producing both cars and wheat, since it can produce more of both. However, it has the comparative advantage in producing wheat, since it is even better at making this product, being able to produce ten times more of this but only five times more cars than the UK. In contrast, the UK has the comparative advantage or lesser disadvantage in making cars, since it is not so bad at making this product, producing one-fifth of the quantity of cars, but only one-tenth of the quantity of wheat, of the USA. Another way of determining in which product a country has a comparative advantage is to examine the internal opportunity cost ratios. A country has a comparative advantage in a product when producing it involves a lower opportunity cost than in another country.

Output will be increased by specialisation, and both countries should be able to enjoy more goods than previously if the exchange rate lies between the internal opportunity cost ratios — in this case, 1 car : 2–4 wheat.

However, the applicability of the theory to international trade has been questioned on a number of grounds. It is often stated in terms of a few countries and a few products, whereas the real world is more complex. It also ignores transport costs. These will reduce the advantages of specialisation and trade — particularly in the case of low-price, bulky goods.

The theory assumes constant opportunity costs as resources are moved from one industry to another, whereas in practice economies or diseconomies of scale may arise. The shifting of resources from one use to another also presumes perfect factor mobility, whereas factors — particularly labour — may be immobile.

Indeed, the theory presumes that perfect competition exists in the international and the domestic markets. In practice, completely free trade does not exist, and the presence of import restrictions reduces specialisation. Also, there is not perfect knowledge, so it may be difficult to calculate comparative advantage. There may also be imperfect competition in the domestic markets. This is likely to mean that at least some prices do not accurately reflect domestic opportunity cost ratios. Countries also have different degrees of economic power and, in practice, exchange rates are more likely to favour developed than developing nations.

The theory concentrates on the supply side. A country may specialise in making a product and yet still import it if home demand exceeds its output potential.

A country may also experience significant unemployment, and it may be considered better to employ factors relatively inefficiently rather than not employing them at all.

The theory of comparative advantage indicates that output will be increased by specialisation and trade, but the simplicity and unreality of some of the assumptions means that it does not fully explain the actual pattern of world trade.

## 17.5 Solutions to Objective Questions

*Solution 17.2   Answer:* **D**

The law of comparative advantage states that international trade is beneficial to two or more countries, provided that there are differences in their opportunity cost ratios. For instance, in the example below the two countries with one resource unit can produce:

| | UK | France |
|---|---|---|
| Cars | 20 | 2 |
| Steel | 5 | 1 |

France has the comparative advantage, or lesser disadvantage, in producing steel. In France the opportunity cost of producing one unit of steel is 2 cars, whereas in the UK it is 4 cars.

*Solution 17.3   Answer:* **E**

In this question it is important to remember that the figures given relate not to the output per resource unit, as is more commonly the case, but to the number of resource units required to produce 1 TV and to produce 1 radio. Country A can produce both goods more efficiently (i.e. with fewer resources) and so it has an absolute advantage in the production of both goods. Options **A** and **B** are both incorrect.

Country A is even better at producing radios, since it requires only one-quarter of the resources that country B does to produce radios, whereas it requires one-half of the resources that B does to make one TV. So country A has the comparative advantage in producing radios and, hence, option **C** is incorrect.

Country B has the comparative advantage in producing TVs, since it requires twice the resources to make TVs but four times the resources to make radios. Thus, option **D** is also incorrect.

*Solution 17.4   Answer:* **B**

Cuba can produce more of both products per factor input and so has an absolute advantage in the production of both goods. Hence, option **B** is correct and options **A** and **C** can easily be rejected.

Cuba has the comparative advantage in producing cigars, since it has a lower opportunity cost in the production of the good than the USA has. In Cuba the opportunity cost of 1 cigar equals 3 units of sugar, whereas in the USA it is 5 units of sugar. The USA has the comparative advantage in the production of sugar, as its opportunity cost is $\frac{1}{5}$ cigar whereas the opportunity cost in Cuba is $\frac{1}{3}$ cigar. So, after consideration, options **D** and **E** can also be rejected.

*Solution 17.5   Answer:* **C**

An exchange rate which will be beneficial to both trading countries must lie between their internal opportunity cost ratios, as established in Solution 17.4. In Cuba 1 cigar equals 3 sugar and in the USA 1 cigar equals 5 sugar. So the only exchange rate which will benefit both countries must lie in the range 1 cigar = 3–5 sugar.

*Solution 17.6   Answer:* **E**

The UK has the absolute advantage in both products. However, as the opportunity costs are the same, a situation of comparative advantage does not exist and the countries will not benefit from specialisation and trade.

*Solution 17.7   Answer:* **E**

A production possibility curve shows the potential output of two commodities which a country can produce with its resources. Country B has the absolute advantage in producing both tractors and wheat and the comparative advantage in producing wheat. It can produce 3 times more tractors than country A but 4 times more wheat. So country B will specialise in wheat and export to country A in exchange for tractors. Country A will concentrate on producing tractors and will export these to country B. As there are differences in the relative efficiencies with which the countries can produce the goods, there is the potential for them to benefit from specialisation and trade.

*Solution 17.8   Answer:* **E**

A reduction in the level of protection faced by domestic producers means that home producers will face more competition from foreign producers.

   At first glance the answer may appear to be option **C**, but a reduction in import quotas would mean that fewer imported goods would be allowed into the country and, hence, protection for home producers would be increased. Options **A** and **D** would also increase protection for home producers, whereas an acceptance of reciprocal tariff concessions proposed by GATT will mean a reduction in taxes on imports, which will make foreign goods more competitive with home products.

*Solution 17.9   Answer:* **B**

The pre-trade domestic production of the good is 0E. With free trade the quantity bought is 0G, where the domestic demand cuts the world supply (SB). Of this quantity, 0C is supplied by domestic producers and CG by foreign producers. When the tariff is imposed and price rises to $P_Z$, the new quantity bought is 0F (where DA cuts what is, in effect, a new supply curve running parallel with $P_Z$). Of this, 0D is supplied by domestic producers and DF by foreign producers. So domestic producers increase their output by CD.

*Solution 17.10   Answer:* **D**

Both a customs union and a free-trade area remove tariff barriers between member countries. However, whereas a customs union also requires member countries to impose a common external tariff, a free-trade area allows member countries to decide their own external tariff policies.

*Solution 17.11   Answer:* **C**

Country A has the absolute advantage in producing both products, since it can produce both products more cheaply than country B. Country A is even better at producing coal than wheat, since it can produce coal five times more cheaply than country B and wheat three times more cheaply. Thus, country A will specialise in coal and export coal in exchange for wheat from country B.

*Solution 17.12   Answer:* **D**

The exchange rate will lie between the opportunity costs prevailing in the two countries. In country Y the opportunity cost of 1 beef is 3 cloth and in country Z it is 1 beef = 5 cloth. Thus, an acceptable exchange rate for both countries will be 1 beef = more than 3 cloth and less than 5 cloth.

# 18 Balance of Payments

## 18.1  Fact Sheet

### (a)  Definition of the Terms of Trade

The *terms of trade* (TOT) is the ratio comparing export and import prices:

$$\text{TOT} = \frac{\text{index of export prices}}{\text{index of import prices}} \times \frac{100}{1}$$

A favourable movement means that the TOT gets larger. Favourable movements are caused by:
   (i)  rise in export prices;
  (ii)  fall in import prices;
 (iii)  rise in export prices and fall in import prices;
  (iv)  export prices rising faster than import prices;
   (v)  import prices falling faster than export prices.

### (b)  Causes of Changes in the Terms of Trade

The TOT change in response to:
   (i)  changes in demand — e.g. rising demand for raw materials during a boom;
  (ii)  changes in supply — e.g. a crop failure;
 (iii)  changes in the value of the currency — e.g. a depreciation results in a fall in export prices and a rise in import prices;
  (iv)  changes in the inflation rate — e.g. an acceleration in the inflation rate will result in higher export prices.

### (c)  Results of a Favourable Movement

   (i)  In the short term, higher export prices and lower import prices are likely to improve the current account balance before demand has had time to adjust.
  (ii)  In the longer term:
        (1)  if demand for exports is elastic, export revenue will fall;
        (2)  if demand for imports is elastic, expenditure on imports will rise;
        (3)  if demand for imports is inelastic, foreigners may experience a fall in income and reduce demand for UK exports;
        (4)  UK subsidiaries abroad may suffer a decline in revenue.

## (d) Composition of the Balance of Payments

The *balance of payments* (BOP) is a record of all economic transactions between residents in the UK and residents in the rest of the world, over a period of a year. The BOP has three components:

    (i) the *current account*;

    (ii) *UK external assets and liabilities*;

    (iii) the *balancing item*

## (e) The Current Account

Particular attention is paid to the current account, which is made up of:

    (i) The *visible balance* (also called the *balance of trade*) shows exports and imports of tangible goods — e.g. cars, radios. A *trade gap* occurs when visible imports exceed visible exports.

    (ii) The *invisible balance* shows the net total of:

        (1) services, including sea transport, civil aviation, travel, banking and insurance, expenditure on embassies abroad and military staff stationed abroad;

        (2) interest, profits and dividends (investment income is included whether it is remitted or retained for investment);

        (3) transfers, including government grants overseas, subscriptions to international organisations (including the EEC) and private transfers in the form of payments to overseas dependants and charitable donations.

Visible balance + Invisible balance = Current account balance

## (f) UK External Assets and Liabilities

This is made up of two sections:

    (i) *Transactions in external assets*   This comprises:

        (1) UK direct and portfolio investment overseas;

        (2) lending to overseas residents;

        (3) drawing on (+) and additions to (−) the reserves;

        (4) inter-governmental loans made by the UK and subscriptions to international lending bodies.

    (ii) *Transactions in external liabilities*   This comprises:

        (1) overseas direct and portfolio investment in the UK;

        (2) borrowing from overseas residents by UK residents and banks;

        (3) inter-governmental loans to the UK, foreign currency borrowing from banks overseas and transactions with the IMF.

Transactions in external assets + Transactions in external liabilities = Net transactions

## (g) The Balancing Item

The *balancing item* represents the net total of errors and omissions in the other items. The BOP always balances, in the sense that the current account balance plus net transactions plus the balancing item must equal zero.

**Table 18.1** The 1986 UK balance of payments

| | £ millions |
|---|---|
| *Current Account* | |
| visibles | − 8 254 |
| invisibles | + 7 154 |
| Current balance | − 1 100 |
| *UK external assets and liabilities* | |
| transactions in assets | − 86 964 |
| transactions in liabilities | + 81 206 |
| Net transactions | − 5 758 |
| *Balancing item* | + 6 858 |

Source: *Monthly Digest of Statistics*, 1986

**(h) Current Account Surplus**

  (i) Consequences: A current account surplus may be taken to be a sign of economic strength, but a large surplus may be considered to be disadvantageous because:

    (1) it involves an opportunity cost in terms of forgone higher living standards;

    (2) it results in an injection of demand into the economy, possibly contributing to demand pull inflation;

    (3) it is likely to increase the money supply, which may contribute to inflationary pressures;

    (4) it may make the country unpopular with countries in deficit.

  (ii) Measures to disperse a surplus:

    (1) Lower interest rates, to encourage a rise in investment abroad and, hence, an increase in transactions in external assets.

    (2) Increase lending abroad, thereby increasing transactions in external assets.

  (iii) Measures to correct a current account surplus:

    (1) Revaluation of the currency. This will increase export prices and lower import prices.

    (2) Reflationary fiscal and/or monetary policy, which will increase demand for imports.

    (3) Reduce or abolish import controls.

**(i) Current Account Deficit**

  (i) Consequences:

    (1) A current account deficit causes a welfare gain, since the country consumes more than it produces.

    (2) A country will eventually be unable to cover a current account deficit by drawing on reserves.

(3) A leakage in domestic demand.

(4) A decrease in the money supply.

(ii) Measures to cover a current account deficit:

(1) Raise interest rates to increase investment and, hence, transactions in external liabilities.

(2) Borrow from abroad, again increasing transactions in external liabilities.

(iii) Measures to correct a current account deficit:

(1) Impose or increase import controls (*protectionism*) to switch expenditure from imports to home-produced goods.

(2) Deflationary fiscal and/or monetary policy to reduce demand for imports and stimulate exports by lowering domestic demand.

(3) Encourage exports by, say, zero rating VAT on exports.

(4) *Devaluation* of the currency. This will decrease export prices and raise import prices.

### (j) The Marshall Lerner Condition

A depreciation of sterling (£s) results:

(i) in a short-run deterioration in the BOP because of

(1) an immediate rise in the price of imports but a constant quantity of imports bought;

(2) a fall in the price of exports but a constant quantity of exports bought.

(ii) in a long-run improvement in the BOP because

(1) eventually UK consumers buy fewer imports;

(2) eventually foreign consumers buy more exports.

It is essential to realise that the overall long-run effect of a depreciation of sterling depends on the Marshal Lerner Condition, which states that a devaluation improves the current account balance if the combined price elasticities of demand for exports and imports are greater than 1. The *J Effect* in Figure 18.1 shows that a devaluation initially causes a deterioration in the current account balance (A to B) before demand and supply adjust to the new prices of exports and imports (B to C).

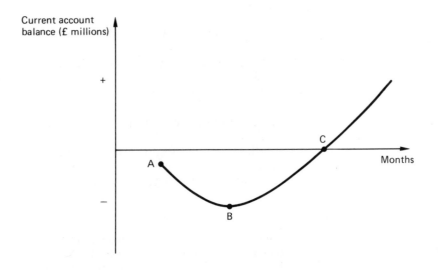

**Figure 18.1**   The J effect

261

## 18.2 Data Response

### Worked Example 18.1

*Singapore: Volume and Price Index of Imports and Exports 1979 (1972 = 100)*

| Commodity section | Volume | Price |
|---|---|---|
| **Imports** | | |
| total | 185 | 210 |
| food | 128 | 187 |
| beverages and tobacco | 103 | 160 |
| crude materials | 142 | 265 |
| mineral fuels | 111 | 634 |
| animal and vegetable oils | 117 | 255 |
| chemicals | 210 | 203 |
| manufactured goods | 163 | 178 |
| machinery and equipment | 243 | 156 |
| miscellaneous manufactures | 154 | 199 |
| miscellaneous | 167 | 225 |
| **Exports** | | |
| total | 227 | 217 |
| food | 149 | 190 |
| beverages and tobacco | 145 | 138 |
| crude materials | 129 | 295 |
| mineral fuels | 138 | 452 |
| animal and vegetable oils | 165 | 350 |
| chemicals | 200 | 270 |
| manufactured goods | 240 | 192 |
| machinery and equipment | 404 | 148 |
| miscellaneous manufactures | 168 | 215 |
| miscellaneous | 262 | 186 |

Source: *Singapore Yearbook of Statistics 1979/80*

(a) (i) Did Singapore's terms of trade improve or deteriorate between 1972 and 1979? Explain your answer. **(2 marks)**

    (ii) How can the information in the table be used to derive the balance of visible trade? **(2 marks)**

    (iii) How did the balance of visible trade change between 1972 and 1979? **(1 mark)**

    (iv) Comment on the relationship between the terms of trade and the balance of trade in this case. **(2 marks)**

(b) (i) Which commodity section grew fastest in terms of both imports and exports between 1972 and 1979? **(1 mark)**

    (ii) How do the data suggest that the relative performance of imports and exports in this commodity section may be influenced by its price competitiveness? **(2 marks)**

    (iii) Singapore has seen a growth in the volume of both imports and exports traded in the same commodity section. How does this fit in with the theory of specialisation in international trade? **(3 marks)**

**(Total 13 marks)**
(Cambridge Nov./Dec. 1985)

(a) (i) The terms of trade are measured by:

$$\frac{\text{index of export prices}}{\text{index of import prices}} \times \frac{100}{1}$$

In 1979 the terms of trade were

$$\frac{217}{210} \times \frac{100}{1} = 103.3$$

As the terms of trade in 1972 were

$$\frac{100}{1} \times \frac{1}{100} = 100$$

there has been an improvement in the terms of trade, caused by export prices rising by more than import prices.

(ii) The balance of trade compares the value of exports and the value of imports. Value is found by volume × price.

(iii) The balance of visible trade position improved, because both the volume and price (and, hence, the value) of exports rose by more than the volume and price (and, hence, the value) of imports.

(iv) In this case, an improvement in the terms of trade was accompanied by an improvement in the visible trade position. This may have occurred because demand for exports was relatively inelastic or because it was the rise in demand from overseas which caused the rise in prices.

(b) (i) The commodity section which showed the most rapid increase in terms of both exports and imports was machinery and equipment. In volume terms, the imports index rose from 100 to 243 and the exports index from 100 to 404.

(ii) In the case of imports, machinery and equipment experienced the biggest increase in volume and the lowest increase in prices. Similarly, the volume of machinery and equipment exported experienced the greatest rise in volume and the second-slowest rise in prices. Thus, price competitiveness would appear to have been important in explaining the rise in volume of exports and imports of the commodity.

(iii) The theory of specialisation in international trade is called the law of comparative costs. It suggests that countries will benefit from specialising in products in which they have a comparative advantage and then trading. In practice, many countries import and export the same products. This is because there may be variations in the types of goods — e.g. the UK imports low-grade oil and exports high-grade oil — and consumers and producers demand a choice of variety of products and equipment both at home and abroad.

## 18.3  Objective Questions

**Example 18.2**

The terms of trade are:
A   the excess of visible exports over visible imports
B   the price of the home currency in terms of another currency

**C** the ratio between the value of exports and the value of imports
**D** the ratio between the volume of exports and the volume of imports
**E** the ratio between export prices and import prices

## Example 18.3

A favourable movement in the terms of trade occurs when:
**A** the price of exports rises relative to the price of imports
**B** the volume of exports rises relative to the volume of imports
**C** the ratio between export and import earnings increases
**D** there is an increase in the value of exports relative to the value of imports
**E** the current account moves into surplus

## Example 18.4

The figures below show a country's terms of trade:

| | | | | | |
|---|---|---|---|---|---|
| 1983: | 120 | 1984: | 115 | 1985: | 109 |
| 1986: | 101 | 1987: | 98 | 1988: | 87 |

Which of the following could account for the movement in the terms of trade from 1983 onwards?
**A** export prices rose faster than import prices
**B** export prices rose while import prices remained constant
**C** import prices fell faster than export prices
**D** import prices rose faster than export prices
**E** import prices fell while export prices remained constant

## Example 18.5

| | Exports | | Imports | |
|---|---|---|---|---|
| | Price per unit (£000s) | Number of units (000s) | Price per unit (£000s) | Number of units (000s) |
| Year 1 | 20 | 20 | 25 | 8 |
| Year 2 | 40 | 12 | 40 | 6 |

What changes have taken place in the terms of trade and the balance of trade between years 1 and 2?

| | Terms of trade | Balance of trade |
|---|---|---|
| **A** | improved | improved |
| **B** | worsened | worsened |
| **C** | improved | worsened |
| **D** | worsened | improved |
| **E** | unchanged | worsened |

## Example 18.6

Which of the following items would appear as a credit item in the invisible balance of the UK balance of payments?
A   the spending of UK tourists in France
B   the purchase by a German company of a china factory in Worcester
C   the hiring of a UK ship by a Dutch oil company
D   profits earned by a Japanese subsidiary located in Sunderland
E   the purchase of UK government bonds by French residents

## Example 18.7

Which of the following will appear in the UK external assets and liabilities section of the UK balance of payments?
A   support costs of UK embassies abroad
B   fees charged by a Welsh insurance company for work carried out in Chile
C   profits earned by British subsidiaries in West Germany
D   lending to Nigerian companies by British banks
E   interest earned on UK funds held in American banks

*Examples 18.8–18.11 are based on the information below.*

|                                | £million |
| ------------------------------ | -------- |
| Visible exports                | 2560     |
| Visible imports                | 2620     |
| Transfers                      | 50       |
| Interest, profits and dividends | 70      |
| Services                       | 90       |
| Net transactions               | − 200    |

A   −£60m     B   £50m     C   £60m     D   £150m     E   £210m

## Example 18.8

What is the balance of trade?

## Example 18.9

What is the invisible balance?

## Example 18.10

What is the current account balance?

## Example 18.11

What is the balancing item?

Example 18.12

The income elasticities of demand for imports and exports in five countries is given below. Which country's balance of payments position will benefit most from a world recession?

| Country | Income elasticity of demand for imports | Income elasticity of demand for exports |
|---------|------------------------------------------|------------------------------------------|
| A | 1.8 | 0.8 |
| B | 1.2 | 1.2 |
| C | 1.0 | 1.6 |
| D | 0.8 | 2.0 |
| E | 0.6 | 2.5 |

Example 18.13

The following information shows a country's national income and domestic expenditure for 3 years.

|  | Year 1 | Year 2 | Year 3 |
|--|--------|--------|--------|
| National Income | 600 | 660 | 720 |
| Consumer spending | 360 | 360 | 390 |
| Government spending | 180 | 180 | 180 |
| Investment | 120 | 120 | 120 |

A balance of trade deficit will be experienced in which year(s)?
A 1 and 3    B 2 and 3    C 1 only    D 2 only    E 3 only

Example 18.14

A current account deficit, in the absence of government intervention, is likely to result in:
A an increase in the money supply in the country
B a decrease in the money supply in the country
C an increase in the level of income in the country
D a decrease in unemployment in the country
E an increase in the exchange rate

Example 18.15

A government may reduce a current account surplus to:
A increase the current living standards of its inhabitants
B increase the domestic money supply
C increase domestic employment
D increase exports

**Example 18.16**

Which of the following policies would a government adopt to reduce a current account surplus and inflation?

**A** devalue the currency  **B** revalue the currency  **C** deflate the economy
**D** raise interest rates  **E** impose import controls


**Example 18.17**

If a UK company keeps the German price of its exports unchanged after a fall in the value of the £, the result will be:

**A** a decrease in the demand for its products in Germany
**B** an increase in the demand for its products in Germany
**C** an increase in the value of German sales valued in marks
**D** an increase in the value of German sales valued in £s
**E** a decrease in the value of German sales valued in £s


**Example 18.18**

Which one of the following policies would be most effective in correcting a current account deficit in a country with a high inflation rate?

**A** revaluing the currency       **B** devaluing the currency
**C** deflating the economy        **D** imposing import controls
**E** reflating the economy


**Example 18.19**

In which of the following circumstances is a devaluation most likely to improve the visible balance?

| | *Demand for imports* | *Demand for exports* |
|---|---|---|
| **A** | price-elastic | price-inelastic |
| **B** | price-inelastic | price-elastic |
| **C** | price-inelastic | price-inelastic |
| **D** | price-elastic | price-elastic |


**Example 18.20**

Measures designed to improve a country's current account balance may be either expenditure-reducing or expenditure-switching. Which of the following is an example of an expenditure-reducing policy?

**A** the imposition of import controls
**B** the granting of export subsidies
**C** the imposition of exchange controls
**D** a credit squeeze
**E** devaluation

*Select your answers to Examples 18.21–18.24 by means of the following code:*
**A** *if 1, 2 and 3 are all correct*
**B** *if 1 and 2 only are correct*
**C** *if 2 and 3 only are correct*
**D** *if 1 only is correct*

**Example 18.21**

Which of the following could result in an improvement in the terms of trade of a country?
1  an increase in foreign costs of production
2  inflationary domestic price rises passed on to overseas customers
3  an increase in overseas demand for the country's products


**Example 18.22**

Which of the following could appear in the UK's invisible balance?
1  spending by UK residents in Norway
2  support costs of British armies overseas
3  the carriage of foreign goods in UK ships


**Example 18.23**

A revaluation of the exchange rate must result in an improvement in a country's:
1  terms of trade          2  visible balance          3  current account balance


**Example 18.24**

Which of the following are included in the transactions in external assets and liabilities section of the UK balance of payments?
1  overseas portfolio investment in the UK
2  lending to overseas residents by UK banks
3  additions to reserves


## 18.4  Essays


**Example 18.25**

Discuss the advantages and disadvantages of the various means by which the government might attempt to improve the UK balance of payments position
(SUJB June 1987)

• Briefly explain what is meant by the balance of payments position.
• Concentrate on three main measures of improving the balance of payments.
• Examine both the internal and external effects of the measures.

*Solution 18.25*

The UK balance of payments is a record of the income and expenditure transactions between UK residents and people abroad. It has three main sections: the current account, UK external assets and liabilities and the balancing item.

A government which is attempting to improve the UK balance of payments position is likely to be trying to reduce a deficit. Thus, the measures it will adopt will be aiming to increase income earned and/or reduce expenditure abroad. In considering which policies to adopt, a government will consider the cause of the weak position and the advantages and disadvantages of the measures.

One possible policy is devaluation or depreciation of the currency. This will mean lowering the price of exports, in terms of foreign currencies, and raising the price of imports, in terms of the home currency. It is essentially an expenditure-switching measure, changing relative prices.

However, whether the policy will be successful in terms of improving the balance of payments position will depend on whether there is elastic demand for imports, elastic demand for exports, elastic supply of exports, lack of import restrictions abroad and a low domestic marginal propensity to import, among other factors.

Lowering the value of the currency will affect not only a country's balance of payments position, but also its internal position. If exports rise and imports decline, there will be a net injection into the circular flow of income, and national income should rise by a multiple amount. This should stimulate output and employment. However, there may be inflationary effects arising from the increase in import prices and the net injection.

While depreciation is associated with an increase in domestic economy activity, deflation is associated, in the short term, with a reduction in economic activity. Deflation involves reducing incomes by restrictive fiscal and/or monetary policy. For instance, a government may increase taxation in the expectation that, if people's incomes decline, they will buy fewer imports. The higher the income elasticity of demand for imports the greater the effect will be. It will also be expected that demand for the home country's products will decline, so home producers will be forced to try to export more of their output. The rate of interest may also be forced up, to deflate the economy and to attract foreign investment. If deflation also reduces inflation, the balance of payments position will be further improved by the increase in price competitiveness.

However, deflation may, even if only in the short term, have an adverse effect on employment and growth. There may also be a longer-term decline in employment if the country is not successful in exporting more and importing less. The Cambridge Economic Policy Group (CEPG) have been particularly critical of deflationary measures.

The CEPG instead advocate a general system of import controls, to allow UK industry to restructure and to ensure that government reflationary policies will result in a rise in demand for UK rather than foreign products. Other economists support selective import controls, to prevent dumping, to assist infant industries, to allow industries to decline gradually, to improve the terms of trade and, of course, to correct a balance of payments deficit.

Import controls may prove to be inflationary. This is because imports are included in the retail price index, costs of production will rise if imported raw materials and components continue to be used and unions press for wage rises to compensate for higher prices. UK firms may also be able to raise prices and remain competitive with more expensive imports. Import controls may also provoke retaliation from other countries.

Among other measures which a country may employ are encouraging exports by, for instance, giving favourable loans to exporters and encouraging other countries to remove some of their import restrictions.

**Example 18.26**

Why might a government eliminate a surplus on its current account balance of payments? What measures could it use to achieve this end?

(L June 1987)

269

- Define a surplus on current account.
- Discuss the main motives for eliminating a surplus.
- Discuss revaluation, reflation and other measures to eliminate a surplus.

*Solution 18.26*

A surplus on its current account means that a country is earning more abroad than it is spending. This could arise as a result of a surplus on its visible balance and invisible balance, a visible balance surplus exceeding an invisible deficit or an invisible surplus exceeding a visible deficit.

A country may wish to eliminate a surplus, to improve the standard of living of its inhabitants. If a country has been experiencing a large current account surplus over a number of years, then the opportunity cost involved is the goods and services which it could have bought with the currency it has been earning.

If a country has been experiencing large current account surpluses, there may be pressure on it from other countries to reduce or eliminate the surplus. Measures which a government may take to achieve this may not only restore its current account equilibrium, but also help deficit countries achieve current account equilibrium. A country trying to reduce a surplus is likely to buy more abroad and sell less. Considerable pressure has, in the past, been put on Germany and Japan to reduce their surpluses.

A country may also eliminate a surplus to reduce inflationary pressures. A surplus can result in an injection of demand into the domestic economy and an increase in the money supply.

One possible measure to eliminate a surplus may be implemented with the prime objective of reducing inflationary pressures. A revaluation of the currency upwards will mean that more foreign currency will be obtained for the same value of the home currency. The home country's exports will be more expensive in terms of foreign currency, while its imports will be cheaper in terms of the domestic currency. The revaluation is likely to result in an increase in import expenditure and a fall in export revenue, presuming elastic demand for exports and elastic demand for imports.

An increase in the value of the currency means that imports are cheaper and these count in the retail price index. There may also be a reduction in the costs of production for home producers, as imported raw materials and components will be cheaper. The rise in the price of exports may force domestic exporters to cut their costs in order to remain competitive. Domestic producers selling in the home market will also have to keep their prices low in order to compete with cheaper imports. However, there is the possibility that foreigners may raise the price of their goods in the knowledge that they may still be competitive.

Reflationary fiscal and/or monetary measures will increase demand for all products. For instance, an increase in government spending will result in a multiple rise in national income and, hence, demand. More imports will be purchased and the rise in domestic demand for home-produced goods may divert goods from the export to the home market.

A country may also seek to increase expenditure on imports by removing or lowering import restrictions. For instance, lowering tariffs will reduce the price of imports on the home market and will result in an increase in expenditure on imports. Subsidies on domestic products could also be removed.

In addition, encouragement for exporters could be reduced or removed. For instance, banks may no longer be directed to give preference to exporters when lending, and indirect taxation may be imposed or increased on exports.

# 18.5 Solutions to Objective Questions

*Solution 18.2    Answer:* **E**

The terms of trade are concerned only with comparing export prices and import prices and not value or volume.

*Solution 18.3    Answer:* **A**

A favourable movement in the terms of trade occurs when the index rises. This situation arises when the price of exports rises in relation to the price of imports. This may result from, e.g., a rise in the price of exports and/or a fall in the price of imports or even export prices falling to a lesser extent than import prices.

*Solution 18.4    Answer:* **D**

The figures in the table show an unfavourable movement in the terms of trade — i.e. the number becoming smaller. An unfavourable movement occurs when the price of imports rises in relation to the price of exports. This could result from import prices rising faster than export prices.

A, B, C, E $\Rightarrow$ In each case there would be a favourable movement in the terms of trade.

*Solution 18.5    Answer:* **A**

The terms of trade in year 1 were:

$$\frac{\text{index of export prices}}{\text{index of import prices}} \times \frac{100}{1}, \quad \text{i.e.} \quad \frac{20}{25} \times \frac{100}{1} = 80$$

and in year 2:

$$\frac{40}{40} \times \frac{100}{1} = 100$$

Thus, there has been an improvement in the terms of trade in the period shown.
The balance of trade in year 1 was:
value of exports (price $\times$ volume) $-$ value of imports (price $\times$ volume)
400 (20 $\times$ 20) $-$ 200 (25 $\times$ 8) = 200 000
and in year 2:
480 (40 $\times$ 12) $-$ 240 (40 $\times$ 6) = 240 000
Thus, the balance of trade has improved with an increase in the surplus of £40 000.

*Solution 18.6    Answer:* **C**

The invisible balance includes services, interest, profits, and dividends and transfers. A credit item on the invisible balance is one which represents money being paid to a UK resident or a firm in the UK, whereas a debit item represents a payment to a foreign resident by a UK resident. If a Dutch oil company hires a UK ship, money will be paid from Holland to the UK.

A and **D** $\Rightarrow$ Represent debit items in the UK invisible balance, since they involve money going out of the UK to other countries.

B and **E** $\Rightarrow$ Are credit items in the net transactions section.

*Solution 18.7   Answer:* **D**

The external assets and liabilities section of the balance of payments includes investment into and out of the UK, lending to and borrowing abroad, inter-governmental lending, and borrowing and drawing on and additions to the reserves. Lending to Nigerian companies by British banks would appear as a transaction in external assets.

**A, B, C, E** $\Rightarrow$ Would all appear in the invisible balance section of the balance of payments.

*Solution 18.8   Answer:* **A**

The balance of trade is visible exports − visible imports — i.e. £2560m − £2620m = − £60m.

*Solution 18.9   Answer:* **E**

The invisible balance is net transfers + net interest, profits and dividends + net services — i.e. £50m + £70m + £90m = £210m.

*Solution 18.10   Answer:* **D**

The current account balance is the visible balance plus the invisible balance — i.e. − £60m + £210m = £150m.

*Solution 18.11   Answer:* **B**

The current account balance plus net transactions plus the balancing item equals zero. In this case £150m + −£200m + the balancing item = 0. So − £50m + the balancing item = 0. Therefore, the balancing item = £50m.

*Solution 18.12   Answer:* **A**

In a world recession, incomes are likely to be falling. To gain the most benefit from a world recession, a country would want demand for its exports to be income-inelastic. Thus, a fall in income results in a smaller percentage fall in demand for its exports. It would, in contrast, want its imports to be income-elastic, so that a fall in domestic income results in a greater percentage fall in demand for imports. If income elasticity of demand for imports is 1.8 — i.e. elastic — and income elasticity of demand for exports is 0.8 — i.e. inelastic — a fall in income will result in a greater reduction in import expenditure than in export earnings. Thus a current account deficit would be reduced or a surplus increased.

*Solution 18.13   Answer:* **C**

The country will have a deficit on the current account when its total demand (consumer spending + government spending + investment) exceeds its output (N.Y.)
   In year 1 output is 600 but demand is 660, so there will be a deficit of 60.
   In year 2 output is 660 and so is demand. Therefore, there will be equilibrium.
   In year 3 output is 720 and demand is 690, so there will be a surplus of 30.

*Solution 18.14   Answer:* **B**

A current account deficit will mean more money leaving the country than entering it. People and firms buying imports may pay pounds sterling, which will directly reduce the money supply in the home country. However, it is more likely that payment will be made in a foreign currency. To obtain the foreign currency, pounds sterling will be given in exchange, and this may reduce the quantity of money in circulation unless the government reintroduces the money into circulation.

*Solution 18.15   Answer:* **A**

A current account surplus has an opportunity cost in forgone consumption. Thus, a government may reduce a surplus to raise living standards. This could be achieved by lowering the value of the currency so that more goods and services can be consumed in the home country.

*Solution 18.16   Answer:* **B**

Revaluing the currency is likely to result in expenditure on imports rising and export revenue falling. This will reduce a current account surplus.

Inflationary pressure is likely to be reduced, since revaluation will reduce import prices, and imports count in the retail price index. Domestic producers are also likely to limit price rises in order to remain competitive at home and abroad.

*Solution 18.17   Answer:* **D**

A company can take advantage of a fall in the value of the currency either by allowing the foreign price of its product to fall and thereby raising demand for it or by leaving the foreign price constant. This latter option will result in an increase in its revenue measured in its own currency. For example, if initially £1 = 10 marks, then a £6 good would sell in Germany for 60 marks. If, when the exchange rate falls to £1 = 5 marks, the company keeps the price in Germany at 60 marks, it will receive £12 per good when it changes its earnings from marks into pounds.

*Solution 18.18   Answer:* **C**

Deflating the economy will involve reducing demand by means of fiscal and/or monetary policy. The reduction in demand is likely to reduce demand pull inflation. It is also likely to improve the current account balance by reducing spending on imports and possibly by stimulating exports, because of the fall in domestic demand.

**A** ⇒ Revaluing the currency will tend to reduce inflationary pressures but increase a current account deficit.

**B** ⇒ Devaluing the currency is likely to reduce a current account deficit but increase inflation, because of higher import prices.

**D** ⇒ Imposing import controls may assist the current account position, but it may raise import prices.

**E** ⇒ Reflating the economy will involve increasing demand, and this may increase inflationary pressure and increase a current account deficit.

*Solution 18.19   Answer:* **D**

A devaluation is most likely to improve the balance of trade position when demand for both exports and imports is price-elastic. If this occurs, the rise in the price of imports will result in a fall in expenditure on imports and the fall in the price of exports will result in a rise in export revenue.

*Solution 18.20   Answer:* **D**

Expenditure-reducing measures seek to improve a country's current account position by reducing demand for all goods and services, both domestic and foreign. The fall in demand for imports will reduce import expenditure and the fall in demand for home-produced goods may encourage firms to switch production from the home to the foreign market.

In contrast, expenditure-switching measures aim to improve the current account balance by switching expenditure from foreign to the home country's goods and services — i.e. from imports to domestic goods and from another country's exports to the home country's exports.

A credit squeeze is a measure designed to reduce demand for all goods bought by the home country's residents.

**A** and **C** ⇒ Are expenditure-switching measures encouraging people to switch from buying foreign to buying domestic products.

**B** ⇒ Is an expenditure-switching measure encouraging foreigners to buy more of the export-subsidising country's products and fewer of other countries' and their own country's products.

**E** ⇒ Is an expenditure-switching measure encouraging residents of the country to switch from buying imports to buying domestically produced goods and foreigners to switch from buying their own products or other countries' products to buying the devaluing country's products.

*Solution 18.21   Answer:* **C**

**1** ⇒ An increase in foreign costs of production will be likely to increase the price of imports, which will cause an unfavourable movement in the terms of trade.
**2** ⇒ Inflation will cause a rise in export prices and, hence, in the terms of trade.
**3** ⇒ An increase in overseas demand for the country's exports is likely to cause a rise in their price and, hence, an improvement in the terms of trade.

*Solution 18.22   Answer:* **A**

All the items will appear under services in the invisible balance. Spending by UK tourists in Norway would be classified as travel, support costs of UK armies overseas would be UK government current expenditure and carriage of foreign goods in UK ships would be classified as sea transport.

*Solution 18.23   Answer:* **D**

A revaluation of the exchange rate results in a rise in export prices and a fall in import prices. This must improve the terms of trade.

It is more likely that a revaluation will reduce the visible and current account balances rather than improve them. However, the outcome will depend on a number of factors — principally the elasticity of demand for imports and exports.

*Solution 18.24    Answer:* **A**

All are included in the UK external assets and liabilities section of the balance of payments.

**1** ⇒ Overseas portfolio investment in the UK is a transaction in external liabilities.

**2** and **3** ⇒ Lending to overseas residents by UK banks and additions to reserves are transactions in external assets.

# 19 Exchange Rates

## 19.1 Fact Sheet

### (a) The Foreign Exchange Rate

The exchange rate is the price of one currency in terms of another currency. An exchange rate can be *bilateral* (e.g. $/£) or *multilateral* (a basket of currencies such as the trade weighted sterling index).

- A *depreciation* of sterling means that one pound now buys fewer units of another currency. The value of sterling has fallen.
- An *appreciation* of sterling means that one pound now buys more units of another currency. The value of sterling has risen.
- A *eurocurrency* is any currency deposited in a financial institution outside its country of origin — e.g. French francs deposited in a bank in Singapore.
- The *London Foreign Exchange Market* consists of all those who deal in foreign exchange but has no formal meeting place.
- The *spot market* is that part of the foreign exchange market concerned with the buying and selling of currencies for immediate use.
- The *forward market* is concerned with agreeing the price of currency now to buy or sell in the future.
- *Arbitrage* is movements of funds to take advantage of differences in exchange or interest rates, and this quickly eliminates any such differences.

**Table 19.1** The demand for and supply of £s sterling

| £s are demanded by | £s are supplied by |
| --- | --- |
| Foreign residents wishing to buy UK exports and pay for UK services | UK residents wishing to buy imports and pay for foreign services |
| People wishing to invest in the UK | UK residents wishing to invest abroad |
| Those wishing to take advantage of a future rise in the value of the £ | Those wishing to take advantage of a future rise in the value of another currency |
| Governments wishing to add £s to their reserves | Governments wishing to replace £s in their reserves with other assets |
| A UK government wishing to raise the value of the £ | A UK government wishing to lower the value of the £ |
| Foreign governments wishing to lower the value of their currencies | Foreign governments wishing to raise the value of their currencies |

- The *Purchasing Power Parity Theory* suggests that the prices of goods in countries will tend to equate under floating exchange rates.

### (b) Exchange Rate Systems

    (i) A *fixed exchange rate* is one which is maintained at a certain level (par) by the government buying and selling currencies when necessary.

  (ii) *Adjustable peg* is when the exchange rate is maintained within agreed limits around a par value but with the possibility that the par value may be changed.

 (iii) *Crawling peg* is a form of adjustable peg where the par value can be changed regularly on the basis of the previous trend in the exchange rate.

 (iv) The *European Monetary System*, which started in 1979, is a form of crawling peg. Member currencies are fixed against each other, with a maximum $2\frac{1}{4}\%$ divergence permitted. This divergence is calculated against a weighted basket of EEC currencies (European Currency Unit).

  (v) *Managed flexibility*, sometimes also called *dirty floating*. The government may intervene in the exchange market to stabilise the exchange rate or move it in a desired direction

 (vi) *Free floating* occurs when the exchange rate is determined by demand and supply, without government intervention.

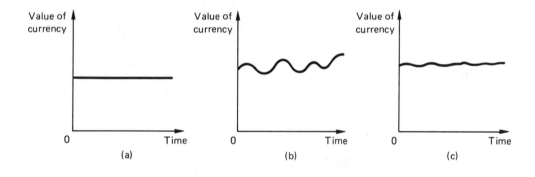

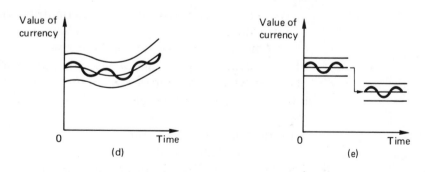

**Figure 19.1**   Exchange rate systems: (a) fixed; (b) floating; (c) managed floating; (d) crawling peg; (e) adjustable peg

### (c) International Liquidity

*International liquidity* is any asset which is acceptable in settling international debts. Internationally acceptable assets are kept in countries' reserves. Forms of international liquidity are:

  (i) Gold.
 (ii) Foreign currencies.
(iii) Reserve positions at the IMF — i.e. the ability to borrow from the IMF.
 (iv) *Special drawing rights* (SDRs) are issued by the IMF, and are specifically created to act as international liquidity assets. They are allocated to member countries on the basis of their quotas, and their value is expressed in terms of a weighted basket of five leading currencies.

### (d) Problems of International Liquidity

The two current major problems are:
  (i) Shortage of international liquidity.
 (ii) What form international liquidity should take. Some economists have suggested:
    (1) Increased use of gold. This view overlooks the opportunity cost of using gold, and its inelastic supply. Some economists suggest *demonetarisation* — i.e. ceasing to use gold as a form of international money.
    (2) Increased reliance on foreign currencies. However, this would mean that the growth of world reserves would depend on national policies. There may be the risk of destabilisation from movements from weakening to strengthening currencies.
    (3) Adoption of completely freely floating exchange rates. This would eliminate the need for reserves.
    (4) Increased international co-operation between central banks, to make more effective use of existing reserves through co-ordinated intervention.
    (5) Increased use of SDRs.

### (e) International Organisations

  (i) The *International Monetary Fund* was set up in 1944, following the Bretton Woods agreement, and now has more than 140 members. Its main aims include:
    (1) facilitating the expansion and balanced growth of world trade;
    (2) promoting assistance to member countries with balance of payments difficulties;
    (3) promoting exchange rate stability.
    Member countries pay a quota based on their National Income and share of world trade. The purpose of quotas is to make available a pool of foreign currency which can be borrowed by member countries in *tranches* — i.e. percentages of their quotas. The right to the first 25% or gold tranche is automatic but the right to subsequent tranches is subject to increasing conditionality.
 (ii) The *International Bank for Reconstruction and Development*, which is more commonly known as the *World Bank*. It was established in 1945 to help member countries recover from World War II. It now gives

long-term loans to member countries for high-priority infrastructure, agricultural, industrial and educational projects.

   (iii) The *International Finance Corporation* was set up in 1956 to encourage private-sector development by providing share and loan capital for companies, encouraging local capital markets and promoting the international flow of private capital.

   (iv) The *International Development Association* lends at low, subsidised interest rates to less developed countries.

   • The IFC and the IDA are members of the World Bank group.

### (f) Overseas Aid

   • *Bilateral aid* is assistance from one government to another.
   • *Multilateral aid* is channelled through international organisations and charities to a number of countries.
   • *Tied aid* is given on condition that the assistance is spent buying goods made in the donor country.

Countries give aid for the following reasons:
   (i) Commercial. Tied aid increases the exports of the donor country. As the assisted country becomes more prosperous, it will tend to buy more goods from 'friendly' countries.
   (ii) Political. Aid is given to win the support and co-operation of strategically important countries.
   (iii) Altruism. Charitable concerns such as Oxfam are motivated by a concern for others.

### (g) Problems of Overseas Aid

Less developed countries argue for trade on more favourable terms than aid, because:
   (i) Aid may involve political interference.
   (ii) Aid may be inappropriate if, say, it promotes capital-intensive projects when labour-intensive activities are better suited to the economy.
   (iii) Loans impose future interest and repayment burdens, particularly if debts must be repaid in foreign currency.
   (iv) Tied aid involves a loss of freedom of choice.
   (v) Aid in the form of products depresses the price of those goods in aided countries. Producers are then unable to sell their own output at a profit.

## 19.2 Data Response

**Worked Example 19.1**

**BANK LETS STERLING BREACH DM3 LEVEL**

The Government's policy of keeping the pound as stable as possible on the foreign exchanges suffered a setback yesterday as the Bank of England finally abandoned attempts to hold sterling below its unofficial ceiling against the West German mark.

In the face of continuing upward pressure, which the Bank had been resisting by selling large amounts of sterling, the decision was taken yesterday morning to let the pound go above the DM3 level. Sterling immediately rose several pfennigs and by the close in London stood at DM3.0455 — its highest level since September 1986, and more than $1\frac{1}{2}$ per cent up on the day.,

The pound also strengthened sharply against a weak American dollar, gaining 4.4 cents to $1.8185. Later in New York it was trading above 41.82 and DM3.05 for a while.

The Treasury stressed there had been no change in policy and the Government was as committed as ever to stable exchange rates. However, officials said stability did not mean immobility, and rates may need to be adjusted from time to time to take account of different circumstances.

Dealers say the upward pressure on the pound is largely due to the high interest rates in the UK compared with other countries, which has attracted savings from around the world.

'The feeling is the pound will go higher. It's just a question of how high', one dealer said.

Although the Government could have eased the pressure on the pound by reducing interest rates, it is reluctant to do this when the economy is growing so fast and there are inflationary dangers such as the high level of pay settlements.

The Bank of England is understood to welcome the decision to allow the pound to rise, in effect tightening monetary policy, at a time when there is concern over domestic monetary conditions. The strong demand for credit in the economy was highlighted again yesterday by the latest figures on consumer credit.

Officials would not want sterling to rise too much, however, and threaten the competitiveness of British industry.

Source: *The Independent*, 8 March 1988

(a) What are the advantages of keeping 'the pound as stable as possible on the foreign exchanges'? **(5 marks)**

(b) What may have caused the 'continuing upward pressure' on the pound? **(3 marks)**

(c) Draw a diagram to illustrate how the sale of sterling can prevent a rise in the value of the pound against the mark. **(3 marks)**

(d) What other action does the article suggest a government could take to stop its currency rising and why may it be reluctant to do this? **(3 marks)**

(e) What are the advantages and disadvantages of a rise in the value of the pound? **(6 marks)**

*Solution 19.1*

(a) 'Keeping the pound as stable as possible' will reduce uncertainty for traders and investors, which may arise if there are frequent and/or large changes in the exchange rate (although uncertainty can be reduced, even in these circumstances, by buying and selling currency in the forward market). Traders, investors and the government can plan more easily on the basis of a stable exchange rate. A stable exchange rate will avoid the problem of a rise in prices which can occur when an exchange rate falls and a reduction in competitiveness when the exchange rate rises. The UK has also been trying to keep its exchange rate in line with other European currencies. It is thought that linking sterling to the currencies of low-inflation countries imposes an external discipline on inflation.

(b) The article refers to one of the causes of upward pressure on the £ — high domestic interest rates. If UK real interest rates exceed those of other countries, there will be an increase in demand for sterling from those wishing to invest in the UK. Upward pressure on the currency can also arise if UK goods and services become more price-competitive or improve in quality, if the government buys £s or if it is believed that the price of the £ will rise in the future.

(c)

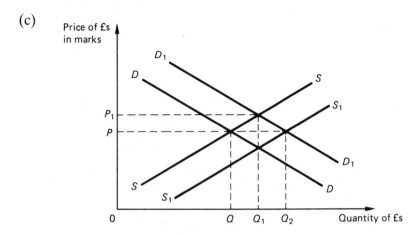

The initial equilibrium price is *P*. A rise in demand for £s would, in a free market, cause price to rise to $P_1$. The government could keep the price at *P* by increasing the supply of £s on the market from *SS* to $S_1S_1$

(d) The article suggests that the government could reduce upward pressure on the £ by lowering domestic interest rates. However, it may be reluctant to do this, since lower interest rates may encourage borrowing and the resulting rise in spending may accelerate inflation.

(e) The two main advantages of a rise in the exchange rate are a reduction in inflationary pressures and an increase in the international purchasing power of the £. A rise in the exchange rate will lower import prices, which will lower the RPI. The rise in export prices may force UK producers to be more price-competitive. The higher value of the £ will also mean that fewer exports will have to be exchanged to obtain the same volume of imports (an improvement in the terms of trade).

However, a high exchange rate will make exports less competitive abroad and imports more competitive in the domestic market. This may result in a reduction in UK output and employment and a worsening of the current account position.

A fall in the exchange rate will also have disadvantages, including the possibility of increasing inflationary pressures. Import prices count in the RPI, and higher import prices may increase some UK producers' costs, may reduce pressure on domestic producers to keep prices low and may stimulate unions to press for wage rises to maintain living standards.

The main advantage of a low exchange rate is that UK goods will become more competitive abroad and at home. This may raise domestic output and employment, and improve the current account position.

# 19.3 Objective Questions

**Example 19.2**

On the foreign exchange market the value of the £ depreciates from £1 = $1.5 to £1 = $1. If a UK exporter allows the price of his goods to reflect this depreciation, by what percentage will the price in the USA of his £20 000 good change?

**A** + 50%   **B** + $33\frac{1}{3}$%   **C** + 10%   **D** − 20%   **E** − $33\frac{1}{3}$%

## Example 19.3

The following diagram shows the market for sterling.

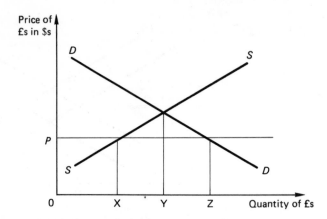

If the government wishes to maintain the exchange rate at OP it should:

A  buy 0X sterling      B  buy XY sterling      C  sell 0X sterling

D  sell XY sterling      E  sell XZ sterling

## Example 19.4

Under a freely floating exchange rate system, which of the following will cause an appreciation of the £ sterling?

A  an increase in the speculative sales of pounds

B  a rise in French interest rates

C  the purchase by a British company of a controlling interest in a company in Germany

D  an increase in Japanese tourist expenditure in London

E  a rise in UK demand for visible imports

## Example 19.5

A British shirt manufacturer sells 60 shirts per week in the USA when the price is £10 per shirt and the exchange rate is £1 = \$1.5. The American market has a unit elasticity of demand for these shirts. If the sterling price is unchanged, what is the maximum number of shirts he can sell in the USA if the exchange rate changes to £1 = \$2?

A  40        B  45        C  60        D  80        E  120

## Example 19.6

Which of the following will impose downward pressure on the pound sterling?

A  a fall in US interest rates

B  a reduction in German import duties

C  a reduction in UK investment abroad

D  a reduction in foreign tourists coming to the UK

E  a reduction in the marginal propensity to import in the UK

**Example 19.7**

Which of the following would be likely to cause a decrease in the UK's reserves under a fixed exchange rate?

A   the issue of SDRs by the IMF
B   a current account surplus
C   an increase in the value of gold
D   a decrease in overseas investment by UK residents
E   support of the pound sterling by the Exchange Equalisation Account

**Example 19.8**

If the UK demand for German TVs is price-elastic, then a rise in their price, under a floating exchange rate system, will cause:

A   an increase in the demand for sterling
B   a decrease in the demand for sterling
C   an increase in the supply of sterling
D   an increase in the demand for German marks
E   a decrease in the demand for German marks

**Example 19.9**

Which of the following is a possible disadvantage of a fixed exchange rate?

A   trade may be diminished because of exchange rate uncertainty
B   there will be an absence of external pressure to control inflationary pressures
C   current account deficits will tend to result in an increase in the country's money supply
D   reserves will have to be held
E   there will be frequent changes in the value of the currency

**Example 19.10**

The Exchange Equalisation Account:

A   finances UK current account deficits
B   assists other countries with current account deficits
C   insures UK exports against currency fluctuations
D   regulates the value of the pound sterling
E   seeks to improve the UK's terms of trade

**Example 19.11**

The exchange rate between country A and country B is £1 = $2.0. To be as well off in country B, a citizen of country A earning £12 000 per annum requires to earn $48 000. What is the purchasing power parity between the $ and £?

A   5 : 1     B   4 : 1     C   3 : 1     D   2 : 1     E   1 : 1

*Examples 19.12–19.15 are based on the following diagram, showing the market for pounds sterling.*

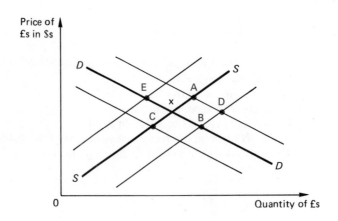

Price of £s in $s (vertical axis)

Quantity of £s (horizontal axis)

The new equilibrium position after each of the changes below, starting each time from X, would be:

### Example 19.12

An increase in spending by foreign tourists in the UK.

### Example 19.13

An increase in overseas investment by British companies.

### Example 19.14

An increase in demand by UK residents for German goods.

### Example 19.15

An increase in the quality and competitiveness of UK cars resulting in a fall in demand for US cars in the UK.

*Select your answers to Examples 19.16–19.19 by means of the following code:*
**A**   *if 1, 2 and 3 are all correct*
**B**   *if 1 and 2 only are correct*
**C**   *if 2 and 3 only are correct*
**D**   *if 1 only is correct*

### Example 19.16

Special drawing rights are:
1   the right of IMF member countries to borrow the first 25% of their quotas
2   a recent form of international liquidity
3   allocated in greater quantities to rich than to poor countries

### Example 19.17

Within the European Monetary System:
1   central banks are expected to intervene to ensure that currencies stay within the permitted limits

2 a depreciation of member countries' currencies will result in a fall in the value of the European Currency Unit

3 the European Monetary Co-operation Fund makes loans to member countries and holds a proportion of their reserves

**Example 19.18**

Which of the following is likely to result in a rise in the exchange rate of the £ sterling?
1 a rise in UK interest rates
2 a rise in the inflation rate of UK competitors
3 an increase in the quantity of foreign currencies bought by the EEA

**Example 19.19**

Which of the following measures may be employed by a government wishing to offset downward pressure on its currency?
1 the sale of its currency on the foreign exchange market
2 the raising of domestic interest rates
3 the reduction of a budget deficit

# 19.4 Essays

**Example 19.20**

Discuss the repercussions for the United Kingdom economy of a significant depreciation in the sterling exchange rate.

(L Jan. 1987)

- Explain the meaning of depreciation.
- Examine the internal and external effects of a depreciation.
- Make use of the concept of price elasticity of demand.

*Solution 19.20*

Depreciation means a lessening of the value of the currency in terms of another currency or currencies. Under a freely floating exchange rate, this would result from demand and supply factors; under a fixed exchange rate, from deliberate government action; and under a managed float, from market forces and government action.

A depreciation will mean that exports, in terms of foreign currency, will be cheaper, while imports, in terms of pounds, will be more expensive. A depreciation not only makes exports more price-competitive, but also increases the competitiveness of UK products sold on the home market which compete against imports.

In the short term, demand for both imports and exports will be inelastic, as there will not be time for the pattern of demand to change. However, if demand for exports is elastic, then total revenue earned from exports should rise, as the fall in price will cause a greater percentage rise in demand. Also, expenditure on imports should decrease, since a rise in their price will cause a greater percentage fall in demand. The Marshall Lerner condition states that, for depreciation of a currency to improve the balance of payments position, the elasticity for exports and imports must be greater than one.

Exporters may take advantage of the fall in the currency either by allowing the price of their goods to fall in foreign markets or by keeping their prices constant, raising their sterling profit margins.

If the depreciation results in a rise in export revenue and a fall in expenditure on imports, there will be a net injection in the circular flow of income. This will cause National Income to rise by a multiple amount.

If more exports are sold and fewer imports purchased and N.Y. is rising, then employment will also be likely to rise. This will occur unless there is already full employment or underemployment or unless a rise in output results entirely from increased capital or changes in technology. The Cambridge Economic Policy Group have advocated using the exchange rate to influence the level of aggregate demand and employment.

While it is believed that demand for UK exports is elastic, it is more doubtful whether some of the other conditions required for a depreciation to improve the balance of payments position will be met. If demand for exports and imports is inelastic, then a fall in the value of the pound will result in more being spent on imports and less being earned from exports. This will cause a deterioration in the balance of payments position and will result in a leakage from the circular flow.

Even if demand for exports is elastic, the country may not benefit if the supply of exports is inelastic. For instance, if there is full employment, then it may be difficult to meet any extra demand. The beneficial effects of a depreciation may also be affected by other countries devaluing their currencies.

A depreciation can accelerate inflation both directly and indirectly. Imports are counted in the retail price index, and a rise in their price will, *ceteris paribus*, raise the RPI. Also, home producers may raise their price because of increases in costs of imported raw materials and components and/or because they can do so while still remaining competitive against more expensive imports. Trade unions may be stimulated to press for wage rises, since higher import prices will probably increase the cost of living.

Investment in the UK may be discouraged, especially if it is thought that there will be a future fall in the value of the pound. Some countries which have kept pounds in their reserves may decide to change to other currencies, and this will put increased pressure on the pound.

The effects of a depreciation are uncertain and may be beneficial or adverse, depending on a number of factors, including the elasticity of demand for exports and imports.


**Example 19.21**

'The problem of international liquidity can be solved by the adoption of floating exchange rates.'

- Define floating exchange rates and international liquidity.
- Discuss why, in theory, reserves should not be necessary under floating exchange rates.
- Discuss why, in practice, international liquidity will still be necessary under conditions of floating exchange rates.
- Discuss the main forms of international liquidity.

*Solution 19.21*

One argument in favour of floating exchange rates is that reserves will not be necessary. This would solve the two main problems of international liquidity, which are its inadequate supply and what form that supply should take. However, as floating exchange rates do not, in practice, guarantee a balance of payments equilibrium and since most governments engage in dirty floating, the existence of floating exchange rates, while possibly easing the problems of international liquidity, does not eliminate them.

A floating exchange rate is one which, if freely floating, is determined entirely by the demand for, and supply of, the currency. In theory, the exchange rate will move to a position to ensure a balance of payments equilibrium. For instance, if a country experienced inflation, demand for its exports would fall and demand for imports would rise. This would cause a decrease in demand for, and an increase in the supply of, the currency. The value of the currency would fall, making exports more, and imports less, price-competitive until export revenue equals import expenditure. If this also occurred, the need for international liquidity would be reduced.

International liquidity is international money and is acceptable in settlement of debts between countries. It is kept by central banks, and is used to cover deficits in international trade payments and investment movements and to influence the value of the currency. These reserves come in four main forms: foreign currency, gold, SDRs and reserve positions at the IMF.

These reserves are still needed under a floating exchange rate system, since, while the rate may move to make a balance of payments equilibrium more likely, this may not be achieved if demand for imports and exports is inelastic and/or capital movements work in the opposite direction.

Also, a government may wish to influence the value of the currency to achieve other economic objectives. For instance, a government may buy pounds in order to raise the exchange rate and thereby possibly reduce inflationary pressures, or a government may sell pounds in order to reduce the exchange rate in an attempt to increase domestic employment.

So, although the problems relating to the provision of international liquidity may be reduced with floating exchange rates, they still exist. Countries have to decide what to keep in their reserves and they have to be able to obtain an adequate supply of reserves. There are a number of problems with all the forms of international liquidity in existence today.

Gold, which is the oldest form of international liquidity, has an opportunity cost, and its supply is controlled not by the needs of world trade but by the decisions mainly of South Africa and the USSR. The problem of supply also relates to foreign currency, since this is under the control of the countries whose currencies are kept in the reserves. In addition, there is the problem that, when the supply of a reserve currency increases, its acceptability is likely to be reduced, since the higher supply is likely to result in countries fearing that the value of the currency will fall.

In the case of reserve positions at the IMF, these may not be considered to be adequate, especially by developing countries, which may have relatively high balance of payments deficits but low reserve positions. SDRs are also the responsibility of the IMF, but these represent the first attempt to provide a form of money for international purposes. All the other forms of international liquidity have other functions and were originally designed for other purposes. However, SDRs have not made such a large contribution to solving the problem of international liquidity as was originally hoped by some economists. This is because the IMF have not issued SDRs on a large or consistent scale, and, as they are issued to countries on the basis of their quotas, they are not always given to those countries which have the greatest need for them.

Although most countries now have floating exchange rates, the problems of international liquidity are still regularly discussed in meetings of the IMF and other forums. In a world of dirty floating and balance of payments difficulties, the problems of the quantity and form of international liquidity are likely to remain important until an acceptable solution is found. At present SDRs seem to be the main hope, but even this latest form of international liquidity has, at the moment, a number of drawbacks, at least for developing countries.

## 19.7   Solutions to Objective Questions

*Solution 19.2   Answer:* **E**

Originally the £20 000 good would sell in the USA for £20 000 × $1.5 = £30 000. After the depreciation it will sell for £20 000 × £1 = £20 000. This is a reduction of ($10 000/$30 000) × (100/1) = 33.3%.

*Solution 19.3   Answer:* **E**

At the exchange rate 0F, demand for the currency exceeds supply by XZ amount. To prevent the exchange rate rising, the government would have to sell XZ amount to ensure that supply matches demand at this artificially low price.

*Solution 19.4   Answer:* **D**

An appreciation of the currency will occur if there is an increase in demand for the currency and/or a decrease in supply of the currency. A rise in Japanese tourist expenditure in London will mean an increase in demand by the Japanese for £ sterling.

**A** ⇒ Selling £s increases supply and, hence, causes a fall in the price of £s.

**B** ⇒ A rise in French interest rates may result in a shift in investment finance from the UK to France. UK residents wishing to invest in France will change £s into francs, thereby increasing the supply of £s. Fewer foreigners will wish to invest in the UK, and so demand for £s will fall.

**C** ⇒ To buy a controlling interest in a German company, a UK firm is likely to exchange £s for marks and, hence, increase the supply of £s on the world market.

**E** ⇒ If UK residents buy more imports, more £s will be sold to gain foreign currency, so again the supply of £s will increase.

*Solution 19.5   Answer:* **B**

The initial price of a £10 shirt in the USA is £10 × $1.5 = $15. Sixty are sold, so the total revenue is 60 × $15 = $900. The change in the exchange rate will cause the USA price to rise to $20. As elasticity of demand for the shirt is unity, a rise in price will cause an equal percentage change in demand and total revenue will remain constant. Thus, as total revenue is $900 and each shirt sells for $20, the number of shirts sold is $900/$20 = 45.

*Solution 19.6   Answer:* **D**

A downward pressure on the £ sterling can arise as a result of an increase in the supply of £s and/or a decrease in the demand for £s.

**A** ⇒ A fall in UK interest rates will be likely to cause a rise in the value of the £ sterling, as fewer UK citizens invest in the USA and more foreigners invest in the UK, as opposed to the USA.

**B** ⇒ If Germany reduces the taxes she places on imports, the UK should be able to export more to Germany and, hence, demand for £s will increase.

**C** ⇒ A reduction in UK investment abroad should reduce the supply of £s on the world markets and so increase the price of £s.

**E** ⇒ A reduction in the UK's mpm will cause a decrease in demand for imports, so fewer £s will be exchanged to gain foreign currency.

*Solution 19.7   Answer:* **E**

If the EEA is supporting the £, it will be buying up £s and using some of the reserves, most probably foreign currencies, to do this.

**A** ⇒ The issue of SDRs by the IMF will increase the reserves of member countries, including the UK.

**B** ⇒ A current account surplus will mean more money being earned abroad than is spent abroad and some of this may be added to the reserves.

**C** ⇒ Gold is one of the items held in the reserves. An increase in the value of gold will not increase the quantity of reserves but will increase their value.

**D** ⇒ A decrease in overseas investment by UK residents may, in the short term, reduce the amount of money going abroad and, hence, may enable less money to be drawn from the reserves or more money added to the reserves.

*Solution 19.8   Answer:* **E**

If the UK demand for German TVs is price-elastic, then a rise in their price will result in a greater percentage fall in demand and a decline in the amount spent on them. Fewer £s will be exchanged for marks to buy German TVs. Hence, the supply of sterling and demand for German marks will decrease.

*Solution 19.9   Answer:* **D**

To maintain a fixed exchange rate, the authorities may have to buy the currency and to do this it will be necessary to hold reserves. Keeping reserves involves an opportunity cost.

**A, B, E** ⇒ The discouragement of trade, absence of external pressure to control inflationary pressures and frequent changes in the exchange rate are claimed by some economists to be disadvantages of a floating exchange rate.

**C** ⇒ A current account deficit will mean more money is spent abroad than is earned and, unless offset, there will be a reduction in the money supply.

*Solution 19.10   Answer:* **D**

The EEA is a department of the Bank of England which operates on behalf of the Treasury buying and selling £s to influence the exchange rate.

*Solution 19.11   Answer:* **B**

The purchasing power parity theory states that the exchange rate between currencies will be such that the purchasing power of the money will be the same in both countries — i.e. the amount which can be purchased with the money concerned. If, in order to be as well off in country B, a citizen earning £12 000 needs to earn $48 000, the value of the currencies is $4 to £1 in terms of what the currencies will buy. Thus, the official exchange rate is not reflecting the purchasing power of the respective currencies.

*Solution 19.12   Answer:* **A**

An increase in spending by foreign tourists in the UK will cause an increase in demand for £s, which, in turn, will result in a rise in price and an extension in supply. The demand curve shifts to the right, intersecting the original supply curve at A.

*Solution 19.13   Answer:* **B**

An increase in overseas investment by UK companies will mean that more £s will be exchanged into foreign currencies to invest abroad. The supply of £s will increase, causing price to fall and demand to expand. The supply curve shifts to the right, intersecting the original demand curve at B.

*Solution 19.14   Answer:* **B**

An increase in demand by UK residents for German goods will cause UK residents to supply more £s in order to purchase marks. Thus, the supply curve will shift to the right, intersecting the original demand curve at B.

*Solution 19.15   Answer:* **E**

If, because of increasing quality and competitiveness of UK cars, fewer US cars are demanded by UK citizens, then fewer £s will be exchanged for dollars on the exchange market. The supply of £s will decrease, causing price to rise and demand to contract. The supply curve shifts to the left, intersecting the original demand curve at E.

*Solution 19.16   Answer:* **C**

SDRs are a form of international liquidity issued by the IMF to member countries.
   **1** $\Rightarrow$ The right of IMF countries to borrow the first 25% of their quotas is known as the gold tranche and not SDRs.
   **2** $\Rightarrow$ SDRs are a recent form of international liquidity.
   **3** $\Rightarrow$ SDRs are issued on the basis of member countries' quotas. Richer countries pay higher quotas and, hence, are allocated more SDRs.

*Solution 19.17   Answer:* **A**

The European Monetary System was implemented in 1979 and includes most EEC countries.
   **1** $\Rightarrow$ There is parity grid with a permitted divergence of $2\frac{1}{4}\%$. Central Banks are expected to ensure that currencies stay within this grid.

**2** ⇒ The permitted divergence of exchange rates is based on a weighted basket called the European Currency Unit rather than against other individual currencies. The fall in the value of one currency will lower the value of the ECU.

**3** ⇒ The European Monetary Co-operation Fund acts as a European Central Bank holding member countries' monetary reserves and making loans.

*Solution 19.18   Answer:* **B**

The sterling exchange rate will rise as a result of an increase in demand for sterling and/or a decrease in the supply of sterling.

**1** ⇒ A rise in UK interest rates is likely to cause more foreigners to wish to invest in the UK. This will result in an increase in demand for £s.

**2** ⇒ A rise in the inflation rate of UK competitors will mean that foreign goods are more expensive in relation to UK goods. This will mean that fewer foreign goods will be purchased by UK residents and more UK goods by foreigners. Thus, the demand for £s will increase and the supply of £s will decrease.

**3** ⇒ To buy foreign currencies, the EEA will use £s. This will increase the supply of £s and, hence, reduce the value of the £.

*Solution 19.19   Answer:* **C**

A government wishing to offset the downward pressure on its currency will increase demand for it and/or reduce its supply.

**1** ⇒ The sale of the currency will increase its supply and lower its price.

**2** ⇒ The raising of domestic interest rates should increase demand for the currency and its price by making it more attractive for foreigners to invest in the country.

**3** ⇒ The reduction of a budget deficit should reduce demand in the economy and, hence, lower expenditure on imports and possibly switch some sales from the domestic to export markets. This will reduce the supply of £s and increase demand for them.

# 20 Managing the Economy

## 20.1   Fact Sheet

### (a) Government Policy

There are three stages of government macro- and microeconomic policy.

  (i) *Objectives*: aims of government policies.
  (ii) *Targets*: variables through which the government attempts to achieve its objectives.
  (iii) *Instruments*: policy tools over which the government has control and which are implemented to influence target variables.

### (b) Economic Objectives

All governments have four main macroeconomic aims:

  (i) *Full employment*, which does not mean zero unemployment, since even in a buoyant economy some workers will be between jobs (frictional unemployment).
  (ii) *Price stability*, which means an acceptable annual inflation rate, since, in a dynamic economy, relative prices will always be changing in response to changes in the conditions of demand and supply.
  (iii) *Current account equilibrium*   Over a period of time a country will aim to avoid a deficit, since reserves and willing lenders are finite. It will also probably try to avoid a long-term surplus, since this involves the opportunity cost of a higher living standard for its residents.
  (iv) *Economic growth* — i.e. increases in output which should ensure higher living standards.

  • Governments may have a number of other macro-objectives, such as a more equitable distribution of income. This requires state intervention through progressive taxation, income-relative benefits, etc.
  • Governments may also have a number of micro-objectives, such as protection of the environment or efficiency in the allocation of resources.

### (c) Macroeconomic Policies

A central issue in macroeconomics is whether or not markets automatically bring about equilibrium. If the free operation of market forces automatically resulted in a full employment level of national income with stable prices and economic growth, there would be no need for government intervention to achieve equilibrium. However, if the economy is unstable or slow to reach satisfactory equilibrium, government economic policies will be required. These include the following.

(i) *Monetary policy*  The two main instruments are changes in the money supply and interest rates.

(ii) *Fiscal policy* or *budgetary policy*  The two main instruments are changes in government spending and taxation.

(iii) *Prices and incomes policy* usually involves a limit on price rises and rises in incomes, particularly wages.

(iv) *Regional policy*, where government measures help influence the location of industry and people.

(v) *Exchange rate policy*, which involves the government managing the exchange rate to achieve its aims.

(vi) *Import controls*, where tariffs or quotas are used to reduce or stabilise imports.

### (d) Policy Approaches

(i) Keynes argued that aggregate monetary demand (AMD) is the chief determinant of output and employment. Therefore, *demand management* through macroeconomic policies is the best method of achieving policy objectives.

- *Reflationary* policies increase AMD.
- *Deflationary* policies decrease AMD.

(ii) Monetarists generally argue that supply is the chief determinant of output and employment. Therefore, micropolicies which increase supply are the best method of achieving policy objectives. Monetarists favour measures such as reductions in tax rates or policies which reduce market distortions:

(1) increasing the gap between earnings from employment and unemployment benefit to reduce voluntary and search unemployment;

(2) increasing, through training, the quality and flexibility of the labour force;

(3) privatising nationalised industries to make them subject to market forces;

(4) removing government restrictions to increase the efficiency of markets;

(5) reducing the monopsony power of unions.

**Table 20.1** Examples of government policies

| Policy | Instrument | Target | Objective |
|---|---|---|---|
| Monetary | Interest rate | Bank lending | Price stability |
| Fiscal | Government spending | Aggregate demand | Employment |
| Regional | Selective grants | Location of firms | Growth |
| Exchange rate | Exchange rate | Price of exports and imports | Current account |
| Supply-side | Privatisation | PSBR | Price stability |
| Supply-side | Union legislation | Labour mobility | Growth |

**(e) Policy Problems**

All governments experience problems in managing the economy.

(i) There may be a conflict between policy objectives. For instance, increasing government spending may increase employment and growth but result in rising prices and a current account deficit. *Tinbergen's rule* states that a government needs to have at least one instrument to achieve each objective. Fiscal policy can be directed at unemployment; exchange rate policy can be directed at the current account; etc.

(ii) Governments are faced with political constraints. For instance, strict monetary policy may cause such high interest rates that mortgage payers refuse to vote for the government.

(iii) Resistance from trade unions and professional bodies may act as a constraint.

(iv) Policy instruments are interdependent. For example, increasing government spending may result in a rise in PSBR and interest rates.

(v) Policy instruments can also become objectives, thereby reducing their flexibility. For example, exchange rates and the money supply.

(vi) There may be time lags between recognising a problem, deciding on the policy, and then implementing that policy. In the meantime, economic relationships may change. For example, if a government tackles unemployment by reducing taxation, only to find that demand is rising anyway, this policy reinforces the cycle rather than acting counter-cyclically.

(vii) The economy may not respond in the way anticipated. For example, entrepreneurs may react to rises in demand by increasing prices rather than output.

(viii) Some target variables are difficult to define. For example, it is difficult to know which assets to include in measures of the money supply.

(ix) External shocks — e.g. a world depression — may undermine government policies.

## 20.2 Data Response

**Worked Example 20.1**

The Chancellor was positively glowing about the merits of a balanced budget, telling the House: 'A balanced budget is a valuable discipline for the medium term. It represents security for the present and an investment for the future. Having achieved it, I intend to stick to it.'

This represents a considerable shift from his previous commitment to a Public Sector Borrowing Requirement (PSBR) of 1 per cent of GDP, or some £4 billion as far as the strategy went, set out in the last set of budget documents.

However, his enthusiasm for balanced budgets has been tempered both in the current financial year and in 1988–9 by his concern that the rapid growth of the economy might lead to rising pay settlements and other domestic inflationary pressures, and to an unsustainably wide current account deficit.

Mr Lawson has thus made a virtue of a prescription straight out of classical Keynesian demand management in aiming for a budget surplus at a time of rapid growth and recovery. The budget surplus, or Public Sector Debt Repayment, as Mr Lawson dubbed it, is estimated at £3 billion this year, or 0.75 per cent of GDP.

He set the same objective for the coming financial year, and thus substantially limited the tax cuts which he would have been able to give away had he aimed for his long-term objective of budget balance and was even more cautious by comparison with last year's £4 billion target for the PSBR in 1988–9.

Mr Lawson has thus achieved once again the triple hat-trick of cutting his original borrowing target, adding to his original plans for public spending, and cutting taxation. The detailed arithmetic in the Red Book published yesterday shows that general government receipts (tax revenues) are expected to be £185 billion compared with a projected £178 billion for 1988–9 in the last budget, despite the greater than expected tax cuts. At the same time, spending is forecast to be £183 billion in the next financial year, compared with a forecast of £180 billion in the last budget. Public corporations are expected to repay £1 billion, leaving a PSBR of minus £3 billion.

Source: *The Guardian*, 16 March 1988

(a) What is meant by a balanced budget? **(2 marks)**
(b) What does the article suggest is the opportunity cost of aiming for a budget surplus for the 1988–9 year rather than a balanced budget? **(2 marks)**
(c) Why may a rapid growth of the economy result in 'domestic inflationary pressure' and 'an unsustainably wide current deficit'? **(5 marks)**
(d) Explain what is meant by 'classical Keynesian demand management in aiming for a budget surplus at a time of rapid growth and recovery'. **(5 marks)**
(e) Why may tax revenues increase despite cuts in tax rates? **(3 marks)**
(f) Why may government revenue turn out to be lower or higher than originally forecast? **(3 marks)**

*Solution 20.1*

(a) A balanced budget is achieved when government expenditure equals government revenue.

(b) The article suggests that one opportunity cost of aiming for a budget surplus for the 1988–9 year was the further tax cuts which could have been made had a balanced budget been the objective instead.

(c) A rapid growth of the economy will raise incomes. If output does not rise in line with incomes, prices may increase. Rising employment may strengthen unions' bargaining power and result in higher wage claims. The high level of demand may also make entrepreneurs more inclined to raise prices.

   The UK has a relatively high marginal propensity to import, and, when income rises, expenditure on imports increases and some UK goods are diverted from the export to the home market. On a number of occasions in the past when the UK has experienced a rise in the growth rate, current account deficits have become a problem.

(d) Keynesian demand management is concerned with the government altering its expenditure and taxation to ensure a full employment level of aggregate demand. If demand is below the desired level, the government will inject extra spending to increase income and employment. On the other hand, if demand is above the full employment level, the government will reduce demand to eliminate the inflationary gap. If private sector demand is rising rapidly and at a rate greater than the government desires, it may seek to reduce aggregate demand by withdrawing more spending power (in the form of taxation) than it injects (in the form of government spending).

(e) Total tax revenue may increase when tax cuts are made. Tax cuts will increase disposable incomes, which may stimulate spending and output. The rise in output is likely to cause an increase in employment. This will mean that previously unemployed people will experience a rise in income as they move into employment. As incomes rise, the total amount of tax paid will rise.

(f) Governments make their forecasts of government spending and taxation on the basis of projections of, e.g., output, growth, employment, etc. If employment rises above the level originally forecast by the government, then revenue from, e.g., income tax and VAT will be higher than originally predicted, while expenditure on unemployment and other benefits will be lower.

## 20.3  Objective Questions

### Example 20.2

Which combination of events might cause a government to lower interest rates and reduce direct taxation?
A   a current account deficit and unemployment
B   a current account deficit and inflation
C   a current account surplus and inflation
D   a current account surplus and unemployment
E   unemployment and inflation

### Example 20.3

According to a supporter of supply-side economics, which of the following measures is most likely to reduce unemployment in the UK?
A   imposing exchange controls          B   increasing labour retraining schemes
C   increasing unemployment benefit     D   increasing public-sector investment
E   increasing the money supply

### Example 20.4

A government is faced with both demand pull inflation and a current account deficit. Which of the following policy measures might simultaneously reduce both problems?
A   devaluation                         B   revaluation
C   deflation                           D   reflation
E   lowering interest rates

## Example 20.5

An example of a restrictionist monetary policy instrument is:
A  a switch of government borrowing from the banking sector to the non-bank private sector
B  an increase in direct taxation
C  a tight prices and incomes policy
D  a decrease in government spending
E  converting long-term government debt into short-term government debt

## Example 20.6

Which of the following is an example of an automatic stabiliser?
A  defence expenditure        B  child benefit
C  education expenditure     D  health expenditure
E  unemployment benefit

## Example 20.7

A government wants to reduce the growth of the money supply and lower direct taxation. Which policy would be most likely to achieve these two aims?
A  the purchase by the Central Bank of government securities from the general public
B  a reduction in interest rates
C  a reduction in VAT
D  a reduction in government spending
E  the release of special deposits

*Examples 20.8 and 20.9 are based on the following information. A country has a progressive income tax system. The first £3000 earned is tax-free. Thereafter the next £9000 of earned income is taxed at 25% and all taxable income above that is taxed at 50%.*

## Example 20.8

A person earns £10 000. What proportion of his income does he pay in tax?
A  50%      B  25%      C  17.5%     D  15.5%     E  10.5%

## Example 20.9

What is the marginal rate of tax paid when a person's income rises from £12 000 to £12 001?
A  0.8      B  0.5      C  0.3      D  0.25     E  0.1

*Select your answers to Examples 20.10–20.12 by means of the following code:*
A  *if 1, 2 and 3 are all correct*
B  *if 1 and 2 only are correct*
C  *if 2 and 3 only are correct*
D  *if 1 only is correct*

**Example 20.10**

Which of the tax systems below is/are regressive?

| Tax system | Income before tax (£) | Income after tax (£) |
| --- | --- | --- |
| 1 | 20 000 | 15 000 |
|   | 40 000 | 24 000 |
| 2 | 20 000 | 10 000 |
|   | 40 000 | 28 000 |
| 3 | 20 000 | 8 000 |
|   | 40 000 | 25 000 |

**Example 20.11**

Which of the following is/are examples of fiscal policy instruments?
1 changes in interest rates
2 changes in employees' National Insurance contributions
3 changes in the price of television licences

**Example 20.12**

In the case of which type of income taxes does/do the amount of tax paid rise with income?
1 regressive        2 proportionate        3 progressive

# 20.4 Essays

**Example 20.13**

Examine the arguments for and against a shift from direct to indirect taxation.
(L Jan. 1987)

- Define direct and indirect taxes.
- Consider the advantages and disadvantages of both indirect and direct taxation.

*Solution 20.13*

Direct taxes — e.g. income tax and corporation tax — are levied directly on a person's or firm's income or wealth. On the other hand, indirect taxes — e.g. VAT and excise duty — are taxes on goods and services and are paid to the government through a third party. They are sometimes referred to as expenditure or outlay taxes.

The argument for moving the tax base towards greater reliance on indirect taxes and less reliance on direct taxation is based on the disadvantages of direct taxes and the advantages of indirect taxes.

It is claimed by some economists that direct taxation, particularly at a high level, acts as a disincentive to effort. However, studies have shown that few people (less than 10%) change the hours they work when income tax rates are altered and that as many work fewer hours as work more hours.

A high level of corporation tax may discourage risk-taking and may discourage investment, since most investment is financed by retained profits. Direct taxation may also reduce savings of individuals, since the rich save more than the poor and since savings may effectively be taxed twice: once when the income is earned and then when interest is received on that part of income which is saved.

In addition to reducing the disadvantages arising from direct taxation, a country would gain more of the advantages of indirect taxation by shifting the tax base. Indirect taxes are relatively cheap to administer and collect. For instance, manufacturers and traders do most of the administrative work involved with VAT.

Indirect taxes can also be adjusted more quickly than direct taxes. While direct taxes can be changed at budget time and may involve complex revision of, e.g., PAYE codings, indirect taxes can be changed relatively quickly.

Indirect taxes are difficult to evade, as they are included in the price of the good. They may provide more freedom of choice in terms of payment, although, if a wide range of goods are taxed, this may not be a significant advantage. Nevertheless, it is thought that many people are unaware of the amount of tax they are paying when they buy goods, and this may reduce the resentment they feel in paying taxes.

Some economists argue that indirect taxes do not discourage effort, since the taxes are linked to spending rather than earning. However, if certain goods — e.g. cars, colour TVs — are highly taxed, this may place them out of the reach of people who would have been prepared to work longer hours to buy them.

Indirect taxation can help to regulate the economy. At times of high demand, spending on goods will go up, which will cause the revenue from indirect taxation to go up, which will reduce demand, although, in real terms, the burden of specific taxes will fall with inflation.

Indirect taxes can also be used for specific aims. Particular goods may be taxed in order to discourage the consumption of those goods, to protect domestic industries and even to encourage the production of certain goods by reducing the amount of tax levied on them. When indirect taxes are placed on goods for which the private costs of production are below the social costs, resources may be reallocated in a way which raises total economic welfare.

However, increasing the percentage of tax revenue accounted for by indirect taxation may give rise to a number of disadvantages. Indirect taxes are regressive, since they take a higher percentage of the income of the poor than of that of the rich. This is thought to be one of the main disadvantages of indirect taxation, and, although certain categories of goods may be zero-rated, the poor are less well protected than under direct taxation.

Indirect taxes may be inflationary, as a rise in indirect taxes will cause a rise in prices. They may also distort consumers' patterns of expenditure and the allocation of resources. If, prior to the imposition of an indirect tax, consumers were maximising their total utility, then the tax would reduce consumer satisfaction. Indirect taxes may reduce consumer and producer surplus, as shown in the diagram.

Some economists would also argue against shifting the tax base, on the grounds that the advantage of direct taxes are greater than those of indirect taxes. Direct taxes provide a high yield, and they are certain and convenient, since most are deducted at source. They also have a stabilising effect, since

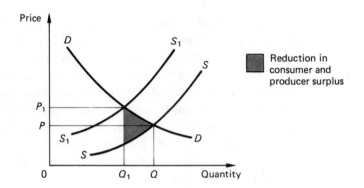

during times of recession tax revenue will fall, while during periods of rising incomes tax revenue will rise. Direct taxes also have the advantage of equity, as most are progressive, so the most able to pay bear the greater burden.

The main arguments advanced for moving towards a greater reliance on indirect taxation are a reduction in the disincentive effect and economy of collection. However, because of the relative merits and demerits of each, the government will continue to rely on both forms of taxation.

Example 20.14

Describe how the level of aggregate demand can be influenced by fiscal policy. Discuss the problems that may be encountered by the use of fiscal policy.
(L June 1987)

- Discuss how fiscal policy can increase and reduce demand.
- In the second part of the question, which should be given more attention, discuss difficulties of adjusting government spending and taxation, time lags, conflicts of objectives, difficulties in forecasting, effects of fiscal policy on other variables and objectives.

Solution 20.14

Discretionary or active fiscal policy is when the government takes a positive decision to alter government spending or taxation to alter demand. This contrasts with automatic stabilisers, which come into effect when tax revenue and government spending change independently of any deliberate government action.

The level of aggregate demand could be raised by an expansionary policy. This could involve an increase in government spending and/or a reduction in taxation. An expansionary or reflationary fiscal policy would represent a net injection into the circular flow and would cause N.Y. to rise by a multiple amount. It may be used to reduce a deflationary gap.

A deflationary or contractionary fiscal policy will result in a multiple fall in N.Y. and will involve a fall in government expenditure and/or a rise in taxation. This may be introduced in order to reduce or eliminate an inflationary gap.

However, there are a number of problems which may be encountered with fiscal policy. Some forms of government spending may not be easy to change. For instance, a government committed to improving educational standards may find it difficult to reduce spending on education. Also, it will be difficult to reduce spending on a long-term investment project once it is under way.

Tax revenues may be difficult to predict. When the government alters indirect taxation, it has to estimate price elasticity of demand. An even more difficult calculation may prove to be the multiplier. If the government gets this wrong, it may inject too much or too little spending into the economy.

There is also likely to be a time lag involved with fiscal policy, which means that the government has to be able to forecast accurately future changes in economic variables. For instance, a government may announce in a March budget a reduction in the standard rate of income tax designed to raise spending. This may take two to three months to come into effect, by which time gross pay and demand may be rising anyway. So the policy will be contributing to the cycle rather than acting countercyclically.

The use of fiscal policy may have different effects on different government objectives. A contractionary policy may reduce inflation and a current account deficit but may have an adverse effect on employment and growth.

There is the possibility that the economy may not respond as anticipated to fine tuning. For instance, a government may raise income tax in order to reduce spending. However, spending may not fall, or may not fall significantly, if, e.g., people choose and are able to work overtime to maintain their current spending patterns and/or if people choose to reduce saving rather than spending.

A fiscal policy measure may also have undesirable effects on other policy instruments and variables or may itself be constrained by these. A rise in government spending, not financed by taxation, may raise the money supply and/or interest rates. The latter may reduce private-sector investment, which may, at least in part, offset the expansionary effect of the increase in government spending. The former may contribute, according to monetarist analysis, to inflation.

When governments in the past have raised government spending to increase demand, they have encountered current account difficulties. This resulted in the 'stop–go' cycles — i.e. governments adopting expansionary policies, N.Y. rising, expenditure on imports rising, governments adopting deflationary fiscal policies to restore current account equilibrium.

Monetarists claim that expansionary fiscal policy aimed at raising employment and growth will have a greater impact on prices than on output. They favour a *fixed throttle* — i.e. aggregate demand being allowed to grow in line with output. They also consider that fiscal policy may have very uncertain effects, as it is difficult to predict future changes in economic variables. They believe that monetary policy is more important and effective.

## 20.5  Solutions to Objective Questions

*Solution 20.2   Answer:* **D**

Lowering interest rates and reducing direct taxation will increase demand in the home economy. This is likely to stimulate domestic output and employment. The increase in demand is also likely to increase imports and possibly reduce exports (as home producers switch from foreign markets to the home market). This will reduce a current account surplus and enable the home country to enjoy more goods and services.

*Solution 20.3   Answer:* **B**

Supporters of supply-side economics urge the use of microeconomic incentives to raise output and employment. They believe that, if the quantity of factors of production is improved and markets operate more efficiently, growth and increases in employment will follow. Retraining schemes should increase the productivity of labour.

A ⇒ Exchange controls would interfere with free market forces.

C ⇒ Increasing unemployment benefit would narrow the gap between unemployment income and earnings. Supply-side economists favour the opposite, ensuring that workers are better off in work. They believe that this will make people seek employment more quickly and settle for lower wages.

D ⇒ Increasing public-sector investment will increase demand. Supply-side economists argue that governments should concentrate on increasing aggregate supply.

E ⇒ Supply-side economists believe that increases in the money supply, if greater than increases in output, lead to higher prices but not higher employment in the long term.

*Solution 20.4   Answer:* **C**

Deflation involves reducing demand, usually by means of fiscal and/or monetary policy. This should reduce demand pull inflation. It should also reduce a current account deficit by reducing expenditure on imports and possibly stimulating exports as a result of the fall in domestic demand.

A ⇒ Devaluation should assist the current account position, but may increase inflationary pressures as a result of the rise in export earnings and a rise in import prices.

B ⇒ Revaluation should reduce inflation by lowering import prices, but it is likely to have an adverse effect on the current account balance as a result of the fall in import prices and the rise in export prices.

D ⇒ Reflation means increasing demand, and this is likely to have an adverse effect on both the current account position and inflation.

E ⇒ Lowering interest rates will also be likely to worsen both problems, at least in the short term. Demand is likely to rise as borrowing becomes cheaper and less foreign investment is likely to be attracted.

*Solution 20.5   Answer:* **A**

When the government borrows from the commercial banks by, e.g., selling treasury bills, it increases their liquid assets and, hence, their ability to lend. In contrast, when the government borrows from members of the non-bank private sector, it merely makes use of existing money. Switching borrowing from the banking to the non-bank private sector will tend to reduce bank lending and, hence, reduce monetary expansion.

B, D ⇒ Increasing taxes and reducing government expenditure are deflationary fiscal policies.

C ⇒ A prices and incomes policy is a direct government policy.

E ⇒ Issuing more short-term government debt is an expansionary policy, since this will increase the supply of liquid assets.

*Solution 20.6   Answer:* **E**

Automatic stabilisers are those which offset changes in N.Y. without any direct government action. If N.Y. is falling, total expenditure on unemployment benefit will rise. This increase will reduce the fall in demand and, hence, will act countercyclically.

A, B, C, D ⇒ will not adjust automatically with changes in N.Y. They are adjusted as a result of government decision and action.

*Solution 20.7   Answer:* **D**

A reduction in government spending may enable both taxation to be lowered and the money supply growth to be reduced. This can occur if government spending is reduced by more than taxation is lowered, thereby reducing any budget deficit. This, in turn, will reduce the PSBR and reduce the need to finance at least part of it by adding to the money supply.

**A, B, E** $\Rightarrow$ Are all likely to increase the growth of the money supply.

**C** $\Rightarrow$ A reduction in VAT is likely to reduce government revenue and, hence, increase any budget deficit.

*Solution 20.8   Answer:* **C**

A person who earns £10 000 will have £3000 tax-free income and taxable income of £7000. The tax he will pay on this will be 25% — i.e. £1750. So the proportion of his income he pays in tax is

$$\frac{£1750}{£10\ 000} \times \frac{100}{1} = 17.5\%$$

*Solution 20.9   Answer:* **B**

A person earning £12 000 will have £9000 taxable income and, hence, he will be in the 25% tax bracket. If his income rises by £1, this extra £1 will be taxed at 50% — i.e. £0.5 will be taken in tax. So the marginal rate of tax is 0.5.

*Solution 20.10   Answer:* **C**

A regressive tax is one which takes a higher percentage of the income of the poor than of the rich. In tax system **2**, people earning £20 000 pay £10 000 tax (i.e. 50%), while those earning £40 000 pay £12 000 tax (i.e. 30%). In tax system **3**, people earning £20 000 pay £12 000 tax (i.e. 60%), while those earning £40 000 pay £15 000 tax (i.e. 37.5%).

**1** $\Rightarrow$ Tax system **1** is a progressive tax, with the higher earners (£40 000) paying 40% of their income in tax, while lower earners (£20 000) pay 25% of their income in tax.

*Solution 20.11   Answer:* **C**

Fiscal policy involves changes in government spending and taxation. Changes in employees' NI contributions and TV licences are both forms of taxation.

**1** $\Rightarrow$ Interest rates are a monetary policy instrument.

*Solution 20.12   Answer:* **A**

While it is only in the case of progressive income taxes that the percentage of tax paid rises with income, the actual amount paid will rise in all three cases.

# Index